WEIRD
NEW ENGLAND

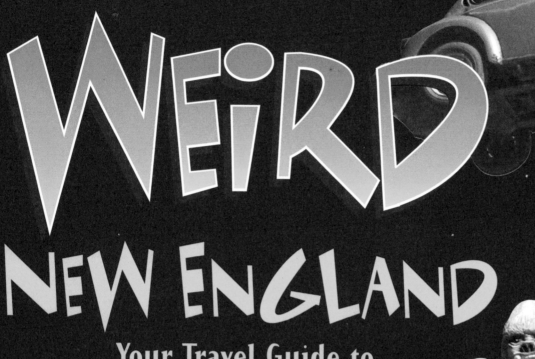

WEiRD

NEW ENGLAND

Your Travel Guide to New England's Local Legends and Best Kept Secrets

BY JOSEPH A. CITRO

Mark Moran and Mark Sceurman, Executive Editors

Sterling Publishing Co., Inc.
New York

Weird New England

Published by Sterling Publishing Co., Inc.
387 Park Avenue South, New York, NY 10016
© 2005 by Sterling Publishing Co., Inc.
Distributed in Canada by Sterling Publishing
c/o Canadian Manda Group, 165 Dufferin Street
Toronto, Ontario, Canada M6K 3H6
Distributed in Great Britain by Chrysalis Books Group PLC
The Chrysalis Building, Bramley Road, London W10 6SP, England
Distributed in Australia by Capricorn Link (Australia) Pty. Ltd.
P. O. Box 704, Windsor, NSW 2756, Australia

10 9 8 7 6 5 4 3 2 1

Manufactured in the United States of America.
All rights reserved.

Photography and illustration credits are found on page 287
and constitute an extension of this copyright page.

Sterling ISBN 1-4027-3330-5

For information about custom editions, special sales, premium and
corporate purchases, please contact Sterling Special Sales
Department at 800-805-5489 or specialsales@sterlingpub.com.

Design: Richard J. Berenson
Berenson Design & Books, LLC, New York, NY

CONTENTS

Foreword: A Note from the Marks

Our weird journey began a long, long time ago in a far-off land called New Jersey. Once a year or so we'd compile a homespun newsletter called *Weird N.J.* to hand out to our friends. The pamphlet was a collection of odd news clippings, bizarre facts, little-known historical anecdotes, and anomalous encounters from our home state. The newsletter also focused on localized legends that were often whispered around a particular town but seldom heard beyond the town line.

Weird N.J. soon became a full-fledged magazine, and we began doing our own investigating to see if we could track down any factual basis for all of these seemingly unbelievable stories. Armed with not much more than a camera and a notepad, we set off on a mystical journey of discovery. Much to our surprise a lot of what we had initially presumed to be just urban legend turned out to be real— or at least contained a grain of truth that had originally sparked the lore.

After about a dozen years of documenting the bizarre, we were asked to write a book about our adventures, and so *Weird N.J.: Your Travel Guide to New Jersey's Local Legends and Best Kept Secrets* was published in 2003. Soon people from all over the country began writing to us, telling us about strange tales from their home states. So we decided to write *Weird U.S.*, in which we could document the local legends and strangest stories from all over the country. For the next twelve months, we set out in search of weirdness wherever it might be found in the fifty states. And indeed, we found plenty of it!

After *Weird U.S.* was published, we came to the conclusion that this country had more great tales than could be contained in just one book. We told our publishers that we wanted to document it ALL, and to do it in a series of books, each focusing on the peculiarities of a particular state or region.

Where to get started was pretty easy.

During our research for *Weird U.S.*, we had found that New England was so rife with strange lore and unusual sites that it was a real challenge to choose just a few to represent the region. It seemed obvious that New England needed a *Weird* book all its own.

Our next step was to find an author who was familiar with all of New England's oddities. Strangely enough, he found us! It happened one day as we

were sitting around the office poring over books on New England's history, mysteries, and folklore. One author's work seemed to rise to the top of the heap again and again—Joseph Citro's. Joe seemed to have a curiosity for the unexplained and a sense of adventure for tracking down the really bizarre tales. As we sat contemplating his work, the phone rang. A glance at the caller ID told us that the *Weird New England* stars must have been coming into alignment. There, printed out in digital letters, the ID read CITRO, JOSEPH.

As it turned out, Joe was calling to interview us for an article he was writing for the *Boston Globe* about the *Weird U.S.* book. We had a wonderful conversation, and by the time we hung up, we knew we had found the right man to tackle *Weird New England*.

Without question, Joe Citro has the "Weird Eye," which requires one to see the world in a different way, with a renewed sense of wonder. And once you have it, there is no going back—you'll never see things the same way again. All of a sudden you begin to reexamine your own environs, noticing your everyday surroundings as if for the first time. And you begin to ask yourself questions like, "What the heck is that thing all about, anyway?" and "Doesn't anybody else think that's kinda weird?"

So come with us now and let Joe show you his New England home as he sees it, with all of its cultural quirks, odd characters, and many mysteries. It's a place we like to call *Weird New England*.

—*Mark Moran and Mark Sceurman*

Introduction

Every American day begins in New England.

The earliest rays of the sun touch down in Maine, so the rhythm is simple: First in sunlight, first in night. I can't honestly say that New England is stranger than any other part of the country, but we get a head start.

In the following pages, we will commence a surreal journey across an area that, over the years, has inspired the dark imaginations of, among others, Nathaniel Hawthorne, Herman Melville, Shirley Jackson, Edith Wharton, H. P. Lovecraft, and Stephen King. Their writings perfectly reflect the New Englander's age-old appetite for the bizarre, the strange, and the unusual.

Clearly there is something different about this place—but what? That question will be the compass of our journey. We are, after all, looking for . . . *something*.

"What's weird around here?" Mark Moran likes to ask. We're not going to try to define "weird." We're like-minded creatures who recognize weirdness when we see it. That's what unites us—writers and readers—in our quest. There are others who simply don't get it, so perhaps this book is not for them. "We don't have anything weird," an employee at the Warren Anatomical exhibit told us. "We prefer to say they're unusual."

Okay. Fine. So we're seeking the unusual, the grotesque, the incongruous, the bizarre, and all the other fascinating qualities that have traditionally been excluded from conventional travel books.

We're tracking New England's unique populations, visible and invisible. We're seeking abandoned and unexplained architecture, alien flora and fauna, citizens demented and divine. We just have to adjust our eyes so we see what's under our feet, in our own backyards, or around the next turn. And we have to see it and record it before it's gone forever.

Before Mark Moran and Mark Sceurman inquired about local weirdness for their seminal *Weird N.J.*, others were asking the same thing about New England. Not just fiction writers, but journalists and chroniclers of the unconventional: Edward Rowe Snow, Alton Blackington, Robert Ellis Cahill, Curt Norris, and many others. Now it is up to you, me, and other intrepid souls like Loren Coleman, Joseph Durwin, Cheryl LeBeau, and Daniel Boudillion.

Luckily, there is still a lot to discover, for New England is a big place. In fact, with our total area of 66,667 square miles, it's far bigger than Old England. (For those of us tuned to meaningful coincidence, one can't help but ask if the first three digits can be accidental.)

The point is, New England not only exceeds the size of most states, it's also bigger than many countries. With a population hovering around 14 million, we have produced more than our share of oddballs, crackpots, and eccentrics. And who knows what manner of strangeness the vast tracts of unpopulated forest may still conceal?

So what's weird around here? A lot. Much of it's still out there waiting to be discovered. All this book can accomplish is to offer a sampling—appetizers, if you will—to whet your appetite for the grand feast that the region contains. We invite you to dine on the same staples that nourished those venerable Yankees already mentioned.

A trip across *Weird New England* is a journey through time and space. Your perceptions are guaranteed to change. So let's get started. The New England day is beginning.

The New England night is close behind. . . .

— *Joseph A. Citro*

Local Legends

Charles Fort once said, "We shall pick up an existence
by its frogs. . . ." Or something like that. I was
never too sure what he meant, because I was always
more inclined to say, "You can pick up on an existence
by its legends." Local legends, folklore, urban myths,
tall tales—they are the metaphorical lens through which
we can examine a population.

So what can we learn about New England by studying its folklore? Your guess is as good as mine, but let's
give it a whirl. In fact, out of respect for Mr. Fort, let's
start with frogs.

Connecticut Croakers

Windham, Connecticut, has a most unusual town seal:
a bullfrog. Odd in itself, but its new bridge over the
Willimantic River features four giant statues of frogs, each
twelve feet tall and weighing a solid ton. Each sits atop
an oversized spool of thread.

A spool of thread?

At first glance this seems like weirdness on top of weirdness. The thread, of course,
denotes the city's history of thread making. But what's with the giant bullfrogs?

It all began just over 250 years ago. During the summer of 1758, Windham was
suffering a terrible drought. At the same time, the town was anticipating an attack by
French and Indian forces from Canada. Probably no one was sleeping too soundly that
dry dark night in July when, just after midnight and following a long stillness, the
citizens were roused from their beds by a frightful caterwauling that filled the stifling
air. Most took cover, fearing infuriated Indians.

The volume of the unfamiliar dissonance increased to the point that people became convinced that Judgment Day was upon them. Many took to their knees, expecting at any moment to hear the blaring trumpets of Armageddon. Certain individuals swore they heard the names of townsfolk being called: "Dyer! Dyer!" "Elderkin! Elderkin!"

Because Colonels Dyer and Elderkin were prominent local lawyers, the general terror increased. People fled into the streets, peering skyward, expecting to meet their maker. Others, less religiously inclined, loaded their muskets, preparing for an onslaught of Indians. These armed citizens mounted a hill at the eastern side of the village, from which the sound seemed to be coming. What would they meet on the far side? Indians? Angels? Demons from the very bowels of hell?

By morning, the answer was all too clear, and without an exchange of bullets and thunderbolts. A certain millpond—forever after to be known as Frog Pond—had nearly fallen victim to the prevailing drought. A seemingly endless population of bullfrogs had apparently been fighting over what little water remained. As John Warner Barber wrote in his 1836 book *Connecticut Historic Collections,* "Long and obstinately [fought] was the contest, and many thousands of the combatants were found dead on both sides of the ditch the next morning."

While the townsfolk had been fearing the world's end or preparing to combat imaginary Indians, the local frogs had been battling over water. Hmmm. Perhaps we can judge a civilization by its frogs after all.

The Buried Bullfrog

In Brandon, Vermont, there's another strange but true frog story. It's even included in the town history. During the summer of 1865, workmen digging a new mine shaft made an impossible discovery: At a depth of 114 feet, they unearthed what appeared to be the petrified body of a giant bullfrog. This oversized amphibian was snugly packed in a pocket of hardened mud that had contoured precisely to its form. Experts guessed it must have been preserved there for thousands of years. Perhaps since the time of the great biblical flood.

The unusual find quickly attracted considerable attention; first, because the specimen was so perfectly preserved. Second, because it was found at so great a depth. And third, because of its remarkably large size. From the tip of its snout to the end of its spine, that frog measured fourteen inches! Unarguably a lot of bull!

As locals admired their find, things got weirder before their very eyes. The Brobdingnagian bullfrog started to twitch and jerk in grotesque spasms. Now fully animated, it began hopping backward in a spastic, convulsive manner.

Finally some sympathetic townsperson managed to seize the frog and transport it to a nearby pond. There it lived happily for many years. During summer nights, Brandon's giant bullfrog bellowed so loudly that it could be heard for miles around.

As a quick aside, the weird business of discovering frog life where no life should be is not unique to Brandon. In 1822, workers digging a well in Bridgewater, Vermont, discovered what they thought was a petrified frog buried under twenty-six feet of solid earth. When they brought it to the surface, it started twitching and hopping around.

And Burlington, Vermont's largest city, offers an interesting pair of stories. In the summer of 1786, on the intervale by the Winooski River, a Mr. Lane decided to dig a well. At twenty-five feet, he unearthed what appeared to be a large number of peculiar small rocks. These, he soon discovered, were actually live frogs. After being exposed to fresh air, they revived, leaped around happily for a while, and then died.

On October 12, 1807, Moses Catlin was digging a well near Burlington's University of Vermont. At a depth of about five feet, workers found six live frogs covered with tiny stones. On October 13, in the same well, they found two more frogs. On October 14, at eleven feet, five more living frogs appeared in hard gravelly soil.

Scientists at the time had no explanation for how frogs could survive while packed solidly in the bowels of the earth. What does it all mean? We can't say. But if you're looking for a pattern, all were found in towns beginning with B: Brandon, Bridgewater, Burlington. But the more important question, if we are to believe Mr. Fort, is, What can we pick up on an existence from these frogs? Well, it is a very deep subject, but it certainly appears that in Vermont, frogs don't croak.

And this brings us to the undisputed granddaddy of all Vermont local legends. . . .

Hibernating Hill Folk

In the not-so-good-old days, certain poverty-stricken Vermonters discovered a novel way of passing the long, grueling winter months: They slept through them. For over a century, whispered tales of the hibernating hill folk have echoed through the Green Mountains. The specifics of this peculiar practice were first publicly revealed in December 1887 on the front page of the state's largest newspaper, the *Montpelier Argus and Patriot.*

The reporter's apparently self-protective byline was simply "A.M." He revealed information from his deceased uncle's diary. Information that, then as now, seems unbelievable and horrifying. Uncle William, he wrote, had witnessed the techniques used by a wretchedly poor family of hill farmers to get their elderly and infirm through the winter without putting a drain on the meager food supply.

Their system was a hybrid of Yankee ingenuity, old-time folk medicine, and sheer gothic horror. Somehow, they had developed a procedure to literally freeze people alive. Like hibernating bears, the poor folk would sleep the winter away, to be revived again in the spring.

A.M. verified his uncle's bizarre claims. "I have been to the place," he wrote, "and seen the old log house where the events . . . took place, and . . . talked with an old man [whose] father was one of the parties operated on."

Although the chemical concoction's specific ingredients were not recorded, the process was thoroughly described. It began by drugging four men and two women, "one of the men," Uncle William wrote, "a cripple about 36 years old, the other five past the age of usefulness. . . ." The unconscious family members were stripped naked. Under the frosty glow of the winter moon, they

were carried outdoors and packed side by side on straw beds encased within a ten-by-six-foot wooden box.

Uncle William watched in horror as their noses, ears, and fingers slowly turned white. He saw their ghastly upturned faces assume a tallowy pallor. When the overseer judged them "ready," helpers placed cloth over their heads and packed more protective straw around them. Then they sealed the box to guard against predators.

Shivering from the cold and quaking from the sight before him, Uncle William ran inside, no longer able to endure the nightmare. In the weeks that followed, twenty-foot snowdrifts buried the sleepers for a quarter of the year.

What Uncle William had witnessed turned out to be more than a crude, perhaps merciful, form of euthanasia. Four months later his May 10 diary entry revealed an unexpected outcome. He returned to the cabin just as the Green Mountains were beginning to warm up, and he watched the sleepers' liberation from their icy crypt. Able-bodied men lifted their stone-stiff relatives into log troughs. Women poured hot water and a hemlock-based potion over them, creating a fragrant, steaming bath. Slowly, pallid faces began to brighten. Muscles twitched. Fingers flexed. Vitality returned. Carefully helped from their baths, the six were carried inside. Warmed by blankets, fire, and a hearty meal, the sleepers slowly revived after their long winter's nap.

The printed version of this remarkable story hibernated for almost half a century. Then, in 1939, Elbert S. Stevens of Bridgewater, Vermont, brought the original clipping to the attention of Bob Wilson of the *Rutland Herald*. The story was soon picked up by the *Boston Globe*, *Yankee* magazine, *The Old Farmer's Almanac*, and numerous books, periodicals, and newspapers from all around the world. Vermont became big news. Vermonters,

on the other hand, were portrayed as having a dark secret. The primitive ritual and the "operator's" apparent indifference to human life cast the state in an unsavory light.

Yet, because the story's grim details seemed like the product of a horror writer's imagination, many dismissed it as an especially grisly mountain myth. At the same time, earnest individuals—including some scientists—believed it. It was, after all, possible.

Researchers like Dr. Temple S. Fay of Philadelphia suggested this arcane Vermont "folk medicine" might someday be used to treat cancer and heart disease. Experiments at the University of Toronto buttressed the story when researchers demonstrated that a dog could be kept alive after freezing. The American Medical Association disclosed recent experiments in which humans were frozen, suspending all bodily functions for hours. An Illinois newspaper reported, "A man was restored to life after having been frozen in an unconscious sleep for five days and nights. . . ."

So the question remains: Had a semiliterate Vermont hill family stumbled on a stupendous medical discovery? Or, as the story jumped from publication to publication, had there been some misinterpretation, misquotation, or just plain mischief?

In his book *Inside New England*, editor Judson Hale relates an anecdote that perfectly illustrates this strange tale's unique position between fact and fantasy. He writes, "I once asked an old Vermont farm couple in the Montpelier area if either one of them truly believed the 'Frozen Death' story.

"'Certainly do,' the husband answered emphatically, without hesitation.

"Then the wife added, 'The only part I doubt is the thawing out.'"

Gray's Anatomy

Massachusetts, too, seems to have its live-forever contingent. Most notable among them is Ephraim Gray (or Graves, as he appears in some accounts).

The story starts during the first half of the nineteenth century in Malden, where Mr. Gray was a reclusive eccentric. Though highly intelligent, he was considered unpleasant, sullen, and rude. He was also mysterious. He didn't seem to have a profession, yet he always had lots of money. He even employed a manservant.

The two men lived in a big dark house near the center of town. Ephraim had no apparent affection for women and never married. He didn't appear at public events, took no interest in politics, and professed no religious affiliation.

But, day or night, people passing his house were likely to see Ephraim in an upstairs window, engaged in mysterious activity. Apparently, he had some kind of laboratory up there. Occasionally passersby recoiled from terrible odors wafting from inside. Sometimes the noxious chemical stench actually made people sick.

Then, in the late 1860s, word got out that Ephraim himself had taken sick. Soon after, news circulated that he had died. His own fault, everyone agreed, breathing those foul chemicals all the time.

Ephraim bequeathed all his worldly possessions to his devoted servant. But there was one catch: The servant had to make sure nothing was done to Gray's body prior to burial. No autopsy, no cuts, no sewing, no embalming. "And why not?" the funeral director demanded to know.

The servant explained that Mr. Gray had been racing against time, trying to develop a chemical formula for eternal life. If he'd lived longer, he might have succeeded. Though his research was cut short, he had nonetheless determined that his formula would preserve tissue perfectly for years. If true, it could replace all commercial embalming products, making the servant a rich man.

So Ephraim's body was placed in a vault at the Malden Cemetery. The servant died soon afterward, and gradually Ephraim Gray's extraordinary claims were almost forgotten.

Almost . . .

Twenty years later, a student at Harvard Medical School heard the story from a friend. Intrigued, a small group of young doctors traveled to Malden, stole quietly into the cemetery, and opened Gray's crypt.

There was something strange about Gray's anatomy. His cadaver displayed none of the corruption associated with two long decades in the tomb. In fact, he looked very much alive. New England folklorist Edward Rowe Snow describes the scene this way: "When they pried open the vault, the investigators found that the corpse was almost as it had been in life, with the exception that it had grown brown and hard, and was truly dreadful to behold. Although in life [Gray] had not been an attractive man, apparently after death he had changed into a hideous, devilish caricature of the being they recalled."

Satisfied, yet eager to leave, the students closed the vault, resealed everything, and returned to Boston. Later, discreet inquiries told them that Gray's chemical formula was lost. And there the whole story might have ended. Except for one thing: The tomb was opened again.

Early in the twentieth century, while relocating certain graves, the Malden Cemetery crew opened Mr. Gray's tomb. His body had vanished! Astonished authorities launched a major investigation. After weeks of questioning, examinations, and head scratching, their findings were frustratingly inconclusive.

Everyone kept coming back to one annoying detail: There was no way the body could have been removed without anyone knowing it. The seal the medical students had used to reclose the crypt remained unbroken. Yet Ephraim Gray was gone.

So where did he go? Had he in fact discovered the secret of prolonged life? After more than twenty years of hibernation, did he get up and walk away? Or, more likely, could the Harvard students have been grave robbers? Had they stolen Gray's well-preserved corpse before resealing the tomb?

In his own vastly different version of the tale, Edward Rowe Snow holds that the medical students removed the corpse's head while studying the cadaver. Immediately moans and phantom footsteps within the tomb ignited fear in the young physicians, so they abandoned the body and fled.

After that, the tomb became a

shunned spot. Mr. Snow writes, "It became known that, in the night at the stroke of twelve, the iron tomb door would fly open. Indeed, few Malden residents dared be caught there to see the fearful thing happen. . . . [The] tomb door would swing ajar. Then the horrific, gruesome remains of Ephraim [Gray] in its mildewed garments would crawl out of the coffin. Pulling itself up by the door ledge, it began to stalk about the cemetery as if in search of its head. At the first sign of daylight, it went back to rest."

During the cemetery relocation, Ephraim Gray's tomb was buried forever, putting an end to his midnight ramblings. But the question remains to this day: When the tomb was finally sealed forever, was Malden's ambulating corpse in or out?

Dreadful Doc Benton

New Hampshire has its own contender for eternal life. For nearly two hundred years, a strangely agile, black-caped figure with long white hair has been spotted occasionally around Mount Moosilauke in the White Mountains. Most agree it is all that remains of Doctor Thomas Benton.

While the figure is definitely not a ghost, it is by no means entirely human. Supposedly, it's the result of an ungodly transformation that started when young Thomas Benton came back to New Hampshire from medical school in Heidelberg, Germany.

Because the town that bears his family name picked up the tab for Tom's education, he dutifully returned to oversee the health of his benefactors. Apparently, he was a brilliant and compassionate physician, and his services were sought by people far and wide. But no offer of a better situation could tempt him from the town and people he loved.

Then, around 1816, something happened. Perhaps he was rejected by the young woman he cherished. Perhaps he lost his fiancée to disease. Or perhaps something went wrong with the wiring in his own brain. Whatever the case, Tom lost interest in his medical practice and took to the woods, where he set up a laboratory in a deserted shack.

There he opened a trunk that had been willed to him by Professor Stockmeyer, one of his teachers at the Heidelberg medical school. In life, Professor Stockmeyer had been shunned by his colleagues because of his research into the forbidden secrets of eternal youth. Now Tom Benton shunned his community to continue those same unholy experiments. Living like a hermit, he made only occasional forays into town for supplies. If anyone ventured to his cabin to beg for medical treatment, Tom would turn them away.

Eventually a series of animal deaths startled the residents of the area. A cow was discovered dead in the barn. Lifeless horses were found in their stalls. Bloated sheep dotted the green hillside like balls of snow. There seemed to be no reason for these numerous deaths, but all shared a single mysterious attribute: Each animal had a fresh wound behind its left ear—a red swelling with a white pinprick in the center.

It wasn't long before people began suffering a similar fate. First, a corpse vanished from the back of an undertaker's wagon. When it was later discovered discarded in some bushes near Warren, there was a second corpse beside it. Each had a wound behind its left ear.

A small cluster of citizens timidly ventured to Dr. Benton's cabin to see if he could shed some light on these medical mysteries, but they found his cabin abandoned. Had he gone missing too? A search was launched for his body, but he seemed to have vanished.

However, in the months to follow, hunters or hikers would see him in some wooded part of the thirty-square-mile Moosilauke area. He was always said to be wearing a black cape, moving rapidly, with long white hair flowing out behind him.

In November 1825, a Benton woman heard her daughter scream. She looked up from her laundry to see a black-caped figure carrying her little girl into the woods. The woman's husband rushed off in pursuit. Neighbors joined him. They followed the footprints to Little Tunnel Ravine, a box canyon from which there could be no escape. Yet weirdly, the footprints ended abruptly.

Suddenly the bewildered men heard laughter coming from overhead. Above them, they recognized Dr. Benton. Somehow, holding the struggling girl, he had ascended the stark cliff. When her father begged for her return, Doc Benton obliged. He hurled the screaming child off the cliff.

Unfortunately, no one was quick enough to catch her, and the child was dashed on the canyon floor.

Sightings of, and confrontations with, the demonic doctor continued. In 1860, two loggers vanished from the mountaintop. One was later found, bearing the odd wound. The other was gone forever. In 1901, Mr. Tomaso, a brakeman on a logging railroad, was found dead beside the track. He hadn't fallen from the train; the only mark on him was that peculiar wound behind his left ear.

In recent years, hikers on the Moosilauke slopes have continued to report seeing a mysterious caped figure in the woods. Is it Doc Benton? One person sees him disappearing behind a tree. Others might spot a wrinkled hand or pant leg moving quickly out of sight.

In the 1970s, a Dartmouth student took a solo hike in Jobidunk Ravine. When he didn't return, searchers went out. They found him easily enough, but he was in a bad way, wandering aimlessly with a glazed look on his face. His friends realized he was in shock. Rescuers transported him to the Ravine Camp, where an emergency vehicle moved him to the hospital in Hanover.

Though he recovered from cuts, bruises, and a fractured skull, he was curiously vague about what had happened to him. Eventually the story came out: He told one of his friends that while he was climbing on a ledge, a hand shot out through an opening in the rocks and shoved him!

In 2002, another student had a near run-in with the doctor. On a solo hike close to the summit of Moosilauke, he found the print of an old-style boot in the mud of an unused trail. It was in a place where there had been no tracks fifteen minutes earlier.

Many people believe that Doc Benton, or whatever he has become, still stalks the slopes of New Hampshire's Mount Moosilauke. They theorize that by kidnapping pets, livestock, and people, his experiments eventually led to the secret of prolonged life.

Today he would be an impossibly old man. Since the murders and organ harvesting seem to have stopped, we must ask, What is he doing now? Perhaps he's looking for that elusive arcane formula that will finally permit him to die.

Water Music

There are many kinds of immortality. We've often heard, for example, that a composer's music can make him immortal. And who can argue? Aren't Mozart, Bach, and Beethoven just as much alive today as they ever were? At least in terms of their tunes. But a wholly different kind of musical immortality seems to be at work in Connecticut: music from the watery deep.

There you'll find a lovely body of water called Gardner Lake. On certain warm, still summer evenings, people near the shore—but especially those in boats—report hearing a strange, faraway refrain that sounds as if it's being played on a piano. No matter how carefully they listen, it is impossible to determine exactly where the music is coming from. But young folks suspect what the old-timers know: It comes from the water itself.

In the past, certain adventurous souls used scuba gear to investigate. What they found more than fifty feet down may explain the mystery, but only in part. There, on the bottom of Gardner Lake, divers discovered a full-sized house, still partially furnished. In fact, they said the furniture inside seemed remarkably well preserved.

The submerged house has been there for a long while. Its only inhabitants now are fish, eels, and an array of underwater houseplants. Nothing there could play the waterlogged piano that still stands in the corner of the parlor.

On the other hand, the mystery of how the house got there is easy to solve. While it was still securely on land, its owner hired a contractor to move the whole thing to a beautiful lot he had purchased on the opposite shore. How to get it there was a perfect example of Yankee ingenuity at work: They'd wait till the lake froze over, then jack up the house, put it on sleds, and slide it across the ice, furniture and all.

In the winter of 1899–1900, the process began. All went swimmingly, but slower than planned. By nightfall, the crew had dragged the building only halfway. Too cold and tired to continue, they decided to complete the job in the morning.

Next day, however, they were horrified to find the house leaning dangerously. It had broken partway through the frozen surface. Obviously, there was no way to pull it out, so they rescued what furniture they could. The piano was too big, too heavy, and too dangerous to remove.

Come spring, everyone in town gathered to watch the house sink. Surprisingly, it floated around for a while, eventually bubbling its way to the bottom. As far as we know, no one was killed in the process, so ghosts are unlikely suspects. But till this day, someone, or something, causes that mysterious music. Those who've investigated say its only source can be that old piano. Those who have heard it can't seem to forget it.

Personally, we suspect the only explanation is witchcraft. After all, Gardner Lake is in the town of Salem.

Lake Bottom Real Estate

In my hometown of Salem, Connecticut, we have a local legend that you can actually hear! The story all started back in 1899 when a homeowner who lived on one side of Salem's Gardner Lake contracted a construction company to move his house to a new plot of land on the opposite side of the water. Unfortunately, the ice cracked under the weight of the building. Today it rests on the bottom some fifty feet beneath the lake's surface. Chillingly, several fishermen have reported hearing the faint strains of piano music floating on still air while alone on the lake in the half-light of the early morning. So be careful where you drop anchor on Gardner Lake. You might just be dropping in on one home's watery grave.—*Dennis M.*

Emily's Bridge to Immortality

In the land of legend and lore, perhaps the most direct route to immortality is simply to become a ghost. Vermont's most enduring and active local legend involves a spirit with enough sense to take up residence in a historic structure, one that is guaranteed perpetual care, a covered bridge.

To the eye, the Gold Brook Bridge in Stowe is not unlike any of the other scenic covered bridges that span New England waterways. Some sources say this one-lane, fifty-foot structure is the oldest covered bridge in the country. Its builder, John N. Smith of Moscow, Vermont, designed it with many unique features and bragged that it would last forever.

Scores of people have had run-ins with its resident specter, known only as Emily. Encounters range from benign to terrifying. On the least menacing end of the scare spectrum are the experiences of tourists with cameras. Photographs taken on the bridge don't come out. Or the photographer will discover that otherwise perfect prints include puzzling, blurry blemishes that weren't there when the photos were snapped. Recently, we received a photograph from a newly married couple who had honeymooned in Vermont. The photo showed the bridge with a young girl standing in front. She looked perfectly human. A girl on a bridge. Only problem is that there was no girl on the bridge when the picture was taken. The photographer intended to shoot the bridge and insisted he would not have snapped the picture if a girl had been in the way.

Other witnesses see inexplicable things like flashing white lights with no visible source. Some visitors swear they hear an eerie voice from nowhere uttering words that can't quite be understood. When the voice can be understood, it sounds like a woman crying for help.

Lights and voices combined in the early '70s when Stowe resident Ed Rhodes and his friend Jim Holden were chasing thunderstorms. Resting in the shelter of Emily's Bridge, they waited for a storm to pass. There, in the semidarkness, Jim became unaccountably frightened. "Let's get out of here," he said.

As he started to drive away, Ed asked, "What's the matter?"

"I heard somebody hollering for help."

"Then wait a minute. Maybe somebody really needs help."

When they turned around, Ed saw what he described as "little tiny specks of light, like strobe lights. But," he added, "the funny thing was, the lights did not illuminate the interior of the bridge."

Sometimes spectral contacts are a bit more aggressive: Hats are whisked away on windless days. People feel inexplicable chills in the summer's heat, or warm spots manifest in the dead of winter. One man witnessed handprints materializing on the foggy windshield of his car—but no hands were there to cause them.

All this sounds pretty benign, but there are more menacing encounters. In the old days, horses and cows crossing the bridge would unaccountably bolt. Farmers would then discover long, bloody gashes left, perhaps, by some ghostly nails. More recently, automobiles occasionally have suffered the same fate when parallel scratches appear in otherwise perfect paint jobs. In 2003, a young woman was videotaping the bridge when she suddenly felt a searing pain in her arm. She looked down to see—and videotape—a gash mysteriously opening in her forearm.

So who is the strange lingering soul who hasn't quite made it across the bridge and into the afterlife? No one seems to know for sure. It is more a matter of convenience than history that she is called Emily, for no

one knows her real name. Many accounts say that she died by her own hand, on that covered bridge, around 1849. The best story holds that Emily was a young Stowe woman who fell in love with a man who, for whatever reason, failed to pass muster with her family. Forbidden to marry, the love-struck youngsters decided to elope. They planned to meet on the covered bridge at midnight.

The appointed hour came and went, but the young man never showed. Shattered, the poor girl didn't know what to do. She couldn't run away alone. Nor could she return to her "I told you so" parents. Perhaps overreacting a bit, the distraught young woman hanged herself from a rafter on the bridge.

Now in spirit form, she's still there, waiting for her lover to return, getting angrier and angrier as time goes by.

Legend or Legit?

There are many types of immortality. Roger Williams, for example, will live forever as the founder of Rhode Island. But he may be immortal in another sense as well. In any event, he is the subject of a great mystery that continues to this day.

History recalls the Reverend Roger Williams as a religious nonconformist, a contentious sort who was always getting in trouble with New England Puritans. He was continually haranguing about some unpopular cause: religious freedom, church and state separation, compensating Native Americans for their land, stuff like that. In consequence, he got himself tossed out of Massachusetts in 1635.

The next year he purchased lands from the Narragansett tribe and founded Providence, where he welcomed religious dissenters and practiced his democratic ideals. By 1654, he'd become president of the combined colonies of Providence, Newport, Narragansett, and Warwick. He died in 1683 and was laid to rest beside his wife on their farm, buried in the shade of an old apple tree.

Almost immediately he became the subject of legend. Folks thereabouts began to say that anyone who ate apples from that graveside tree would become as contentious as Roger Williams. They'd fuss, question things, and become generally ornery and outspoken. But there were far stranger legends to come.

Flash forward to the spring of 1860. Members of the Roger Williams Monument Association decided Rhode Island's founder deserved a grander gravestone in a finer spot. But when they set out to disinter Mr. and Mrs.

Williams's remains, they were in for a shock. The bodies were gone! No casket, no flesh, no bones. Nothing.

Where did they go? Had they joined the ranks of Rhode Island's famous vampires? Were they the victims of a grave robbing? After so many years, people feared it would be impossible to solve such a mystery. But as it turns out, the culprit was standing right in front of them. It was a shady character indeed: the old apple tree!

The bodies were there after all, but in a much altered state. In the passing decades, the tree's roots had penetrated the couple's coffins, taking nourishment from their rotting remains. One large root now filled the spot formerly occupied by Roger Williams's head. It also penetrated the chest cavity, traveling along the spine and continuing to form legs. There it angled upward, creating feet. An identical process had displaced the body of Mrs. Williams. The hungry roots had completely absorbed the couple, leaving twisted wooden replicas in their place. To the amazement of all, the distended tubers bore a remarkable resemblance to recumbent human forms. The thick main shafts with their weave work of veiny branches looked for all the world like the circulatory system of the human body.

Today these historic roots are said to be preserved by the Rhode Island Historical Society: the Reverend Roger Williams and his wife are hidden in the basement of the John Brown House at 52 Power Street in Providence.

So is this story legend or legit? Well, this sort of investigation takes courage. Here's the historical society's phone number: 401-331-8575. Are you brave enough to call and ask?

A Fiery Phantom

In compiling a smorgasbord of New England's local legends it would be a mistake to exclude ghost ships. These vexing vessels are generally spotted from the seacoast, but even rivers and landlocked lakes can support them. But how can a ship have a soul? That seems to argue against the notion that ghosts are the spirits of the departed. Yet evidence of ghosts-of-things-that-never-lived is deeply rooted in local lore.

The world's most famous ghost ship is the so-called *Flying Dutchman,* whose captain and crew are cursed to sail the seas till doomsday. But America's most illustrious example comes from New England. She's called the *Palatine,* though that was probably not her registered name. For over two hundred years, she has appeared in a well-defined stretch of water off Rhode Island. This Yankee *Flying Dutchman* is easily recognized because it's eternally ablaze.

Before sailing into the spirit realm, she was most probably a British ship, called the *Princess Augusta,* heading for Philadelphia in 1738. Her decks were crowded with German immigrants from the Palatinate region, eager for a new life.

After the ship was three months at sea, food and fresh water were scarce. During Christmas week, somewhere in that Devil's Triangle formed by the mainland, Montauk Point, and Block Island, the vessel was menaced by a murderous snowstorm. Weak from hunger and stressed beyond reason, the crew mutinied, murdered the captain, plundered the ship, then took off in the lifeboats. The ship tossed helplessly at the mercy of wind and wave until she rammed the rocky shore of Block Island.

Block Islanders, we may be sure, have their own version of the story. But, thanks to John Greenleaf Whittier's 1867 poem "The Palatine," the islanders are portrayed as looters who stormed the beached vessel. Finding nothing of value, they torched the ship, then sent it and its passengers back out to sea.

A more humane telling, one that's closer to the truth, says the Block Islanders helped the seventeen survivors by transporting them to Simon Ray's farm on the island. Some regained their health, but most perished. It is a fact that their marked graves may be seen on the island. The ship, damaged beyond repair, would soon become a navigational hazard, so the islanders burned it. A freak wind sent the flaming vessel back to sea.

This gentler rendition of the story has an especially gothic detail. As the ship sailed away, screams echoed from deep within the flames. One woman was still on board. Rescue attempts failed because, terrified and perhaps mad, she refused to leave the deck. The islanders watched helplessly as the blazing wreck, with its sole crazed occupant, drifted slowly out of sight.

But not for long . . .

The ship is still spotted, generally on the anniversary of the fire. It is perceived as a queer crimson light on the darkening horizon. As newsman Edwin C. Hill reported in 1934, "There are people living on Block Island who will tell you, with their hand on the Book, that they have gazed seaward in the blackness of the night, startled by a bright radiance at sea, and have watched, with straining eyes, while the *Palatine,* blazing from trunk to keelson, swept along the horizon.

"For many years [the abandoned woman's] screams were said to accompany that queer crimson light on the darkening horizon—the light of the *Palatine* forever burning, yet never consumed."

Whatever it may be, this extraordinary luminous phenomenon has been witnessed frequently enough to keep the *Palatine* afloat for over 250 years.

Violent Violette

Just about as far north as you can go in the state of Maine, way up in northern Aroostook County, by the border with New Brunswick, Canada, lies the historic town of Fort Kent. While many of the local legends of this remote region have never been committed to paper, it is an area rich in history and mystery.

There, at the end of a dirt road that runs perpendicular to the St. John River, you will find Violette Settlement, part of the original Acadian French settlement between the Madawaska and Fish rivers. The whole small village is regarded as haunted, but the preternatural entities involved are not the typical ancestral-type ghosts of New England lore. Culturally, the area is French Catholic and Maliseet Indian, so a hybrid of supernatural suspects has to be considered, for much of the activity seems more demonic than ghostly. In fact, certain people will tell you that the whole town is not haunted, but demon infested.

Around 1950, a farm family in Violette Settlement came under supernatural siege, perhaps attracted by the godless activities of the father. He was habitually violent and abusive toward his wife and children. He dabbled sexually not only with his daughters but also with certain of his farm animals. Eventually the women either ran off or, as some people believe, were murdered one by one and stashed in shallow graves in the woods.

No doubt the devil saw an amiable companion in this ghastly man.

For the children, the only respite had been to attend the local schoolhouse. But even that escape route was cut short when the oldest boy turned sixteen. His father ordered him to quit school and work full-time on the farm.

But the boy had excelled at school. Unlike his socially and intellectually challenged siblings, he had a will to

learn that might have taken him far from Violette Settlement. Now that avenue of escape was gone. At home full-time, there was no getting away from his unrelenting father. The lad was a veritable slave, forced to work from sunup to sunset without food or rest. If he stopped even for a moment, his father would beat him unmercifully.

One night the boy reached his breaking point. He cried out, "If this is God's will, then give me the devil! I am sick to death of drudging for my father. Since I am in hell already, I will become the devil if I must!"

Since demonic entities were never far from his father's farm, one must have overheard the boy's invitation. Shortly afterward he became possessed by a demon. It was obvious in his behavior. He was able to work harder, faster, and

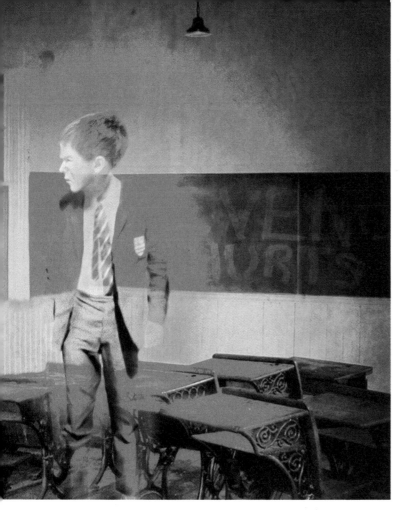

longer than any other man. Stranger still, he never grew tired or hungry. Unfortunately, this demon-driven labor eventually took a toll on the son's body. Though it made the demon inside stronger and stronger, it killed the boy.

After he was laid to rest, the hatred and anger that had been trapped inside were released. These malignant forces remained as a malevolent, lingering presence around the farm.

Soon after, the father was discovered dead in his barn. Although no cause of death could be determined, some suspected he had been blasted away by the pent-up rage released when his son expired. When the farmhouse burned to the ground, people were certain the devil was behind it all.

Its fury spent, the son's spirit now returned to the only place he had ever felt comfortable: the Violette Settlement schoolhouse. There are those who believe his benign ghost still haunts the old school's third floor. And some say that on certain nights the father's ghost can be seen as well, angrily patrolling the grounds outside, walking around and around the building while the boy's wounded spirit remains safely inside.

As further evidence that Violette Settlement may be demon infested, consider the incidents that took place around 1970. An "invisible bad man" did, or rather didn't, appear on the scene. His MO was to play with the local children. But his idea of playing was covering the kids with scratches, then sending them home in tears, bruised and battered. No description was possible, because he was invisible; several victims said so. And there was no evidence of collusion among the nonwitnesses.

Remember, this is a strong Roman Catholic community, so the village priest had the remedy for such shenanigans. Violette Settlement's invisible bad man was finally driven away through exorcism. The priest would show up at the homes of the afflicted children, bless the house, then instruct the mother to open all the doors and windows and drive the entity outside with a broom. Apparently, it worked.

Around 1980, a more tangible entity arrived in Violette Settlement. A number of people reported seeing some kind of unfamiliar creature. Descriptions all agreed that it had a beastlike face, but it stood upright on its hind legs, like a man. In every case, it was described as wearing a hood. One housewife swore it was a ghost, but its description makes it sound more demonic than ghostly. Again the village priest came to the rescue, suggesting exorcism through the ritual of opening the doors and windows and sweeping the evil away.

Satan's Kingdom

New England has no shortage of locales named in honor of the Evil One. In Connecticut, for example, there is the Devil's Kitchen in Burlington, the Devil's Pulpit in Hamden, and the Devil's Mouth in Redding. You can taste the Devil's Dripping Pan in Branch Brook, jump the Devil's Gap in Brookfield, and spit into the Devil's Gorge in Weston. There's a Devil's Jump in Derby, a Devil's Plunge in Morris, and a Devil's Rock in Old Saybrook and another in Portland. There are five Devil's Dens, four Devil's Back Bones, and two Devil's Footprints.

Just outside New Hartford is an area known by perhaps the most colorful and majestic name of all of the abodes of the Prince of Darkness—Satan's Kingdom. What is today a recreation area famous for its hiking and canoeing adventures was once seen as an infamously dangerous land and a bastion of the lawless. Local clergy gave the area its name centuries ago. Descriptions from the eighteenth century tell of the sort of people who were attracted to its forbidding wilds: "Indians, Negroes, and renegade whites" claimed the area as their own home turf, from which they would venture out to rob, steal, and otherwise terrorize the law-abiding local citizens. Legends say that Satan himself once claimed the area as his own, until the angel Gabriel decided the area was too idyllic and cleared out the dark lord and his band of demons.

These days Satan's Kingdom is a tranquil and scenic state recreation area. Though it no longer seems to deserve its demonic nickname, it still does offer canoeists some wicked Class III rapids to shoot along the West Branch of the Farmington River.

The Devil's Hopyard

Just a few miles north of the point where Routes 82 and 156 intersect in East Haddam, Connecticut, is a notorious spot known as the Devil's Hopyard. Stories have been told of its strange nature since even before European settlers moved into the area in the seventeenth century. Native Americans claimed that this 860-acre area, which features the Chapman Falls of the Eight Mile River, was home to a god. Upon arriving and hearing this, Puritan settlers actually thought that the wild land was more apt to be home to the devil and gave it its present moniker.

Under the Chapman Falls are rocks that have perfectly round potholes in them. While geologists might tell you that these strange pockmarks are the result of swirling eddies of water boring away at the stone, local lore tells a more diabolical tale. Legend has it that these curious depressions were drilled into the stone by the tail of none other than Satan himself.

Some stories say that the evil one has been seen sitting on a boulder at the top of the Chapman Falls. Others have seen and heard strange moving shapes, and in 1999 five men claimed to have been accosted by demonic creatures.

Devil's Den

Within the town of Sterling, Connecticut, is a large cave said to be the home of the devil, due to its strange features. Known as the Devil's Den, the cavern is circular, one hundred feet around, and has two fifty-foot-deep fissures, one of which serves as the entryway into the lair.

Curiously, this entryway also features a depression that extends to the outside, forming a natural chimney. There is also a natural staircase within the den that extends from the top all the way to the bottom of the rock wall. The constantly cold cave has often been explored, and many stories have been told of sightings of evil beings within it.

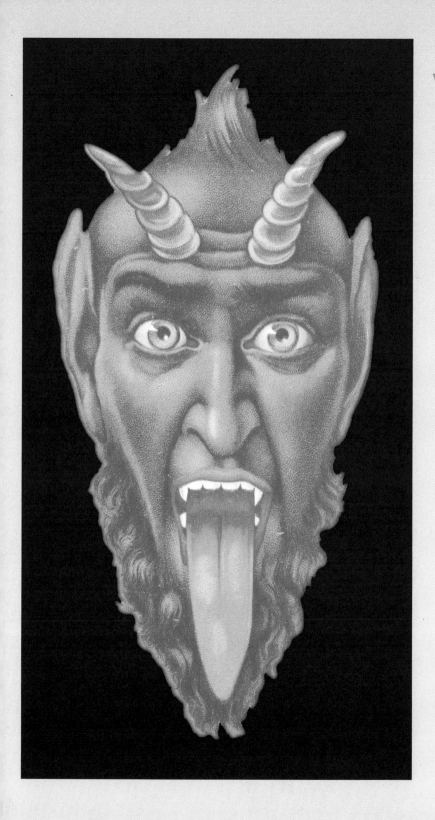

The Devil's Footprint

Manchester, Maine, is the home of a legendary piece of stone known as the Devil's Footprint. The story goes like this: Construction workers were laying down a new road in Manchester when they hit an unexpected snag. A large boulder blocked their path, and no amount of effort or equipment could get it to budge. Fed up, one man began cursing and proclaimed that he would give his soul to the devil if the rock was moved.

The next morning the workers trudged back to the spot where their progress had stopped. The rock had miraculously been moved yards away, onto the property of a local cemetery across from the Manchester Meeting House. Imprinted on it were some strange shapes. One was a man's footprint, and the other was a three-toed footprint. Supposedly, this is the footprint of Satan himself.

The man who challenged the devil was never seen again.

Efforts have been made over the years to chisel down or sandblast away the footprints. No amount of work has been able to remove them.

Another version of the Devil's Footprint story tells of a local farmer who had fallen upon some very hard times. He made a deal with the devil to sell his soul if he would be able to harvest enough crops to pay off all of his debts. He did so, but when the devil came to collect his soul, he refused. A chase ensued, and the man wound up climbing atop a structure on his property. The devil followed. Both of them jumped off at the same time, landing on top of a large stone next to the building. Their footprints have been embedded in the stone ever since. –*Chris G.*

Ancient
Mysteries

ew England is a misnomer. There is really nothing new about the hills and dales of the Northeast. Sure, common wisdom is that it all began when the Pilgrims collided with Plymouth Rock in 1620. But the question is, What did they find when they picked themselves up and looked around? Overwhelming evidence suggests Miles Standish and the crew were just one of myriad groups who blundered through, many traveling from places far more exotic than Merrie Old England. (And if it was so merrie, why did they leave in the first place?)

Berkeley's Sign-in Rock

A lot of pre-Pilgrim pilgrims may have signed in at a mysterious rock once situated near the mouth of the Taunton River in Berkeley, Massachusetts. As far as anyone can tell, it is the oldest inscribed rock in North America. Known as Dighton Rock, this forty-ton boulder has been puzzling people for centuries. Its western surface is completely covered with a variety of organized markings: writing, pictures, dates, and the like.

We know it is old because it was first studied and sketched by Dr. John Danforth in 1680. Later, Cotton Mather became fascinated with it. Around 1712, he copied the complex hodgepodge of inscriptions and sent them off to the Royal Society in London to be deciphered. Apparently, the London guys are still working on a translation; they have yet to send it back.

Since then, innumerable scholars here and abroad have taken their turn trying to crack the strange hieroglyphics. According to various interpretations, they have been attributed to Native Americans (unlikely), English settlers (didn't they have better things to do than spend hours creating puzzles for subsequent generations?), the Vikings (specifically, Leif Eriksson), the Portuguese

(Miguel Corte Real, whose signature seems to have been identified), the Italians (Verrazano, before he went on to build the bridge in New York), nameless Phoenician explorers, and, of course, hoaxers, who always step in just in time to save the day whenever experts are baffled.

Some individuals venture that the markings might even be the collected work of all of the above, comparing Dighton Rock to a graffiti-covered boulder along a highway, where every passing pre-Columbian left his John Hancock.

On the off chance that Dighton Rock is not the product of prehistoric hoaxers, and to preserve what may have been a favorite tourist spot for thousands of years (or possibly to maintain any revenue flow it is capable of generating), the state of Massachusetts moved Dighton Rock in 1974. Today, protected from erosion and modern graffiti artists, the rock is installed in a small museum along with other exhibits and explanations of the carvings.

Countless Conundrums

Even if we were to join the naysayers and brand Dighton Rock a hoax, how are we to explain countless other out-of-place oddities that keep popping up throughout all six New England states . . . and all over North America?

There is the carved Celtic head found in Searsmont, Maine, now exhibited at the Sturbridge Village Museum. And the puzzling Bourne Stone once used as a step in an Indian church on Cape Cod. Someone turned it over to reveal Celtic-Iberic characters that translate as "Hanno takes possession of this place." (Hanno was a Carthaginian explorer of the Atlantic circa 425 B.C.) Two Roman spoons and a Roman coin were dug up in Ipswich, Massachusetts, in the nineteenth century, and then there's the granite head that was unearthed in Essex, Massachusetts, in 1810. Then presumed to be Roman, today it has been reinterpreted as an ancient Celtic carving. Four Roman coins that date from the fourth century B.C. were found on the Dane Street Beach at Beverly, Massachusetts.

And the list goes on and on and on.

An Ancient Stone Keeps Its Secrets

One of the most puzzling and mysterious out-of-place objects now resides at the Museum of New Hampshire History in Concord. It is commonly referred to simply as the Mystery Stone, a perfect appellation because no one has any idea what it is.

It was discovered in 1872 by laborers digging a ditch not far from Lake Winnipesaukee, in the town of Meredith, New Hampshire. Embedded in a clump of earth about three feet down, it might have been summarily tossed away had not Seneca Ladd, a collector of Indian relics, realized there was something unusual about it. He carefully broke away the encrusting soil to discover a smooth, egg-shaped stone decorated with finely carved designs.

The object is four inches long and weighs just eighteen ounces. Its surface is covered with ten distinctly different designs carved with extraordinary precision. Within a small perfect circle, which could represent the sun or moon, are images of a bird or a bee in flight, a deer's leg, and what might be a bear's paw or a tooth. Above the circle there's a three-sided Indian teepee and an artfully formed ear of corn with seventeen perfect kernels in each row. There is also a delicate spiral and a precisely executed eight-pointed star. Four arrows, or perhaps spears, are crossed, seeming to form the letter M.

Hmmmmmmm…? For Mystery, maybe?

What some people consider to be the stone's most puzzling feature covers one entire side: a human face that is definitely not Native American. The features seem to be Aztec, Eskimo, or possibly Polynesian.

But its most vexing feature is a tapering hole running through its center, top to bottom. It's roughly one-quarter inch wide, narrowing to about one-eighth inch. The reason for the strange shape is still unknown.

Seneca Ladd kept the stone in his collection until his death, when it was purchased by D. V. Coe, whose widow donated it to the New Hampshire Historical Society. Questions still surround the Mystery Stone: Who made it, and for what purpose? When was it created? Do the odd, seemingly unrelated images convey some code or message?

And perhaps most mysterious of all: Why would someone take the time to create the intricate carving, only to abandon his handiwork in a wild, untraveled part of the New Hampshire wilderness?

The Mysterious Mounds Root Cellars or Ancient Dwellings?

As puzzling as the smorgasbord of odd objects found all around New England may be, what really confounds the imagination is mysterious structures—from isolated buildings to what must have been whole villages—all made from stone.

My own experience with New England's megalithic mysteries began when I was in high school back in Chester, Vermont. Around 1965, my pal Rick Bates and I were tromping around in the woods up behind my family place: boys in the act of being boys. The first oddity we noticed was a series of low rock platforms. They were slightly raised rectangles of small stones on the forest floor, roughly the size of graves. At the time, they piqued our curiosity a little, but we quickly dismissed them as burial places and were too respectful, or lazy, to start digging them up. We continued hiking.

After a while, we came upon what appeared to be a mound of earth. It was a little out of sync with the rest of the landscape, like a bump on an otherwise perfect behind. So we moved closer to get a better look.

What we found was an earth-covered structure, roughly ten feet high, with small trees and wild shrubbery growing from it. It looked something like an igloo, made not of ice but of stone. As we circumnavigated the thing, we got the surprise of our lives: There was an opening in it! Could this be a tunnel leading to the very bowels of the Vermont hills?

Naturally, we climbed in. We found that the interior walls were fitted stones free of mortar; the roof was massive stone slabs. Each must have weighed several tons. This was no random deposit of stones; it was definitely man-made. The place gave us an uncomfortable feeling because we had no idea what we were looking at.

Much later I discovered that Chester's stone structure, like nearly a hundred others throughout the state, is at the heart of an archaeological controversy: No one knows who made it, when, or why. And how do we explain the strange markings on many of these mounds? Who carved the stone faces, wildlife, and fertility symbols often found in their proximity?

Mainstream archaeologists insist these igloolike sites are nothing more than Colonial root cellars and the markings are scrapes from passing glaciers or the scars of Colonial plows.

Dr. Cook's theory was that Vermont is dappled with the remains of mining settlements constructed by prehistoric Celtic copper-seekers.

Other archaeologists, however, have different theories. The late Dr. Warren Cook of Castleton State College was one of a growing number of scholars who feel that ancient sites suggest ancient settlements.

Dr. Cook proposed that much of Vermont and many parts of New England had been colonized by seagoing Celts during the Bronze Age, a time when European copper supplies seemed nearly exhausted. Dr. Cook's theory was that Vermont is dappled with the remains of mining settlements constructed by prehistoric Celtic copper-seekers. It makes sense: The Green Mountains are full of copper; Vermont was the country's leading producer during the Civil War. In short, Vermont and much of New England may have been settled by Europeans at least two thousand years before Columbus.

Or Vermont's mysterious stone sites might be religious structures, shrines, or communal mausoleums, places for returning the ashes of the dead to the womb of mother earth. Many sites have been irrefutably shown to have astronomical significance. As with Stonehenge in England, archaeoastronomers have confirmed astronomical alignment during solstices and equinoxes.

And the strange markings etched on the rock walls? They might be a language, called ogham, that is also seen on similar structures in Europe and can be translated. If so, perhaps retired Harvard professor Barry Fell's interpretation of an inscribed stone in Royalton is Vermont's original name. The inscription says, "Precincts of the gods of the land beyond the sunset."

Has a nice ring to it, doesn't it?

Short Stairway to Confusion

In Jim Brandon's wonderful book *Weird America,* he makes brief reference to a mysterious site in South Windham, Maine. The entire entry reads, "A rocky bluff on private land here contains a flight of stairs, about 25 feet off the ground, beginning and ending nowhere."

Weird New England set out to find those stairs. Oddly, local folks didn't seem to know anything about them. Even elderly volunteers at the local historical society who had heard of them couldn't say exactly where they were. But we kept looking: Something about a flight of carved stone stairs "beginning and ending nowhere" really piqued our imagination.

Applying a good bit of Yankee stick-to-itiveness, we finally found them behind a brand-new housing development and on private property. Tucked away now, overgrown, and apparently forgotten, the steps were being treated just like any other bit of glacial flotsam or jetsam.

But to the true seeker of curiosities, they are a vision to behold. What you see is a boulder as big as a tractor-trailer, with a stone stairway carved right up the center. The stone is obviously very old and crumbling a bit. Still, it has the ability to mystify.

A little research revealed that the Stairway to Nowhere was firmly in place when South Windham's first settlers arrived. They called them the Indian Steps, but local Native Americans were as puzzled as the newcomers: They didn't build them either.

Simply put: The steps have been there longer than anyone can remember. Since South Windham's founding in 1732, ongoing and inconclusive discussions have persisted: Who made them? When? Why there? And what was their purpose?

For years, it was a wonderful puzzle. Then geologists stepped in, trying to spoil the fun. They said Mother Nature built the steps about two hundred million years ago. They are, say the scientists, a naturally occurring formation known as a basalt dike.

Well, maybe. But they sure looked like steps to us.

Deep Dark Tunnel to Nowhere

Of the many puzzling structures throughout New England, our personal favorite is locally known in Massachusetts as the Goshen Mystery. It is unique. Nothing else like it has been discovered anywhere in these parts, so it must serve as its own frame of reference.

Goshen's 920 residents and their ancestors have been scratching their heads over the Mystery since it was first discovered "sodded over" in the late 1800s. Nothing about its origins survives. There is no mention of it in town records or in the diaries of founding fathers. All theories have been weighed and—for one reason or another—discarded.

The Goshen Mystery is a cleverly designed underground stone tunnel, built without mortar. The main shaft is three and a half feet wide, descending straight down for fifteen feet. The knee-jerk assessment is that it is a well, but look again. There's no water. And it is carved out of dense clay hardpan where no water would be expected. To further deep-six the perception of a well, there are horizontal tunnels branching off from the sides. One, at the bottom, leads eastward for about seventy-five feet. It's about three feet in diameter: big enough to crawl into but not big enough to stand in, unless, of course, one is very very short.

A higher tunnel, branching out about three feet up on the main shaft, has a larger diameter but extends only about fifteen feet. Some examiners suspect that at one time this shaft may have been longer; it appears to have been truncated by a cave-in. What lies beyond it is anybody's guess.

But one thing is certain: This unfathomable oddity was constructed in the days of hand tools. Cutting and placing the innumerable tons of stones would have required countless hours of slow, backbreaking labor. The horizontal shafts would have been especially difficult to engineer and build.

If it was constructed in Colonial times, how did it escape the notice of the town's residents? And most important, what was it? Theories include a den for thieves or counterfeiters, an underground railroad stop, a root cellar, a place to store ice, a hideout from the Indians, and an abandoned treasure pit. But most likely it will turn out to be an eternal puzzle.

Whatever it is, or was, the people of Goshen, Massachusetts, say, "It's always been there."

Bulldozing History

"Only three miles out of Stamford, Connecticut, there is a cluster of thirteen . . . drywall huts. They were long thought by the locals to be Indian dwellings, but in 1870 an old Stockbridge Indian named Joe returned to the site of his ancestors. . . . Joe said that his ancestors had told his people that they had found these huts when they first arrived in Connecticut. They were not comfortable to his people, so they moved across the Ripowam to the high ground to live. Therefore, these stone huts were there before the Colonials came in the 1600s and before the Indians came. But then, who built them? At this writing they have been bulldozed away to make room for modern buildings." —Robert Ellis Cahill, *New England's Ancient Mysteries*

The risk to New England's ancient stone structures is clear. How many of them have already been destroyed? Because of some peculiar cultural myopia, we tend to believe there was no civilization here before the historic arrival at Plymouth Rock. But as we have seen, other rocks suggest otherwise.

It is clear that many of the stone buildings under discussion in this chapter are at least as old as the original colonies. So why are they not afforded the same protection as other Colonial buildings? Even today a landowner can bulldoze one into oblivion, and there is little or nothing to prevent it. A sad case in point is the endangered structure in Upton, Massachusetts.

"A Deserted Haunt of Unknown Origin"

The Upton Tunnel is one of the largest stone chambers in New England. It is also one of the most perfectly preserved. Like all the others, its origin remains a mystery.

The town of Upton, Massachusetts, was founded in 1720, though settlers had drifted in before that time. On April 26, 1893, Daniel Fiske, writing in the *Milford Journal*, called the chamber "A Deserted Haunt of Unknown Origin."

"We venture to assert that on account of its secluded location there are not fifty living citizens who have ever been within this mouldering enclosure and many hundreds born in Upton for a period of fourscore years, were ignorant of its existence. . . . From our youth we have occasionally sought information of the oldest citizens whose ancestors

lived on this road from 150 to 200 years ago and they were as ignorant of its origin as we of today."

Little has changed since Fiske's day. The tunnel is still there and still an unsolved mystery.

The entrance to the odd structure is an opening three by four feet square. To go inside, you enter a narrow passageway that extends fourteen feet until it connects with an interior, circle-shaped room, some twelve feet in diameter and about eleven feet high. The room is big enough to shelter twelve to fifteen adults. Overhead, a dome was achieved by laying flat granite stones, tier upon tier, overlapping inwardly and gradually culminating with a twelve-hundred-pound circular capstone at the top. No mortar was used in its construction; gravity holds everything in place. There are no indications of tools, drills, or inscriptions on the walls or ceiling. Obviously, the structure is the work of skilled and hardy artisans.

Though it is nearly identical to a prehistoric stone site found in Ireland, some authorities date its construction as recently as A.D. 710. Visitors have found that if they stand inside and look out through the entrance tunnel as if it were a telescope, certain star configurations line up precisely with three stone cairns on nearby Pratt Hill.

There are myriad theories to explain the Upton structure. The most conservative says it is nothing more than an icehouse, a root cellar, or a leather-tanning site. Each of these is unlikely: First, the labor and skill involved in the vast stone construction far exceeds any needed for those three applications. Plus, the entrance is too narrow and cramped to move stored goods in and out easily, and the interior is too wet and poorly ventilated to serve as a vegetable bin.

More exotic explanations have more appeal. Was the Upton Tunnel constructed by Vikings? Irish Culdee Monks who, like the Puritans, sought the New World for religious freedom? Or by some unknown race of pre-Colonial Europeans lost to history?

In addition to the mystery of its purpose and its builders, the site hints at other secrets within:

There is an area on an interior wall where the stonework is inconsistent with the rest of the structure. Some speculate that this is a bricked-up exit or the entrance to another chamber or tunnel as yet unopened and undiscovered.

Snow outside the structure melts at varying rates, implying that underground temperatures are not uniform and perhaps indicating the presence of tunnels.

Voices of people within the chamber can be heard up to seventy-five feet away, again suggesting an undiscovered system of caves or a design that, for some reason, deliberately enhances sonic properties.

A strange blue light emitted from the opening, photographed by Cathy Taylor of the Upton Historical Commission, seems to add credence to the site's alleged otherworldly or supernatural properties.

Personally, we'd rather see unexplained blue light in front of the entrance than the present gate and NO TRESPASSING sign. The former portends mysteries yet unsolved. The latter suggest an end to problem solving and possibly destruction of this magnificent mystery. A developer has bought the property. The town's citizens are fighting to preserve the structure, but right now the future of Upton's deserted haunt is every bit as uncertain as its past.

The Weird Windmill (Maybe) of Newport

By contrast, the city of Newport, Rhode Island, takes good care of its resident enigma.

In the middle of busy downtown, smack dab at the center of Truro Park, stands what may be the most puzzling architectural structure in the United States.

The first question is what to call it. Over time, it was known by different names: the Mystery Tower, the Old Stone Mill, the Norse Tower, the Viking Tower, the Truro Tower, or simply the Tower. Nowadays it's usually just called the Newport Tower.

It is a massive building—twenty-four feet high—constructed of small slabs of unfinished stone held together by mortar comprised of shells, sand, and water. It's estimated to contain more than six thousand cubic feet of stone weighing almost one million pounds.

The tower appears to be round, but isn't. One diameter is twenty-two feet two inches, another measures twenty-three feet three inches. Such a discrepancy is puzzling, and it could not have been accidental.

It is a two-story structure, the lower comprised of eight columns defining eight arches that support a second floor containing a double-flued fireplace and several double-splayed windows.

Controversy has surrounded the structure for centuries; no one has ever been able to explain it. That it is old is not disputed. Evidence suggests it was standing when the first colonists arrived. On the other hand, some experts think it was constructed around 1675 to be used as a windmill by Governor Benedict Arnold, traitor Benedict Arnold's grandfather. Maybe, but it appears on a map of Rhode Island dated 1630.

Beyond that, we have all the usual suspects: twelfth-century Vikings, Portuguese, Norwegians, Swedes, or seagoing Celts. The newest suspect was fingered by Gavin Menzies in his book *1421 – The Year China Discovered*

America. He suggests the tower was built by fifteenth-century Chinese explorers who used it as a lighthouse. He backs his unexpected conclusion by comparing Newport's tower to an ancient lighthouse in the port of Zaiton in southern China. Point by point, the sheer number of similar design elements is astonishing.

To further complicate things, in 1994 the Early Sites Research Society found previously unknown shapes and plots under the ground throughout Truro Park. Then, in October 2003, 3-D imaging discovered two objects underground—one apparently a flat slab, the other possibly a wall. This suggests that the tower may once have been part of a complex of buildings. Maybe what is now Truro Park was the site of a fort, a church, a monastery, or a whole village.

Windmill, watchtower, fort, lighthouse, or cathedral—over the years, numerous theories have been advocated, considered, and discarded. Whatever else it may be, Newport's tower remains a mystery that may never be solved.

America's Stonehenge

Less than fifty miles away from Boston's crowded urban chaos lies the comparatively sedate seclusion of Salem, New Hampshire. There, on a desolate granite hilltop, generations of scientists and sightseers have pondered what may be North America's greatest and most gigantic megalithic enigma. It could be a whole stone village, perhaps America's first man-made construction, built in an unknown past.

Today it is known as America's Stonehenge, but its former name seems more appropriate: Mystery Hill. The site is so weird that H. P. Lovecraft used it in scenes in his story "The Dunwich Horror." It has eluded understanding since farmer Jonathan Pattee discovered it around 1826. We don't know exactly how the place looked when Mr. Pattee found it, because he helped himself to whatever he fancied from the site. But what he and subsequent owners left undisturbed has been sufficient to puzzle archaeologists, historians, and astronomers for almost two centuries.

The Granite State's claim to megalithic fame covers some thirty acres. There are low, rambling stone walls, primitive cavelike buildings, and a series of tunnels that seem to run helter-skelter. Yet the structures were erected with painstaking care. The stones, some weighing up to eleven tons, were shaped and placed with precision.

What it all means and how the structures were used is a complicated conundrum. Though it lacks the intricacy and elegance of the English Stonehenge, both were built by people knowledgeable in stonework and astronomy. The two share many astronomical alignments and can be used as observatories to determine specific solar and lunar events.

But its other purposes remain a mystery. Was it a settlement? A village? Or some kind of cathedral? Evidence suggests it was never inhabited, though somebody certainly passed through ages ago. Fragments of pottery found at the site date back to 1000 B.C. Charcoal from a firepit was radiocarbon-dated to be 4,000 years old.

Most likely it was used for long-forgotten, perhaps best-forgotten, religious ceremonies. Consider the so-called Sacrificial Stone altar that seems to be a main feature of the complex. It's an enormous flat stone table supported by four stone legs.

Though it lacks the intricacy and elegance of the English Stonehenge, both were built by people knowledge-able in stonework and astronomy.

A carefully carved groove runs around its surface and leads to a spout. Though the gutter could have been used to collect rainwater, more likely it was intended to drain the blood of animal, or even human, sacrifices.

This religious interpretation is buttressed by another design oddity. Beneath the Sacrificial Stone there is a hidden tube eight feet long. It leads to an underground chamber. A priest hiding in the chamber could have spoken through the tube, creating a mysterious, spectral voice that uttered predictions, commands, and curses.

But who were those priests? We just don't know. New England's Native Americans didn't build with stone. And the Sacrificial Stone certainly doesn't conform to any Colonial religious beliefs we've heard of.

What we can say for sure is both accurate and intriguing: America's Stonehenge was built in ancient times by an ancient people we know nothing about.

At present the site is privately owned by the appropriately named Stone family. Robert E. Stone of Derry, New Hampshire, bought the place and opened it to the public in 1958. The admission charge goes for maintenance and research. Though it is administered by the America's Stonehenge Foundation, to us the most appropriate name will always be Mystery Hill.

Gungywamp in Groton

Though the word Gungywamp may sound Indian, it's actually ancient Gaelic, meaning "Church of the People." It refers to over twenty mysterious acres of indisputably ancient ruins sitting atop a steep thirty-foot cliff in Groton, Connecticut, just six miles north of Long Island Sound and two miles east of the Thames River. Like the other ancient structures, Gungywamp poses seemingly unsolvable mysteries about its purpose and origin. Yet clues are all around, leading . . . where?

Part of the difficulty in determining who built Gungywamp is that since it was constructed, many different peoples have used it. Paleo Indians were there (arrowheads and pottery fragments, 2000–770 B.C.). Colonists used it, as did post-Colonials (buttons, coins, clay pipes). The astute observer can even find elusive indications of modern tenancy (beer cans, broken glass, plastic bags, and the ubiquitous graffiti).

Near the center of this complex is a double circle of massive quarried stones positioned end to end. Archaeological digs have revealed stone flooring between the circles. Charcoal found there (dating to approximately A.D. 455) and burn marks suggest use as an altar. Then again, it might have been a mill for grinding apples, seashells, or bark for leather tanning. If so, one would expect to find a central post to support the axle for the crushing wheel. No indication of any post can be located.

Nearby, a handful of standing stones and a single slab are positioned along astronomical lines, indicating that, like the Salem, New Hampshire, site, Gungywamp functioned as a calendar.

Part of what makes this location so unusual is the variety of structures. There are earthen mounds, stone piles, petroglyphs, and four stone chambers similar to dozens of others scattered throughout New England forests. The largest is eighteen feet long.

But Gungywamp has one weird feature all its own: a rock ledge known as the Cliff of Tears. Certain people walking past this ledge become inexplicably sad or depressed. Some may begin weeping without knowing why. A few individuals even report unaccountable nosebleeds or bleeding gums. On-site electromagnetic readings attest to wild activity, which may serve as a partial explanation. Perhaps whoever built the complex realized they were on mysterious, if not sacred, ground. In modern quasi-scientific, New Age speak, we could say that perhaps Gungywamp is seated on the vortex of some as yet unexplained electromagnetic field that generates earth energy once channeled for some as yet undisclosed purpose.

That's the scientific guess. The ancients may have come to a different conclusion: Perhaps Gungywamp, the Church of the People, is in reality the seat of God.

Not-So-Old New England

Some New England oddities may not be as old as the ones already discussed — in fact, they can be comparatively recent. But in their own way, they are just as puzzling as the ancient sites. For example:

Thresher Road's Mystery Stones

There are some who say that every New England town has some kind of skeleton in its closet. Not necessarily something sinister, maybe just something strange. Then again, it could be a mind-blowing malignancy.

Let's start with the little mysteries, those tiny puzzles that, in some cases, even the locals can't figure out. Take the town of Hardwick, Massachusetts. Its 2,800 residents have a private puzzle that's been baffling them for generations. Just off Route 32A is a line of equally spaced marked stones. They begin at the Rod and Gun Club and follow Thresher Road for about one third of a mile, ending at Deer Spring.

Someone, sometime, chiseled numbers into the stones, beginning with 1 and ending with 32. Why, you ask? Good question, no good answer.

Thresher Road is quintessentially rural: dirt, narrow, generally undisturbed since the town was settled around 1730. Its sides are thickly overgrown, making the marked stones difficult to find. When we visited recently, accompanied by Mr. Leon Thresher (whose family gives the road its name), we could locate only a few of them. But that was enough to reinforce the mystery: When were the stones put there? By whom? And for what purpose?

Nothing is readily revealed by studying them. Each is about the size of the footstone on a grave. The numbers are carved into their fronts, facing the road. And small holes are drilled into the tops.

In some ways it is easier to determine what the stones are not. For example, they are not mile markers; they're too close together. And it's unlikely they are graves, lined up as they are so close to the roadside. Thirty-two stones in such a limited area also shoots down the idea of address or property markers. No homes or foundations correspond to their placement. If they had in fact marked building lots, this would have been a crowded neighborhood indeed. But it never was a neighborhood — not now, not ever.

Some people guess the stones once had religious or ritualistic significance. The depressions at their tops might have been for candles, and, some are quick to point out, the number thirty-two corresponds with the highest degree of Freemasonry.

To make the whole matter more vexing, the markers are obviously very old. They may be older than the town; however, they are not unfathomably ancient, like some of the sites discussed in this chapter, since the numbers they bear are in recognizable script. Some are moss covered, some have tumbled, others have been crowded or displaced by trees. All are severely weatherbeaten.

The stones are not Hardwick's only oddity. It's also home to a number of stone cairns — those baffling beehives that punctuate all of New England with question marks and may, in fact, be truly ancient.

And what may seem stranger still, the town also has a bridge in the middle of nowhere. No road runs to or away from it. Yet there it sits like a teleported causeway provoking spooky questions. This apparent mystery, however, is a little easier to solve. It's a trackless railroad bridge built in anticipation of a railroad that never came through.

The Andover Rock Pile Timeless Turtle or Modern Folly?

At a casual glance, the mound of rocks in Andover, Massachusetts, appears to be nothing more than a heap of stones left by some long-ago farmer as he cleared his field. There's none of the beehive symmetry and conspicuous design elements that define some of New England's other megalithic structures. However, certain attributes have made attentive people take a second and third look—ultimately leading to a revelation.

In 1939, William Goodwin and Malcolm Pearson examined and photographed the mound. They perceived tunnels and cavities, passages, and tiny rooms within it, all of seemingly deliberate design. But the big revelation came in 1944 when Mr. Goodwin took another look at his notes and pictures. He then made what he called an "extraordinary discovery." What had appeared chaotic from ground level took on design if viewed from

When we examined it, certain things bothered us. The arched entryways didn't seem consistent with other ancient sites.

above. Mr. Goodwin suggested that the Andover rocks, like the famous Serpent Mound in Ohio, were carefully placed, in the shape of a snapping turtle. Since then, Andover's rock pile has been referred to as the Turtle Mound.

Well, maybe so. It might also be called the Rorschach Heap or Ink Blot Pile. From Mr. Goodwin's diagram, one can see how it could be seen as a turtle, but so can clouds and cliffs. Perhaps a better question is, Is it really ancient?

When we examined it, certain things bothered us. The arched entryways didn't seem consistent with other ancient sites. Masonry was contoured around relatively new trees, which strongly suggested new building. And the marks of a modern drill above one of the doorways implied something other than ancient architects.

Andover's mysterious mound might have been constructed by a former owner of the property, a nineteenth-century landscape gardener. He had definitely built a platform on top of the mound on which he served tea, hot chocolate, and snacks to tourists and skaters who came by railroad to a nearby pond. Another property owner, a French Canadian Roman Catholic named Harnois, had retrofitted a shrine into the existing rock pile. For a while, Turtle Mound had been known as Harnois's Shrine.

Some people suspect that the whole thing is a "folly," something new made to look old, something intended to puzzle and delight. Perhaps it wasn't originally constructed to deceive, but as time passed, memories faded until today only the mystery remains.

Then again, in 1959 archaeologist Frank Glynn investigated the mound. While excavating the floor of one of the two chambers, he claimed to have discovered a Neolithic burial. Mr. Glynn reported his findings in the *New England Antiquities Association Newsletter* in December 1969.

It is beyond the scope of this book to try to clear things up. But whether the Turtle Mound is old or new, and whether its alleged reptilian shape is deliberate or accidental, it still tickles the imagination. And it is weird.

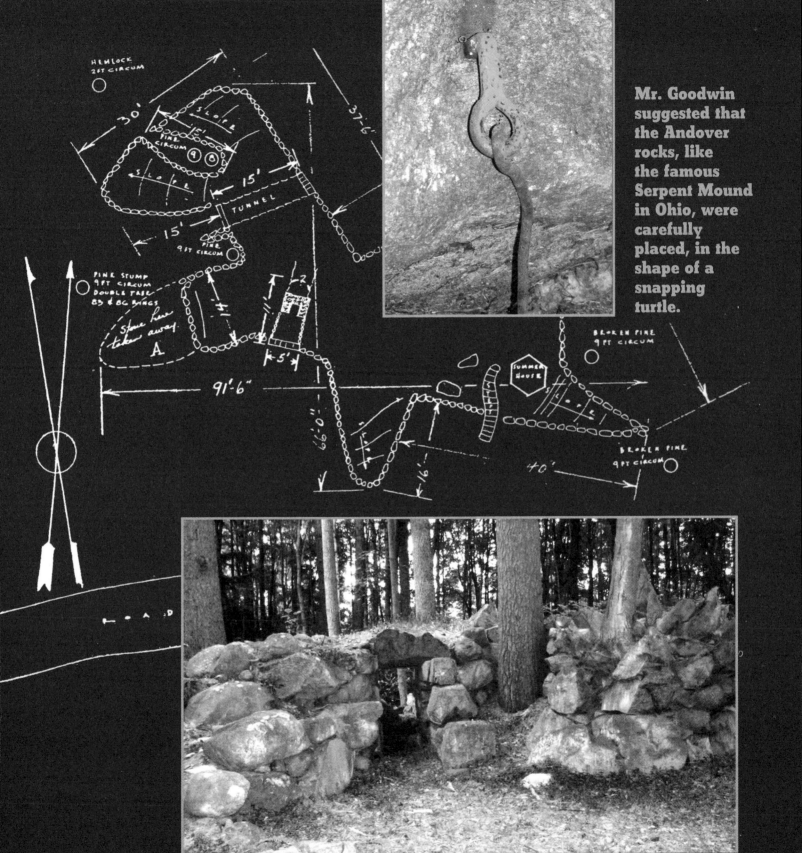

Mr. Goodwin suggested that the Andover rocks, like the famous Serpent Mound in Ohio, were carefully placed, in the shape of a snapping turtle.

Fabled People and Places

To the outsider New England has always been a fabled land, a vast and varied theme park designed by whimsical architects such as Norman Rockwell and John Greenleaf Whittier.

But New England's wildly diverse topography makes it a perfect setting for the weird. The landscape ranges from the desert wasteland of Freeport, Maine, to the arctic tundra atop Mount Washington, New Hampshire, where the most powerful winds on record blow so fiercely that buildings have to be chained to the earth. Some New England forests are so big you could discharge a mortar shell into the sky and not have to worry about where it lands. Certain caves are so deep and serpentine that a man could become lost forever—or run into something he never expected to meet. Our mystical land is dappled with castles and crevasses, hollows and hills, and enough characters to populate four centuries' worth of poems, stories, novels, and tall tales.

There is New England legend and New England truth. And where truth is lacking, a real Yankee seeks it just the same. Proceed with caution, for we're about to enter the fabled terrain of *Weird New England*, where some of its equally fabled residents may linger, waiting for your visit.

The Golden City of Norumbega

New England might not have been New England. It might have been New France. In olden times, both countries laid claim to the virgin world north of Spanish Mexico, until the British won the prize. One of the minor attractions of the new land appeared on a 1529 map by Girolamo Verrazano: Norumbega. Some rumored details were published in 1539 by a French sea captain. But what started out as enticing legend gained the weight of truth when validated by a marooned British sailor, David Ingram.

In 1568, Mr. Ingram sailed aboard a slave ship convoy commanded by Captain John Hawkins. After Captain Hawkins lost four ships during combat with a Spanish fleet in the West Indies, his two surviving vessels limped into port on the Gulf of Mexico, where they were repaired. But he had to abandon some of his men, David Ingram among them.

The intrepid Mr. Ingram set out on foot, commencing a 2,000-mile journey up the Atlantic coast that eventually brought him to Maine. From there, he was transported safely home to England. But the tale he brought with him resounds to this day. He offered a detailed report of a fabulous place where he had been a guest for a while: the gem-encrusted, golden-walled city of Norumbega, whose territory, he reckoned, was situated somewhere in what we now call the state of Maine. It was ruled by the great Bashaba, who resided in its capital, Arembec. Mr. Ingram said he was so generously treated that he hated to depart when natives escorted him to a nearby ship bound for Europe.

Here at last was the Ophir, the El Dorado, the New World's answer to the seven cities of Cíbola. Suddenly rumors of a glorious kingdom in the wilderness had been validated. Buildings were plated with gold; gemstones decorated the walls. City gates were pillars of crystal or lapis lazuli. Pearls and precious stones were as common as cobblestones. As near as Mr. Ingram could recall, this fabulous city was located on the Penobscot River about where Bangor is today. It appears on certain sixteenth- and seventeenth-century maps, including one by the great explorer Samuel de Champlain.

But Norumbega may have been built by the same architects who conceived Brigadoon. Although many people reported seeing it, no one has ever been able to locate it. And David Ingram's directions were anything but precise.

In the late nineteenth century, Harvard professor Eben Norton Horsford took an interest in the matter. An amateur archaeologist, he identified Norumbega—not in Maine, but on the Charles River at Watertown, Massachusetts. Professor Horsford didn't find any gold or jewels (surely those had been covertly removed by earlier treasure-seekers), but he found stonework and artifacts enough to satisfy himself that he had identified an ancient settlement. It predated European arrival, he was certain, and was dissimilar to the work of Native Americans.

Eventually Professor Horsford became convinced that Vikings had settled the Charles River Basin around A.D. 1000. At what is now the Charles River Reservation in Weston, he unearthed what he thought was evidence of a Viking fort. He christened it Fort Norumbega and, in 1889, built an imitation Viking edifice to commemorate his find. This imaginative monument contains a stone that Professor Horsford believed Vikings used to grind grain—but does not hold a single gem, gold nugget, or pearl. He went on to elaborate on his findings in a series of largely forgotten books containing maps, photographs, and theories. Though today Professor Horsford is generally dismissed as an imaginative crackpot, his monument to a myth still stands.

And legends about the fabled city of Norumbega just won't go away. Even today visitors to Maine will hear references to it. It's out there, someplace, the faithful believe.

Eventually Professor Horsford became convinced that Vikings had settled the Charles River Basin around A.D. 1000.

Gentlemen of the Highway

No one knows New England better than its Gentlemen of the Highway. Neither heroes nor villains, these legendary sojourners have inspired speculation and myth that, in time, took on the sheen of truth. Presumably they possessed local insight unrivaled by our most accomplished scholars. The trouble is, they aren't talking. Instead, they made their solitary way along the invisible highways of *Weird New England*, whatever wisdom or misery they knew locked forever inside.

Old Leatherman

The best-known of this vanished breed is still as puzzling as he was when he wandered his routes through Connecticut and eastern New York State. Because he was invariably seen dressed entirely in leather, everyone simply called him the Leatherman. We're not talking a macho Davy Crockett–style buckskin suit, but a crude patchwork of leather scraps and discarded boot tops awkwardly held together by leather thongs.

The Leatherman caught people's attention because of his extraordinary predictability. Every thirty-four days he completed a circuit of about 365 miles. Invariably he traveled in a clockwise direction. In fact, the Leatherman was so regular in his habits that people knew the very day and exact hour to expect him. It was said that "housewives could set their clocks by him."

In time, people began to make small gestures of kindness, offering food or refreshment, even tobacco and matches. These he would accept willingly, expressing his appreciation with animated gestures, for, it seems, the Leatherman never spoke. He refused money and alcohol and would never accept accommodations in anyone's home. In fact, he never slept in buildings. He had staked out a series of caves along his repetitious route.

The era of the Leatherman lasted almost a third of a century. He first appeared in the early 1860s and continued his unwavering rounds till his death in Briarcliff Manor, New York, in 1889. Although there are many theories—some stated with certainty and conviction—no one actually knows who the Leatherman was or where he came from. One story goes that he was a Frenchman who brought ruin to himself and dashed his hopes for marriage to the woman he loved when he mismanaged her family's leather business. (He bought too much leather!) Whether true or not, his legacy to us includes a few photographs, diverse recollections, and even sightings of his ghost!

But many questions also remain: How could one seemingly so irresponsible adhere to such a fixed and rigorous routine? What compelled him to repeat this particular route? And most fundamental, why did he always dress in leather? Over the years, there have been many theories, of course, but we can never expect an answer. Who or what drove the Leatherman has vanished along with the solitary creature himself.

Old Darn Man

Everyone called him the Old Darn Man because no one knew his name. He began his unpredictable trek around 1820, traveling through Connecticut, Massachusetts, and Rhode Island. Those who met him described him as a "man of good breeding"—gentle, highly intelligent, well-read . . . a trained violinist with a sad, lost air.

Like the Leatherman, the Old Darn Man is remembered for his distinct apparel. Rather than tattered swatches of leather, he wore a formal suit with tails. At the beginning of his wanderings, it looked brand-new. With vest and gold watch fob, he appeared to be a distinguished gentleman out for a stroll . . . a stroll that continued for over sixty years. In all that time, he never changed his suit.

Yet he always kept his clothes clean and in good repair. When approaching a house for food or shelter, the first thing he'd ask was, "May I borrow a needle and thread to mend my clothes?" Then, with a skillful hand, he'd stitch up the torn or worn spots. Darning clothes was how he got his nickname. When a hostess offered to do the repairs, he'd always decline and politely explain, "I refuse because these are my wedding clothes and they are sacred. My bride will be here soon."

As decades passed, the fine formal wear became blemished and patched, but the Old Darn Man would never permit a spot or tear to go unattended. He'd repay a family's hospitality by reading to them, playing his violin, or doing light housework.

There was much speculation about why his life had taken this odd, endless turn, and—in some ways more mysterious—where he'd disappear to in the wintertime. He'd say he'd gone to his "mansion" during the cold months.

Speculation was that his condition resulted from an unhappy love affair that—considering his clothing—may have ended at the altar. But the fact is, no one ever learned his story.

When he died an old man (the year is uncertain), he wore the same tattered suit, now a crazy patchwork of mismatched cloth and surprisingly skillful stitchery. Supposedly, his last words were, "My bride will come tonight. Surely she will not disappoint me."

A Genuine Highwayman?

A "Gentleman of the Highway" should not be confused with a "genuine highwayman." And that is exactly what the people of Brookline, Vermont, may have had in their midst. He left his peculiar mark on the town—a round schoolhouse that is a true curiosity. And he left a story that has never had a satisfactory ending.

Brookline's round schoolhouse—possibly the only one in the country—built in 1822, was designed by its founding instructor, Dr. John Wilson, a distinguished-looking British gentleman who was also the town's part-time physician. Solidly constructed from red brick, with windows facing all directions, the school is a unique piece of Vermont architecture. Its architect is no less unique, for Dr. Wilson—if that was indeed his name—was indisputably a man of mystery.

Why, the locals wondered, would such an aristocratic gentleman work as a lowly schoolteacher? And why would he hole up in tiny Brookline when his medical skills could earn him a fortune in Brattleboro or Burlington? His behavior was an ongoing puzzle. Though brilliant and eloquent, he would never talk about his past. And why did he occasionally walk with a noticeable limp and invariably wear high collars or thick scarves when neither fashion nor weather required them? And, the ladies wondered, why was he so charming yet remote?

In May 1847, when Dr. Wilson passed away, the answers finally came. As he lay dying, he summoned his closest friend,

exacting a promise that he should be buried in the clothes he was wearing, including his scarf and boots. Fortunately for collectors of New England legend and lore, the friend disregarded the doctor's dying wish. Undressing the corpse revealed a cork prosthesis where Dr. Wilson's heel had been shot away. There was a nasty scar of a musket ball on his withered leg, and his neck was horribly disfigured, as if he had been slashed, shackled, or unsuccessfully hanged. Someone discovered a stiletto concealed in his walking stick. An examination of his home revealed an abundant cache of swords, guns, and ammunition.

Eventually people in the town put two and two together: Their reclusive schoolmaster was none other than the infamous British highwayman Captain Thunderbolt. For over a decade, he and his accomplice,

Mr. Lightfoot, had terrorized the Irish countryside and the England-Scotland border. Known as a swashbuckling Robin-Hood-like rogue, Captain Thunderbolt was said to have robbed the rich, given to the poor, and squirreled enough away to escape to the wilds of America. There, hiding in rural Vermont, he became a model citizen. But he never stopped peering warily in all directions from the windows of his lookout—Brookline's round brick schoolhouse.

The story of Captain Thunderbolt is many layered and fascinating. But if it all sounds like fiction to you, it can be easily verified. Just stop in the Brooks Library in Brattleboro. Its Vermont Room displays some of Dr. Wilson's possessions that were recovered after his death. Among them are his false heel, his medical instruments, his photograph, and his intriguing sword cane.

Cling-Clang, the Vaulting Peddler

One of the more bizarre of New England's wayward wanderers was known simply as Cling-Clang. The name reflected his profession: selling and repairing pots and pans. His merchandise clanged as he moved, announcing his arrival at remote farms or villages.

Cling-Clang traveled the coastal towns of Maine and New Hampshire. As with other members of this breed, he had his peculiarities. For example, he'd never sleep in anyone's house. When invited for an overnight, he'd curl up in the barn or shed. If no invitation was forthcoming, he'd find a comfortable spot near a stone wall or under a tree. He would, however, accept a meal in exchange for a service. Those who offered him this boon would find that Cling-Clang had an odd mode of eating. He'd finish one item before tackling the next. First, he'd eat all of his potato, then all his vegetable, then his meat. He'd eat bread, then eat the butter. If coffee or tea followed, he'd drink it straight. Then he'd eat two spoonfuls of sugar.

Cling-Clang's many idiosyncrasies included a terrible aversion to the sound of a rooster crowing. If a farmer had a rooster, the peddler would meekly request that it be covered so it wouldn't crow in the morning. Needless to say, mischievous boys often used this weakness to torment him. He'd react by screaming and running away.

But the truly unique thing about Cling-Clang was his peculiar mode of locomotion. He traveled by poling himself along. He had two long, brass-tipped poles that he grasped near the top. He used them to leap, or pole vault, making rapid ten- to twelve-foot jumps that allowed him to travel six or seven miles an hour. He easily sailed over fences, creeks, or other obstructions, making an awful racket in the process.

Cling-Clang's wanderings came to an end when someone found him one winter's day beneath an overturned boat in Sullivan, Maine. When he didn't respond to a gentle nudge, they discovered the old man was dead, frozen solid in his sleep.

Roaming Roadside Robots

Of course Cling-Clang's adventures took place a long time ago. More recently other odd denizens of *Weird New England* have made themselves known in the most unexpected places.

For example, on September 5, 1967, the *Hartford Courant* reported that something uniquely out of the ordinary was prowling the shadows atop Talcott Mountain in Avon, Connecticut. A number of motorists phoned town police with stories of a roadside robot that was trying to flag down passing cars along a deserted stretch of highway.

The first report came in at eleven thirty Sunday night. The unidentified motorist said the "robot" — or maybe a "spaceman" — signaled his car as he drove along Route 44. The driver chose not to stop.

Similar reports quickly followed, each identifying the same robot at the same spot. All witnesses agreed that the robot (or spaceman) wore a one-piece silver suit that concealed its hands and feet. Also a reflective metallic-looking helmet or hood obscured its head. It moved stiffly, everyone said, as it awkwardly went about its task of trying to stop vehicles. Avon police hurried to the scene. After a thorough search, they could find no trace of the mysterious visitor.

Consulted the next day, Donald LaSalle, Director of the Talcott Mountain Science Center, found the report amusing. Without investigating, he tossed the whole thing off as a joke or prank. Guesses included all of the usual suspects: tricksters, motorcyclists in metallic suits with crash helmets, students undergoing fraternity initiations. What no one doubted is that all

the motorists had actually seen something of a highly unusual nature.

Unwavering from his initial evaluation, Mr. LaSalle said, "This is obviously a joke, but wouldn't it be something if we did get a visitor from outer space. . . . Who knows what else exists out there."

What amazes us here at *Weird New England* is that so many people leaped to the conclusion that Avon's

metallic visitor was something extraterrestrial. Maybe it came from right here. Maybe there's a whole colony of them hiding in the woods. And maybe if it had lifted its mysterious helmet, we'd have seen one of New England's many and varied crypto-critters. Repeated evidence confirms they can be just as mischievous as fraternity boys.

Birth of the Melonheads

One of the most reported-on enclaves of humanity's outcasts are the Melonheads, well-known to trackers of the weird in other parts of the country. We had always dismissed them as a non–New England phenomenon, so you can imagine our surprise when we began to hear reports that Melonheads are living here, in staid old New England. We decided to investigate.

In 1991, Marie Guglielmo, a staff writer for the *Bridgeport Post* (now the *Connecticut Post*), collected reports regarding these bulbous-headed beings. Apparently, New England Melonheads reside only in Connecticut, mostly in Fairfield County. There are essentially two accounts that explain their origins.

One version holds that it all began around 1860. Apparently, at that time a high-security institution for the criminally insane was situated deep in the woods of Fairfield County. After a century or so in business, in the fall of 1960, the place burned to the ground. Strangely, all staff members perished in the conflagration, as did most of the inmates. However, about ten to twenty inmate bodies were never recovered. An all-out manhunt did no good; it was as if they had vanished entirely.

Some theorize that the fire and escape were deliberate. The fugitives hid in the woods, successfully surviving an especially grueling winter . . . until their food ran out. Rather than return to civilization and incarceration, they embraced a landlocked version of "The Custom of the Sea": They turned to cannibalism. Supposedly this modified diet—perhaps exacerbated by indiscriminate inbreeding—sparked a metabolic chemical reaction. Their craniums began to swell. And so did their appetite for human flesh.

That's one version. The alternate explanation, which lays the whole thing on the intolerance of our Puritan forefathers (and mothers), claims that in Colonial times a family from the Shelton-Trumbull area was accused of witchcraft and banished from civilization. Apparently, the expelled assemblage was large enough that brothers and sisters were able to begin repopulation efforts in the wild. In time, mental and physical mutations became obvious. The undesirable outcasts evolved into Melonheads.

Those who have seen them say they are small in stature, frail looking, with long spindly arms and fingers. Their teeth are crooked, blocky, and discolored. Their heads, their most conspicuous feature, are bald and bulbous and out of proportion with their stooped torsos. Some observers say their eyes are red.

Melonheads don't seem to have developed the knack of raising food. Rather, they survive in the woods by dining on whatever they catch—fish, frogs, bugs, moles, or roadkill. That is, between their occasional human flesh feasts. Local legend holds that people sightseeing, biking, or hiking in the vicinity of any Melonhead habitat are likely to vanish, never to be seen again. Bikes, backpacks, and cars may be recovered, but never the people.

Did these vanished folk encounter the vastly mutated grandchildren or great-grandchildren of the original Melonheads? Were they initiated into the Melonhead society or turned into Melonheads themselves? Or was their fate a little less . . . appetizing?

A Case of Survival

Megan O'Connell recalls a terrifying incident from the early 1980s when she was a student at Notre Dame High School in Fairfield, Connecticut. After a Friday night football game, Megan and some other girls piled into her friend Debbie's baby-blue Granada. Deciding that a few thrills would only enhance the evening, they headed over to Trumbull's creepy Velvet Street, known locally as Dracula Drive. This is the area where the Melonheads were known to lurk.

With music blaring, the girls turned onto a narrow dirt path. When they could drive no farther they parked and switched off the engine, music, and lights. Then, in the quiet darkness, Megan led Sue, Kim, Deb, Jen, and Karen into the woods looking for Melonheads. Somewhere around here, they knew, was a house in which a group of Melonheads was thought to live. A full moon lit their way as they giggled, whispered, and jumped at the occasional snapping branch or hooting owl.

Then they heard another sound, a loud mechanical roar behind them. Deb's car was starting up!

The horn blared, headlights flashed from high to low

and back as the engine growled. The vehicle leaped to life and bore down on them like an avenging monster. It swerved from side to side, spitting dirt, as the girls scrambled out of its way. Safely cowering behind rocks and trees, the six watched in horror as the car rumbled past. Inside they could plainly see a cluster of the big-headed beings they heretofore had truly believed to be legendary. But it was no legend that howled and screamed from the car's interior as it sped away.

Abandoned in the shadow-crowded woodland, the girls ran breathlessly along the deserted road until they reached a highway. From there, they commenced the long walk home.

To this day, on the back roads and quiet streets of rural Connecticut, a group of Melonheads is occasionally spotted driving in the night. Their vehicle is much the worse for wear, but anyone with an eye for classic cars can recognize it as a bumped and battered baby-blue Granada.

Melonheads Still Live on Dracula Drive

We here in Trumbull, Connecticut, have our own Melonheads, who lived on Dracula Drive! As an adult, I was told Dracula Drive really existed and was called Velvet Lane. I pretty much forgot about all this until I got lost tag-saling and ended up on Velvet Lane and realized just why this awful place had inspired the legend. I promised myself I would never go back there. –*Georjean M. Fraina*

My Dad's Seen Melonheads

When my father was a teenager, he and his friends would go to Velvet Street. People would say Melonheads lived in the nearby woods. One night for a joke, his friends pushed my dad out of the car on Velvet Street and drove off. My dad was running like mad to get out of there. His friends came back and picked him up. Later that month my dad and one of his friends saw a mother and a baby in a car in a parking lot. The baby had a huge head as big as a garbage can lid. That was the first Melonhead my dad had ever seen, which is why he believes in Melonheads.
–*Shannon Noonan*

The Farm of the Faceless People

Somewhere, on a rutted, nearly impassable back road in rural Monroe, Connecticut, stands what locals call the House of the Faceless People. This ancient, ramshackle farmhouse is surrounded by swamps and marshland, partially enclosed within a forest of gnarled, bent, and bony-looking trees. All its windows are boarded up. Since faceless people have no eyes, they have no need of windows. But there is another dimension to this architectural modification: security. The house is fortlike—impenetrable—as if designed to keep something out, or in.

If visited at night—and that's the only time to experience the full effect of the place—the house will appear gray in the moonlight. It will be entirely dark. To the eyeless, interior lighting is as useless as windows. But, we're told, on certain occasions a dim kerosene lamp will be visible through the slats covering the window of one room at the downstairs left front corner. This, it is said, is the caretaker's room. He's an old man who oversees the faceless ones. Though he is occasionally spotted working around the yard or chasing away cars that pass by too slowly, his faceless charges remain a mystery.

But there are a few rare individuals who have chanced to glimpse them. These unfortunate witnesses tell a haunting tale of featureless white-domed men, with stretched membranes where their eyes should be, colorless lips, bumps for noses, and holes for ears. But their senses seem strangely heightened, for they will quickly duck out of sight when strangers are nearby, alerted by—who knows?

A cluster of Melonheads? A family of freaks? A pod of earthbound aliens? Or a pathetic population of congenitally malformed? We just don't know. The answer lies in the realm of legend. Or in some elusive swampy hollow on the uncharted back roads of mysterious Monroe, Connecticut.

The Frog People of Danbury and Bethel

They live alone in a desolate compound that no outsiders dare enter. Due to years of inbreeding, they bear hideous features that make them look more like amphibious creatures than human beings. They come out only at night. They are the Frog People.

The *Fairfield County Weekly* ran a short mention of the strange population in 1998. While most reports say that the Frog People live in Danbury, Connecticut, the newspaper placed them in nearby Bethel. "For years, rumors of an inbred family of large-eyed freaks have been circulating throughout the town, even seeping into the gossip of neighboring burgs," the article read. "It is said that this mysterious family lives together on a decrepit compound not far from Bethel's center, and that members of the clan have been observed milling about the place, spilling from open doors and windows, and performing various bizarre, unspecified acts. They even venture into town from time to time, we hear, for the occasional shopping trip."

One of the most pervasive legends regarding the Frog People is that they do not take kindly to outsiders, so few dare to venture near their secluded enclave. But I managed to locate a man who bucked this trend and personally visited the homes of the Frog People. This is Redding native Curtis Gwinn's take on these local legends he has seen with his own two eyes.

"When I was growing up," Curtis said, "I heard about them from other middle school kids. The way they

One of the most pervasive legends regarding the Frog People is that they do not take kindly to outsiders, so few dare to venture near their secluded enclave.

described them was that their eyeballs were on the sides of their heads, that they had thin crusty lips and wide mouths, and sunken noses with nostrils that were just thin slits. They had patchy hair that sat on heads that were too big for their bodies. Their bodies were frail and weak. They wore clothes from the Salvation Army and came out only at night because they were afraid of being tormented. Supposedly, they looked that way because of years of inbreeding.

"The summer before my junior year of high school a friend of mine's mother was running a version of meals-on-wheels at a local Catholic church. I volunteered to help. We would go around in Danbury door-to-door to give out lunches to unfortunates. I had two houses. One was a ten-year-old kid who weighed 250 pounds. His family was never around. He used to try to bribe us into bringing him junk food. He would put hot dogs in his cereal.

"Anyway, my other house was the Frog People. They all share a family name that I can't remember. We'd drop food off for them. They literally wouldn't come to the door. We were told to knock on the door a few times and then leave the food there. Being the mischievous kids we were, we would knock, then hide or drive the car around. It was like condominiums but crappy, like projects. We'd pull around to their unit and wait and watch. The door would crack open, and a hand would come out. They would snatch the food. I never got a great view, but I knew it was them.

"Cut to a year later. I'm doubting they are mutated. I figured they were some destitute family and the rumors were all fake. So I'm at my local Finast grocery store one night at around eleven p.m., with the same two friends from the meals-on-wheels program. We were in the canned goods aisle, by the soups, and there's a Frog

Person in the bright lights of the Finast—those fluorescent lights. It was a guy. He has penny loafers and a short-sleeved dress shirt tucked into khaki pants. We audibly gasped. He turned and saw us, and I'll tell you what—it was not as horrific as described.

"His head was lemon-shaped. He had a very bad lazy eye. His face was sort of stretched, and his eyes and nose did look far apart. He really did have a very froggy appearance. However, he had a normal head of hair. I'd go so far as to say it was even sort of nice, parted on the side. He had a bobble head sort of appearance and was very gangly.

"Then a girl Frog Person came around the corner—blond hair, pretty well groomed. That added to the creepiness of it. If you saw them from behind, they would look totally normal, but if you turn them around, it's a monster!

"They looked up. I know it sounds mean, but they did look like two frogs. Their heads darted away quickly, and they quickly made their way out of the aisle. We got our stuff and left."
—Chris Gethard

Isle of the Wee Folk

Somewhere in the Connecticut River there is said to be an island that, at least briefly, hosted a peculiar population. We first learned of the story in an article written by Betty Hill. But in a later interview she told us that her memory of the details was vague and she could not vouch for her informant. Still, for those interested in what folklorist Michael Bell calls "legend tripping," this one could be a real bonanza. The island in question could be anywhere in the river, which is approximately 410 miles long. Mrs. Hill recalls that it is somewhere near Springfield, Massachusetts.

Events developed roughly as follows:

From the shore, people started to notice activity on an otherwise unpopulated island. Watching through binoculars, folks were surprised to see a number of small, primitive-looking individuals moving about. No boats were seen that might have brought them there. People said the mysterious individuals looked "prehistoric" and guessed the population numbered as many as fifty. Members of this fabled "tribe" were spotted on and off for about three years; then they vanished entirely.

Whether they existed in this world or the fairy realm is part of the mystery, because no one was ever able to get close to them. People—including police—ventured to the island, but the tiny individuals scampered away before they could be accurately observed. It was said they could outrun anyone! Some people swore they vanished into thin air. Others guessed they darted into a system of caves that honeycombed the island. No one could figure out how they survived there for three years, especially during the winter. There was no food source on the island. No fire was ever seen, nor was evidence of a fire ever discovered.

In her article "Bigfoot in New England," Mrs. Hill says, "It was as though somebody had picked up a group of early cavemen and had set them down on the island in a New England countryside. Planes and helicopters had flown over the area, hoping to get pictures, but these little people—they're not really tiny people, but maybe four feet tall or so—would just take off running at such speeds that no one could even get pictures of them. These prehistoric-looking people would be there one instant, then would start running, and in the next instant, they would just disappear!"

So again the question, Were they part of this world, or some other?

The Half-Men of the Connecticut River

When I was growing up, in Chicopee, Massachusetts, my Uncle Joe used to tell us about the half-men who lived in caves down by the Connecticut River. They were part human and part wolf and lay in wait for anyone foolish enough to enter their domain after dark. They were well known in our area. Naturally, since my uncle told us not to go down to the river, my sister, brother, and I had to go. We saw plenty of strange things there. There were giant eels, as wide as a man's thigh. Things we couldn't identify would brush past in the night and go crashing through the woods behind us. One night we saw thousands of strange lights. They might have been fireflies; we were never sure. We never saw the half-men, and I eventually concluded it was my uncle's way of keeping us away from the river. Or was it?—*Tom C.*

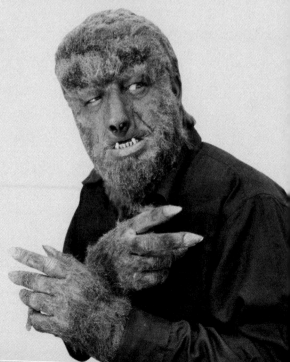

Mysterious Men in Black

Ever since the 1997 blockbuster science-fiction comedy *Men in Black,* people have mistaken the dark-suited heroes for a Hollywood contrivance. But that's not so; MIBs are real. And they're definitely not funny.

Though we may wonder who—or what—they are, perhaps the bigger question is, Where do they come from? If not Hollywood, then where? Are they from the government or some other planet or maybe a parallel dimension? Wherever they may have originated, their point of entry seems to have been New England. More specifically, Bridgeport, Connecticut.

It's true that they dress up when they come calling. Wearing dark suits with broad-brimmed black hats, sunglasses, black ties, and shoes polished to an ebony sheen, they usually arrive in threes, driving big black cars that are several years old but appear brand-new. They are often described as dark skinned, possibly looking Oriental, Italian, or like gypsies. Sometimes they walk awkwardly and speak in various peculiar ways.

It all started in the early 1950s, when Albert K. Bender, a Bridgeport factory clerk, took an interest in the relatively new phenomenon of flying saucers. He studied them, conducted private investigations, and eventually founded the International Flying Saucer Bureau. With Mr. Bender as editor, the group's newsletter, *Space Review,* was mailed to an ever-increasing number of subscribers.

UFO study was in its infancy then, so believers automatically assumed the saucers were spaceships carrying visitors—or maybe enemies—from faraway planets. What could these alien beings want? *Space Review* subscribers were understandably delighted when, in September 1953, editor Bender wrote, "I know what the saucers are." He had solved the mystery! He wasn't revealing details, though—not yet.

Disappointment soon followed. His next issue said, "The mystery of the

flying saucers is no longer a mystery. . . . [But] any information about this is being withheld by orders from a higher source. We would like to print the full story . . . but . . . we have been advised in the negative." Then he issued an ominous warning: Anyone engaged in flying saucer research should be "very cautious." Subsequently Mr. Bender stopped publishing his magazine and closed his research bureau.

So what happened? Some of Albert Bender's acquaintances guessed he'd run out of money and didn't want to admit it. Closer associates, however, noticed that he was acting strangely, suffering disabling headaches whenever the topic of UFOs came up. In a newspaper interview, Mr. Bender later told an astonishing tale. He said he had described his UFO revelations in a private letter mailed to a friend. Then three Men in Black showed up and returned his letter—unopened. Their extraordinary visit began as Albert was resting on his bed. He said he became aware of "three shadowy figures in the room. . . . All of them were dressed in black clothes. They looked like clergymen but wore hats similar to Homburg style."

Their behavior was so intimidating that Albert Bender actually feared for his life. Apparently, they told him something so menacing that he would never speak about UFOs again. Today, living in California, he still holds his silence.

Though Mr. Bender never explicitly said so, many people guessed the MIBs represented some branch of government that was charged with covering up the truth about UFOs. Others thought that they were emissaries from the flying saucers themselves.

The Albert K. Bender episode seems to be the first modern example of intervention by the seemingly sinister Men in Black. Soon other UFO witnesses were receiving visits from these intimidating intruders.

MIBs in Maine

At first glance, it might appear that the strange black-clad messengers' only purpose is to silence anyone who has information about UFOs. However, further study reveals that MIBs also harass individuals who simply have an elevated curiosity about the UFO question. One of the most puzzling cases on record occurred in Old Orchard Beach, Maine.

On September 11, 1976, Herbert Hopkins, a healthy fifty-eight-year-old medical doctor, was tape-recording a session with a hypnotized patient. They were trying to reconstruct the events of an apparent UFO abduction. Later that evening, alone in his home, Dr. Hopkins received a phone call from the vice president of the New Jersey UFO Research Organization. The caller said he'd heard about Dr. Hopkins's abduction case and wondered if he might stop by to discuss it. Dr. Hopkins said he'd be grateful for the help.

Immediately after hanging up, Dr. Hopkins heard the man already climbing the front steps. How the outsider had heard about the case and his quick trip from New Jersey didn't strike Dr. Hopkins as odd at the time. What he noticed was how strangely the man was dressed: black suit, black socks, black shoes, black tie, and a white shirt. The trousers were sharply creased. The clothing looked brand-new and wrinkle-free.

When the man politely removed his black hat, Dr. Hopkins saw that he was not only completely bald, but also completely hairless: no eyebrows, no eyelashes, no stubble of facial hair. The man's skin was as white as his shirt. His mouth was a brilliant red. At one point during their conversation, the man's hand brushed his lip. To Dr. Hopkins amazement the lips smeared, staining the pallid hand with lipstick.

The weirdness level quickly escalated. Somehow the stranger seemed to know everything about the UFO case—even information that had never been released. Then, at some point during their discussion, the man made an incongruous observation: He said that Dr. Hopkins had two coins in his pocket. The doctor agreed it was true.

"Take one of them in your hand and stare at it," the man instructed. Expecting an ill-timed parlor trick, Dr. Hopkins complied. As he concentrated on the coin, it seemed to change. First it became hazy, while the lines of his hand remained in perfect focus. Then it seemed to change color. Finally, unbelievably, it faded from sight,

vanishing entirely from the doctor's open palm. As the disbelieving man gaped, the stranger said, "Neither you nor anyone else on this planet will ever see that coin again."

At some point in their convoluted discussion the man asked if Dr. Hopkins knew about Betty and Barney Hill, a Portsmouth, New Hampshire, couple who supposedly had been abducted by aliens in 1961.

"Yes," Dr. Hopkins said. "Mr. Hill recently passed away, didn't he?"

"That's right," said the man. "And do you know what he died from?"

"I'm not sure," said Dr. Hopkins. "I think it was a heart attack."

"That's not entirely the case," the man replied. "He died because he knew too much."

As the weird, wandering dialogue continued, Dr. Hopkins noticed that the stranger's speech was slowing down. Soon, with great effort, the visitor struggled to his feet. "My energy is running low," he said. "Must go now. Good-bye."

He crossed unsteadily to the door and left abruptly. Alone again, Dr. Hopkins slowly began to understand how bizarre the entire experience had been. As he replayed it in his memory, his terror mounted. Clearly, he had been threatened.

Later, when his wife and children returned, they found Dr. Hopkins in a locked house, with every light in the place burning brightly. He visibly shook as he sat at the kitchen table with a gun beside him. Ultimately, the good doctor went along with the two "requests" his black-suited visitor had made: He erased the tapes of the hypnosis sessions, and he withdrew from the UFO abduction case. After that, he never saw the strange man again. When he tried to contact the New Jersey UFO Research Organization, he learned that it had never existed.

Triangular Terror

It may be possible that certain geographical areas are prone to paranormal activity. In *Lo!*, while discussing a baffling unexplained disappearance, Charles Fort speculated that there may exist "a transporting current through so-called solid substance, which 'opened and then closed,' with no sign of yawning. It may be that what we call substance is as much open as closed."

In other words, Mr. Fort was talking about holes in the universe. Various writers have used other labels to describe these holes. New England horror visionary H. P. Lovecraft discussed "dimensional gateways." Rod Serling called them "twilight zones." And zoologist Ivan Sanderson introduced the slightly more ominous "vile vortices."

But it was the Fortean writer Vincent Gaddis who coined the term "Bermuda Triangle" when describing the most famous of these mystery-charged regions.

Today the Triangle is part of our language. It has come to designate any area where anything can happen. Anything weird, that is. Pterodactyl sightings. Flying saucers. Shambling man-beasts. Vanishings. Time slips. Whatever. They all seem to congregate in certain topographical ghettos known as Triangles.

Perhaps the Roadside Robots slipped in through one of these triangular gateways. Perhaps the Old Darn Man's mysterious mansion was situated somewhere on this unreal real estate. Maybe the Melonheads are there right now. Just beyond the tricornered threshold. Peeking through. Ready to come in.

And maybe there's a break in the veil between this dimension and another right here in New England.

The Bridgewater Triangle

Take a map of Massachusetts. Draw lines connecting the towns of Abingdon, Freetown, and Rehoboth. You have just outlined what researcher Loren Coleman identified as the Bay State's Bridgewater Triangle, an area of some two hundred square miles. Dead center in the triangle is the largest swampland in all New England — the murky, shadow infested, quicksand dappled, 6,000-acre Hockomock Swamp. It is a vast primeval horror-scape, unchanged for five hundred years, and just forty minutes from Boston.

In the language of the local Indians, "Hockomock" means something like "place of spirits." For them it is and has always been both sacred and evil.

In his book *Mysterious America*, Loren Coleman described an 8,000-year-old burial ground discovered by archaeologists on Grassy Island in Hockomock Swamp. As the graves were excavated, the red ocher within began to bubble and dissolve. There was no known reason for this odd chemical disturbance. Stranger still, all attempts to document the event were frustrated; every photograph failed to come out.

On the riverbank across from the Grassy Island burial ground stands the mysterious Dighton Rock with its unfathomable markings (described earlier in this volume). During Colonial times, the normally blue skies over the Triangle occasionally glowed a mysterious yellow. These so-called Yellow Days have never been explained.

Even today, every January right on schedule, elusive spheres of incandescence known as spook lights zip along the railroad tracks near the dog-racing stadium in Raynham. Pulsating baseball-sized ghost lights are frequently witnessed along Elm Street in Bridgewater. They change color — red, blue, and orange — as they bounce along and vanish.

Bigger lights, shaped like more traditional UFOs, are frequent visitors to the Triangle's skies. Boston newsman Jerry Lopez saw one on March 23, 1979, and reported it on WHDW radio. He said it was shaped like home plate on a baseball field. It sported bright red lights on top and rows of white and red lights around the sides. His sighting was at the intersection of Routes 24 and 106, right at the center of the Bridgewater Triangle.

In January 1991, witnesses in Bridgewater reported a green flying disk about fifty feet up and moving slowly. It was silent as its brilliant spotlight illuminated the ground below. It seemed to be looking for something.

Though the objects described above seem to be mechanical, other UFOs appear to be alive. A giant bird is occasionally seen. The number of reports suggest that a whole flock of them might reside within the Triangle. About two o'clock one summer night in 1971, for example, Norton police sergeant Thomas Downy was patrolling along Winter Street in Mansfield. On a place known as Bird Hill, he spied a gigantic winged creature flying straight upward. It was over six feet tall, with a wingspan of eight to twelve feet.

He was not the first to see such feathered phantoms at that particular spot. Perhaps such sightings explain why it's called Bird Hill. But doesn't it seem odd that the officer's name was Downy?

In 1988, two Bridgewater boys followed man-sized, three-toed tracks . . . until they saw the bird that was making them. It had a black, wrinkled face, dark feathers, and long brown legs that dangled behind it as it flew off into the forest. The wingspan, they estimated, was greater than twelve feet. In 1992, in Taunton, the bird was seen again. Witnesses described a wingspan of ten to twelve feet. Odder still, some people have asserted it looks less like a bird and more like a man with wings.

Bigfootlike critters also roam the Bridgewater Triangle. They are routinely blamed for the unearthly screeching that issues from the depths of the swamp. Though they are generally described as docile and retiring, in the early 1970s, one of the shambling hairy bipeds seemed to go haywire, making war on farm animals. For no apparent reason, it killed and mutilated pigs and sheep belonging to several local farmers. Police with attack dogs searched the swamp for two days and nights, but found nothing. Of course they didn't say they were hunting for Bigfoot. They called it a bear hunt, though residents and police alike know that no bears have been in the region for many years.

Maybe the creature got chased away by the giant dogs that inhabit the swamp. One oversized, vicious hellhound was reported in Abingdon, where it ripped out the throats of two ponies. Witnesses said it was as big as the animals it killed. This crypto-canine went on to terrorize the community for several weeks, evading every attempt to capture it. Police officer Frank Curran did get off a shot at it. Unfazed, the dog turned slowly away and sauntered off down the railroad tracks. Admittedly, Officer Curran could have missed. Then again, maybe he should have been using silver bullets.

Visits by these weird critters are invariably short, dramatic, and puzzling. Somehow they manage to elude all attempts to kill or capture them. Can it be coincidence that such a wide variety of seemingly paranormal occurrences take place in such a defined area and have been doing so for so many years?

One is almost forced to believe that within these so-called Triangles of Terror there really are gateways to the beyond, and unusual animals from some other place have somehow tumbled into our world. But what happens when one of us trips through a gateway and stumbles into unknown and alien terrain—the other side of the Triangle?

Bennington—The Triangle of No Return

In a 1992 public radio broadcast, your author swiped the term Triangle to designate the mysterious area around Glastenbury Mountain, near Bennington, Vermont. It was then that the name Bennington Triangle was coined, but this rugged wilderness area had long been the scene of some of the state's most terrifying mysteries.

In fact, Glastenbury Mountain has always been considered a haunted place. Indians said it was cursed, and the earliest settlers experienced strange lights, eerie sounds, and unidentifiable odors. Some had run-ins with monstrous unknown animals and lived to tell the tale. And others . . . well, their fate is uncertain. They vanished.

Not so very long ago, in the late 1940s and early '50s, at least six people disappeared from the Bennington Triangle. It's as if they stepped off the edge of the earth. This recent cluster of vanishings started with a man named Middie Rivers, a seventy-five-year-old hunting and fishing guide. A lifelong native of the region, Mr. Rivers led four hunters up the mountain on November 12, 1945. Returning, he got a little ahead of the others. They never caught up to their guide; Middie Rivers vanished completely. Volunteers and police combed the area for a month, but no trace, nothing, was ever found.

An eighteen-year-old Bennington College sophomore was the second to go. On Sunday, December 1, 1946, the petite Paula Welden set out for a short hike on the Long Trail. She never came back. The next day the sheriff's department was joined by four hundred students, faculty, and townspeople for a thorough, well-conducted search. Later FBI teams combed the mountains for weeks. In spite of a $5,000 reward, hundreds of volunteers, and the aid of a famous clairvoyant, nothing turned up. The official search ended on December 22 with no results.

A third person vanished in December 1949. Perhaps coincidentally, it was on the third anniversary of Paula Welden's disappearance. Jim Tedford had been visiting relatives in St. Albans and was returning to Bennington by bus. Impossible as it may sound, witnesses saw him get on the bus, but apparently he never got off. Poof! Gone without a trace. As usual, no one saw anything. Even the bus driver could offer no explanation.

In the fall of 1950 it was Freida Langer's turn. While hiking with her cousin on the Glastenbury slopes, Freida slipped and fell into a stream. In spite of her stumble, Freida was an experienced outdoors person and gun-handler, thoroughly familiar with the area. Her cousin waited while she ran the short distance home to change clothes.

But she never came back, and she never reached home. And no one saw her come out of the woods. Again, there was a long hunt involving hundreds of well-practiced searchers; again nothing. The local newspaper, the *Bennington Banner,* summed up what many people were feeling: "One of the things hard to explain is how Mrs. Langer could have become so completely lost in an hour's time before dark in an area with which she was so thoroughly familiar."

A few days after the search ended, Frances Christman left home to visit a friend a half mile away. Somewhere on that brief hike she too vanished without a trace.

All those people vanishing between 1945 and 1950. Gone as if they'd blinked out of existence. How can we possibly explain it? Did big hairy monsters carry them away to the caves and swamps of Glastenbury Mountain? Did tiny aliens whisk them off to faraway galaxies? Or could they have slipped through some interdimensional trapdoor, some New England equivalent of the Bermuda Triangle?

Then again, the solution could be something more mundane, something with which police were not so familiar in 1945: a serial killer. Even then locals speculated about a particularly cunning madman alternately called the Bennington Ripper or the Mad Murderer of the Long Trail. But the fact is, no murder was ever proved, and no evidence of murder ever came to light.

We'll probably never find an answer. All we can say for sure is that the mysterious vanishings in the Bennington Triangle took place over a limited amount of time: five years. And mostly during the last three months of the calendar year. Victims' ages spanned from an eight-year-old named Paul Jepson to seventy-five-year-old Middie Rivers. Half were women. Though no reasonable theory to explain the disappearances has ever been put forth, there is one grisly footnote to the story. On May 12, 1951, the body of Freida Langer reappeared! Seven months after she'd vanished, her corpse was discovered among tall grasses near Somerset Reservoir, right out in the open and easily visible. The original teams of searchers simply could not have missed her—they had repeatedly combed that area for weeks. In fact, the hunt for Freida Langer had probably been the most thorough of all. It is as if she had been snatched away and then put back.

But the whole thing remains unexplained. The reappearing corpse offered no clues. As the local newspaper reported, Freida's remains were in "gruesome condition."

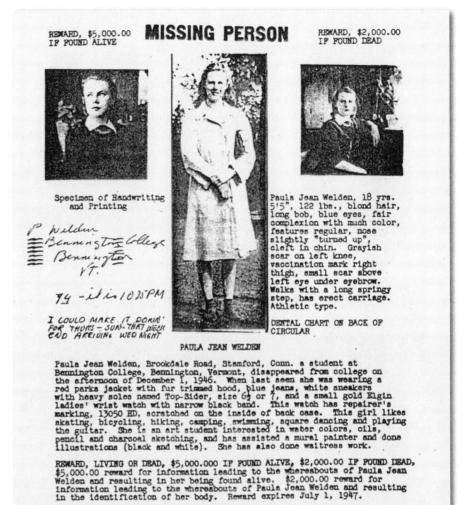

In spite of a $5,000 reward, hundreds of volunteers, and the aid of a famous clairvoyant, nothing turned up.

Unexplained Phenomena

Anyone *reading this book* has probably made the literary acquaintance of Charles Fort, who is considered the father of all collectors of weird phenomena. Having grown up in Albany, New York, he was almost a New Englander.

But Fort had some notable predecessors. Perhaps the great-great-grandfather of oddity collectors was none other than John Winthrop, first governor of the Massachusetts Bay Colony. In March of 1639 he recorded an incident of incontestably high strangeness. He saw a bright luminous object zipping around the skies over what is now the Back Bay section of Boston. This CUFO (Colonial Unidentified Flying Object) seemed to play zigzag games in the sky. Certain witnesses— and there were many—said its actions resembled those of a pig trying to elude capture as it raced "hither and yon."

It vanished for a while, only to return in January of 1695. This time it brought a companion—two moon-sized luminous objects seeming to play tag over Boston Harbor. And now there was an elevated degree of strangeness: Witnesses heard a voice in the sky repeating, "in a most dreadful manner," the words "Boy . . . boy . . . come away . . . come away."

Two weeks later the aerial orb returned, intoning the same unearthly summons. No one has ever determined who—or what—was doing the calling, who the boy was, or where he was being called to.

A mystery, yes, and it goes to show one thing: New Englanders have been observing, experiencing, and collecting unexplained phenomena for a good long time. And, as we shall see, only a small portion of them take place in the skies. Some occur right under our noses.

Boom in Burlington

Let's take a new look at an aerial event that occurred about a century ago in downtown Burlington, Vermont. Since it happened long before jet airplanes were ever dreamed of, sonic booms can't be the culprit. Indeed, on the morning of the occurrence, July 2, 1907, there were fewer than five airplanes in the whole U.S.A. But something unnatural took place in the skies above Burlington.

On that morning, just before noon, hundreds of people heard a terrific explosion. Windows rattled. Animals howled. Bewildered pigeons zigzagged through the air. A gunshot, perhaps? A cannon? Some premature Independence Day fireworks? No, it was too massive a sound for such trifling explanations.

The impact was loudest in the business section, near Church and College streets. The first people on the scene found a horse flattened in front of the Standard Coal and Ice Company. Several men rushed to it, only to discover the dazed animal struggling to its feet. One individual was sure he had seen a mysterious flying object, a glowing ball, strike the center of College Street, bounce, knock down the horse, then soar off into the sky.

Alvaro Adsit, co-owner of Ferguson and Adsit's Store, saw a "ball of fire" descending in front of Hall's Furniture Store. When the ball was about fifteen feet above the ground, Mr. Adsit reported, it "exploded with a deafening sound." He said it had been eight or ten inches in diameter, with a surrounding halo measuring about ten feet.

Mr. W. P. Dodds of the Equitable Life Insurance building said the ball "was moving . . . from the northwest [over the Howard Bank building] and gradually descending."

Recently an international scientific research organization called the Center for the Study of

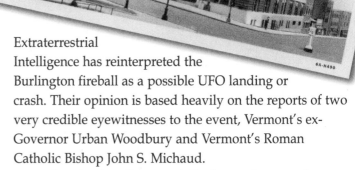

Extraterrestrial Intelligence has reinterpreted the Burlington fireball as a possible UFO landing or crash. Their opinion is based heavily on the reports of two very credible eyewitnesses to the event, Vermont's ex-Governor Urban Woodbury and Vermont's Roman Catholic Bishop John S. Michaud.

Bishop Michaud reported, "I observed a torpedo-shaped body some 300 feet away, stationary in appearance and suspended in the air about 50 feet above the tops of the buildings. . . . It was about six feet long by eight inches in diameter, the shell-cover having a dark appearance, with here and there tongues of fire issuing from spots on the surface resembling red-hot unburnished copper.

"Although stationary when first noticed," he continued, "this object soon began to move, rather slowly, and disappeared over Dolan Brothers' store [on the corner of College and Mechanic streets, heading] southward. As it moved, the covering seemed rupturing in places and through these the intensely red flames issued. . . ." He added, "I hope I may never hear or see a similar phenomenon. . . ."

So today we're still left with a major puzzle: Exactly what did Burlingtonians see on that otherwise clear July morning? If the Center for the Study of Extraterrestrial Intelligence is correct, it was some variety of otherworldly craft. And if they're right about its crashing, then we must ask — what happened to its remains?

The Perforated Pond

And what happened to the remains that should have been recovered from the bottom of Bill McCarthy's pond in Wakefield, New Hampshire?

Around noon on January 10, 1977, farmer McCarthy looked out his window and saw something extraordinary: a big hole in the ice of his pond. A month earlier he might have thought nothing of it, but now everything around Wakefield was frozen up solid. The pond ice was a good eighteen inches thick.

Upon inspecting the mysterious opening, Mr. McCarthy found it perfectly round and about three feet in diameter. The puzzled farmer found a long stick and began poking around under the ice. He definitely struck something submerged in the water. As he peered below the murky surface, he "saw what appeared to be a square black object." Not sure what else to do, Mr. McCarthy phoned the police.

Big mistake. That innocent phone call touched off a national furor. The police showed up with a bunch of Civil Defense workers, their Geiger counters clicking like crazy. Radiation was so high that officials ordered everyone to stay clear of the pond. They also instructed the McCarthys not to tell anyone about the incident.

But word got out. Suddenly an army of photographers, TV crews, and journalists were crawling all over the place. By the end of the afternoon, the National Guard, the Attorney General, and even the Pentagon were in on the act.

Every airfield within one hundred miles was checked.

No military or civilian craft had dropped anything over New Hampshire. Experts ruled out meteors, natural thawing, hot springs, satellite debris, and giant ice fishermen with oversized augers. By nightfall, after hours of chaos and confusion, everyone but the official guards gave up and went home.

Next morning the underwater mystery plunged a few fathoms deeper. New readings showed that the radioactivity had vanished. And so, apparently, had the black box Bill McCarthy said he had seen. However, certain eyewitnesses maintained that National Guardsmen had removed something from the pond and hauled it away in the back of a truck. State officials said that a chemist had taken samples of water and soil, which he'd carried away in a black box. But no one admitted taking anything else.

In the days to come, amid de-escalating confusion, Mr. McCarthy noticed another oddity: The hole never seemed to refreeze. Even after a windy subzero night, only a slush would form in the opening.

And that's the story. We can be certain of only one indisputable fact: *Something* made that hole. Could it have originated beneath the water, shooting up and out like an underwater cruise missile? Or should we believe something crashed down through the ice, then reversed direction, exiting through the same perfectly round hole?

We don't really know if this occurrence was UFO-related. But other New Hampshire weirdness is less ambiguous.

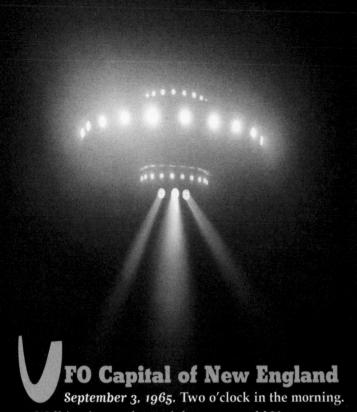

UFO Capital of New England

September 3, 1965. Two o'clock in the morning. Walking home alone, eighteen-year-old Norman Muscarello spots something in the skies above Kensington, New Hampshire. When the bright object seems to make a beeline toward him, he ducks, flags down a passing car, and reports the aerial oddity to the police station in nearby Exeter.

Officer Eugene Bertrand accompanies Norman to the field where he had been "attacked" by the unidentified flying object. There they both see something bright moving above the treetops. Fearing it might rush them again, both men take shelter in the police cruiser. Soon Officer David Hunt joins them, and all three watch the bright, silent object soar noiselessly south toward the sea.

This event marked the beginning of an avalanche of UFO sightings that culminated in John G. Fuller's well-known book *Incident at Exeter.* It also went a long way toward establishing New Hampshire as the UFO capital of New England.

Adventure on a Flying Saucer

The queen of New England's UFO capital is, of course, the late Betty Hill. Her 1961 UFO abduction was made famous in another of John Fuller's best-selling books, *The Interrupted Journey: Two Lost Hours Aboard a Flying Saucer* (1965). The story of the Hills' dramatic abduction in New Hampshire's White Mountains is so well known, so thoroughly documented, and so ridiculously complex that we can only summarize it here.

On September 19, 1961, Mr. and Mrs. Hill were heading home to Portsmouth, New Hampshire, after a Canadian vacation. It was dark, around ten o'clock at night. Near the town of Lancaster, Barney became extremely nervous when he noticed a bright object in the sky. It seemed to be following their car. At some point, the object passed directly overhead. In front of them now, it wavered slightly, with attached yellow lights glowing.

Barney stopped and tried to get a better look with his binoculars. As he got out of the car, Betty heard strange beeping sounds. Suddenly Barney jumped back into the car, crying, "Let's get out of here!" As he sped down the road, the terrified Barney said he had seen a man watching him from the mysterious craft.

When the beeping started again, their whole vehicle began to vibrate. Barney tried to escape the UFO by turning down a side road. But the beeping continued. Then they saw a sign saying seventeen miles to Concord. It seemed to the Hills that they had traveled an awfully long way entirely too quickly. From there on, the trip home was uneventful. But the more they thought about it, the more they realized that about two hours were unaccounted for.

Soon Betty began experiencing nightmares involving little men with big heads and slanty eyes. Barney became uncommonly nervous, silent, and moody. In time, the couple decided to visit a psychiatrist, Dr. Benjamin Simon of Arlington, Massachusetts. Though he didn't believe in

Betty and Barney Hill

beginning when Barney turned onto that side road to escape the saucer.

First, the car died. Then six small, thin men approached. They wore dark uniforms; some had hats. Their eyes appeared Oriental and spaced farther than normal on the sides of their large, hairless heads. They had tiny noses and lipless slits for mouths.

Barney panicked, but somehow Betty remained calm as the creatures removed them from their car. "They aren't so awful-looking," she kept telling herself. As the aliens walked the Hills through the woods, one of the little men repeated to Betty in clumsy English, "Don't be afraid. We're just going to do some tests. . . ."

They moved into a clearing, where a ramp led up to the grounded saucer. Inside, the Hills were separated and each of them was examined. The little men collected samples of their skin, fingernails, and hair. They inspected the couple's eyes and throats. All the while the abductors jabbered away in a language the Hills could not understand.

The most terrifying part of Betty's exam was when they unzipped her dress and placed her on an examining table. There one of the little men inserted a long needle into her navel. This was the only part of the exam that was truly painful. Betty screamed and began crying. When the alien placed his hand over Betty's eyes, the pain vanished. "It's just a pregnancy test," he explained in broken English.

Betty recalled a humorous incident that contrasted with her moment of horror. Three excited little men hurried into the room and began tugging on Betty's teeth. They were amazed that Barney's came out and Betty's didn't. Apparently, their science didn't include an understanding of dentures.

After some time, the Hills were released and the modern age of UFO abductions began.

UFOs, Dr. Simon was convinced he could employ hypnosis to discover what had really happened that mysterious night.

In trances, Barney and Betty told their stories separately. Dr. Simon was so shocked by their disclosures that he would puzzle over them until his dying day. He was convinced the Hills were not fabricating the episode, but he could find no way to explain it. Here's what they said happened during the two hours of missing time,

Biopsy of an Alien Bump

Have human beings really *been* abducted by aliens? That may be the most vexing mystery of the last half century. It all comes down to proof. The scoffers say, "Where's the evidence?" The believers say, "There's plenty of evidence if you would just look at it."

These abduction experiences seem to have hit a full range of New Englanders. We have interviewed a former entertainer, an ex-policeman, and a recreation worker, all claiming they were spirited away by tiny, frail-looking alien beings. But the question remains, What happens to the evidence? One Vermonter's story may give us some insight.

Jack Weiner is one of four men who went camping in the wilds of Maine's Allagash region. There, over a lake, the men saw a light in the sky. After that, things got weird.

Later the men had no memory of what had happened, only a vague sense of unease. Plagued by bad dreams and physical symptoms, the four began to realize that the light had been a UFO. As with the Hills, hypnosis revealed that its occupants had taken the campers aboard and performed what seemed to be medical examinations.

In time, Jack discovered a lump under the skin of his lower right leg. When the apparent growth didn't go away, he visited a local doctor. The puzzled M.D. referred Jack to a specialist at Brattleboro Memorial Hospital. This specialist decided that whatever it was had to come out and removed it surgically. The object, Jack says, was "pinkish in color and looked like chewed-up bubble gum."

The Brattleboro lab wanted a more detailed analysis than they could give, so they said they were sending it off to the Centers for Disease Control in Atlanta, Georgia.

Time passed. After about two months, an understandably anxious Jack asked if the doctor had any

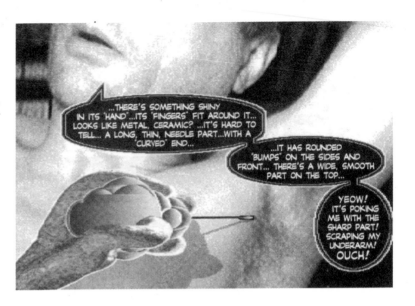

news from the Georgia lab. No, he didn't, the doctor said.

Two more worry-filled months passed before the doctor finally gave Jack the lab results.

"Nothing to worry about," he said. But apparently, the consulting lab had been unable to identify the sample.

Could the lump have been related to Jack's confrontation with the UFO? Massachusetts UFO investigator Ray Fowler wasn't sure. He asked Jack to get his medical transcript from the Brattleboro hospital. The records clerk checked the computer and asked, "Were you in the military when this happened?" When Jack said no, the clerk seemed perplexed. "Gee," she said, "they sent [your material] to a military institute. . . ."

It was true; the report was signed by William R. Cowan, colonel, U.S. Air Force, director of the Armed Forces Institute of Pathology in Washington, DC. This most decidedly was *not* the Georgia lab Jack had been told about. Stranger still, there was no transmittal letter to explain why it had been sent to Washington.

Next Mr. Fowler asked Jack to obtain copies of his X-rays for examination by another medical doctor. "Okay," said a friendly nurse in radiology. But, Jack says, when she called up his file on the computer, her friendly attitude suddenly changed. She began grilling him about who wanted the records and why. Finally she had no choice but to agree, but said he'd have to pick them up the next day, which he did.

At this point, Jack must have felt like a character in an *X-Files* episode. Implants? Secret testing? Military involvement? Was Jack's mysterious lump evidence of an alien abduction? We'll probably never know. But even without UFOs, this chain of events is pretty puzzling.

What we find especially disturbing is that someone in a small Vermont hospital would know enough to send the mysterious pink object to a specific air force pathologist. If, as some people believe, there really is a conspiracy to cover up military-alien contact, it must be pretty widespread to have reached Vermont. But then, we don't really know how widespread it is, do we?

The Elusive Hum-m-m-m-m-m-m

Certain Vermont residents in Newark and the surrounding towns have been hearing a mysterious sound— an elusive low-pitched hum often described as resembling the distant drone of a diesel engine. No one has any idea what it is.

Newark is in Caledonia County, part of Vermont's fabled Northeast Kingdom. But that is as close as anyone can come to determining the exact source of the sound. It is also difficult to pinpoint exactly when people started hearing it, but it first reached public attention in March 1997, when the *Caledonian Record* reported it. Oddly, as if to contradict the article, the hum immediately stopped. But after a few days, it started again, steadier now and slightly higher pitched.

There are many puzzling attributes associated with Vermont's mysterious hum:

1. It occurs in places where there's no electricity, so we can eliminate dehumidifiers, blenders, milking machines, and pump motors submerged in wells. Even during power outages, the hum keeps humming along.

2. Not everyone can hear it. Those who can are often sharing a room with people who cannot. Even more weird: In some cases, deaf people can hear it while someone with perfect hearing cannot.

3. Different people describe it in different ways. In general, it's perceived as low pitched, like an electrical motor running in a distant room. Sometimes it sounds deeper, turning on and off at unpredictable intervals. Sometimes it fades in and out.

In the old days, speculation might have gravitated toward the supernatural. But this is the twenty-first century; surely science can explain this odd noise. But the laboratory lets us down. The hum cannot be detected by microphones or special low-frequency antennas.

The mystery of Vermont's hum broadens when we realize this puzzling phenomenon is not confined to the Green Mountain State. Similar low-pitched sounds are heard all over the country and all over the world: New Jersey, Florida, Minnesota, Michigan, New York, England, and northern Europe. Explanations range from UFO interference to stresses in the earth's crust, to epidemic ear problems. Some scientists even speculate that certain people are hypersensitive to the growing volume of electromagnetic noise from microwave communications, cordless phones, and the like.

But the truth is, no one knows what causes the hum. As mysteries go, this one's a humdinger.

Moodus Noises

If we travel farther south, to East Haddam, Connecticut, we find the grand-daddy of New England's unaccountable clamor—the venerable Moodus Noises. There the earth rumbles and shakes as if Mother Nature is in continual gastrointestinal distress.

The original Native Americans knew the cause: It was that old devil Hobomoko who sat in his underground chamber and, as devils will, raised a ruckus. Indians called the area Machemoodus, which translates as something like "place of noises." Apparently, the underground rumblings got worse when white settlers started showing up around 1670. The Indians said that their god was upset because the English god had moved in. Perfectly understandable.

In 1729, Haddam's first minister, Rev. Stephen Hosmer, wrote, "Oftentimes I have heard [the sounds] to be coming down from the north, imitating slow thunder, which shakes the houses and all that is in them." Then Rev. Hosmer adds, "Now whether there be any thing diabolical in these things, I know not. . . ."

It was easy for New England Puritans to believe their trek into the wilderness had delivered them to the very gates of hell, what with wild animals and hostile Indians and who knew what else running around in the primeval woods. During the crazy witchcraft era of the 1690s, a story developed involving a local conflict between the "black" witches of Haddam and the "white" witches of Moodus—or maybe it was the other way around. Anyway, their battle took place in the vast cave under Mount Tom. The sounds of their warfare became the Moodus Noises. Illumination of the battlefield was supplied by a so-called Great Carbuncle. The carbuncle apparently was a pearl, though how it got into a cave under Mount Tom is a mystery on top of a mystery.

Around 1760, King George sent an alchemist by the name of Dr. Steel to Connecticut to end the curse of the noises. One night the good doctor was seen leaving his house carrying a glowing red "something," presumably the cursed carbuncle. He tried transporting the rock back to England, but his ship sank. Poor Dr. Steel had been misguided; the noises continued after the offending "pearl" returned to the oysters.

In 1923, Charles Fort wrote about the strange noises in his book *New Lands.* His attention moved the matter slightly toward natural science, but he concluded that "no satisfactory explanation" existed. And as recently as 1988, Walter Sullivan wrote about the sounds in *The New York Times.* His article was titled "A Connecticut Mystery Still Defying Scientists," which pretty much sums up his conclusion.

Today's belief is that the Moodus Noises are the product of mini-earthquakes that occur close to the surface. But the cause of the quakes is a mystery, and so, strictly speaking, the noises remain unexplained.

Beware the Celestial Symphony

Reports of a mystical musical phenomenon heard by very few people—a so-called Music of the Spheres—have been around for centuries. Supposedly, on unpredictable occasions, certain individuals hear beautiful, awe-inspiring harmonies that seem to come from nowhere. The music is so exquisite some have said they would gladly die just to hear those heavenly harmonies again.

One example happened in Barnet, Vermont, in 1812. One bright July morning fourteen-year-old Elizabeth McCallum set out on horseback to visit the John McNab family, who lived several miles east through a thickly wooded section of Blue Mountain, not far from the Connecticut River.

When she arrived at the McNabs', Elizabeth was in a state of excitement and wonder. She told them that something marvelous had happened in the woods. She described the spot with precision, and it was a place John McNab knew well. Breathlessly, the girl explained how, virtually in the middle of nowhere, she had heard strange and beautiful music, like nothing she had ever heard before. It seemed to come from every direction, filling the air, displacing all other sounds.

Now, Elizabeth was known to be a trustworthy young woman, so John McNab and his family were quite taken by this fascinating account. But no one could offer an explanation for the mysterious sounds. Elizabeth had lunch with the McNabs, then hurried home to tell her own family about her wonderful experience. She followed the same trail, hoping to hear the beautiful sounds again.

But Elizabeth never arrived home.

As twilight thickened into darkness, her parents grew alarmed. Mr. McCallum summoned a few neighbors, who grabbed lanterns and torches before setting out along the darkened path toward the McNab place. Within an hour, they found Elizabeth's horse—without its rider. Then the girl was discovered lying beside the trail, dead. There were no marks or bruises on her body, and no blood or broken bones. In fact, there was nothing to give the searchers any clue about how Elizabeth McCallum had met her end.

Later, John McNab and his wife told the McCallums about the music Elizabeth said she had heard. Recalling Elizabeth's description of the spot, Mr. McNab was able to determine that her body had been discovered exactly where she had heard the mysterious melody.

But a puzzle remains: What did poor Elizabeth hear? Music from some passing spaceship? Woodland elves in concert? Or perhaps a recital by a celestial choir of angels?

Lord knows visits from divine entities are just business as usual in New England and have been for a long time. It was here that prophet William Miller predicted the end of the world—three times! Mary Baker Eddy began the Christian Science Church in New Hampshire, while Vermont's John Humphrey Noyes came up with the notion of Perfectionism. And Joseph Smith, founder of the Mormon Church, was born in Vermont. But few people have heard of another New England prophet: Melissa Warner of Bristol, Vermont. This modest farmwife got an important message directly from God, but was too timid to pass it along.

Mrs. Warner's Warning

In March 1843, while working alone in her house, Melissa Warner experienced a startling encounter. According to testimony recorded by her minister, Rev. Calvin Butler, she saw two entities descend "quick as lightning from heaven " and hover near the roof. One seemed to radiate a golden glow as he sat, half reclining, in midair. A wound in his chest convinced Mrs. Warner she was looking at Jesus Christ. The other, a luminous cloud, she recognized as God the Father.

Then Jesus spoke, saying, "You see I am coming [and] have advanced almost to the earth and shall soon be there." He then commanded Mrs. Warner to "warn the impenitent of their danger[;] instruct them to prepare for my coming. Tell all of my speedy approach for they are stupid and insensible of it."

Then, as she stared directly at Him, He disappeared.

Meanwhile, the cloud descended. Mrs. Warner noted a peculiar detail: Part of it opened and closed like a mouth as God went on to explain how mankind's stupidity and disbelief arose from human reason, vain philosophy, and worldly logic. With that, the cloud vanished, leaving the astonished woman alone.

Soon, as might be expected, doubt began to set in. What she had seen was impossible; who would believe her? Telling such a story could ruin her family's reputation. At the same time, the tortured woman feared that if she didn't speak up, the "blood of souls" would be on her hands. She cogitated several days before—ever so cautiously—she mentioned the event to her family. The next week she wrote letters to distant friends, telling them to prepare for the end.

On Sunday, March 19, hoping for some much needed sleep, the poor woman retired at midnight. Around two a.m., she was awakened by a gentle stroke on her face. It was Jesus, reprimanding her for disbelief and inaction. He departed, vanishing as quickly as a puff of smoke.

Melissa Warner hemmed and hawed another ten days, until, finally determined to do her duty, she told Rev. Calvin Butler, who wrote the account from which this is taken.

But apparently, Jesus neglected to put in the promised appearance, the world failed to end, and our reluctant prophetess faded into the obscurity she no doubt desired.

The Jesus Door

A more recent New England miracle might have taken place in January 1999, in Wareham, Massachusetts. There certain members of the Episcopalian Church of the Good Shepherd thought they had received a visit from the Good Shepherd himself.

It all started when a group of parishioners gathered to help make improvements to the church. Several women were on the third floor, staining doors. Suddenly Father Cuthbert Mandell heard someone exclaim, "Jesus!"

Cussing in the church? Father Mandell hurried to discover the culprit and found Roseanne Leverone staring in amazement at the door she'd been staining. Other women surrounded her. The minister immediately saw what all the fuss was about: A likeness of Jesus had somehow appeared on the two- by three-foot closet door. The new stain had heightened the grain of the wood, and its swirls and lines seemed to form a recognizable image.

The shape is shadowy, almost a silhouette, facing directly forward. One can see what appears to be long hair parted in the middle. The eyes, nose, and mouth are discernible and positioned correctly. A beard seems to surround the mouth, cover the chin, and descend to the top of what might be perceived as a robe. Even *Weird New England* has to admit the likeness is quite convincing. As Father Mandell said, "People are just pulled into it."

But is it a true miracle? As one woman reminds us, Jesus had been a carpenter, so a door was a likely place for Him to appear. Another lady marveled, "The eyes are so penetrating. . . . [It's] like He's looking right through you." She was also able to point out Jesus' sacred heart, with thorns around it, and a cross on top of the heart.

But what about the priest? Does Father Mandell himself believe it's a miracle? "If nothing else," he says, "it's a natural piece of art."

But he adds, "Of course, it's not signed."

JESUS IMAGE – Visitors point out an image of Jesus that appeared on a freshly stained wooden door at the Episcopalian Church of the Good Shepherd in Wareham, Mass., Sunday.

Some see image of Christ on stained church door

WAREHAM, Mass. (AP) – Some parishioners at the Episcopalian Church of the Good Shepherd say an image of Jesus Christ has appeared on a freshly stained wooden door.

The image appeared last Wednesday night when women were staining doors for a room on the third floor of the church, said the pastor, the Rev. Cuthbert Mandell.

"A group of women were staining some doors, and I was talking to another group of people when all of a sudden I heard, 'Jesus,'" he told the Boston Herald.

Asked about divine intervention, Mandell said, "I don't like to speculate on what I don't know about. It's so unusual, we're still sorting it out."

A Bloody Miracle or a Mistake?

For a while it seemed as if the twenty-first century was kicking off with an avalanche of New England miracles.

On Thursday, June 1, 2000, something miraculous seemed to happen in the little town of Berlin, New Hampshire. On that day, between six thirty and seven thirty p.m., Mr. George Arsenault, a eucharistic minister at St. Joseph's Catholic Church, came face-to-face with the supernatural. Or at least he thought he did.

During a meditative part of the service he was attending, Mr. Arsenault noticed something peculiar behind the altar. As he watched, tiny red dots began to appear on the wall directly under a crucifix. Oddly, they were precisely positioned beneath the wounds on Jesus' hands and feet. Not wanting to disturb the service, Mr. Arsenault waited until the end. By then, however, the dots had expanded into red lines. It looked as if blood were flowing down the wall.

Convinced he was seeing something out of the ordinary, Mr. Arsenault called other people to have a look. Soon a group of perplexed parishioners were clustered around the statue, all trying to understand exactly what they were seeing: Could the crucifix be bleeding?

Mr. Arsenault checked the attic to see if something was dripping down from above. Everything was absolutely dry.

At around nine o'clock, Father Roberge, the pastor of the church, inspected the scene. With a white linen cloth, he wiped some of the mysterious substance off the wall. Then he and Mr. Arsenault used a ladder to climb to the statue and determine if the fluid was actually flowing from it. They found the crucifix to be "dry and dusty," but red trails were still visible below.

News traveled quickly. Hundreds of people arrived with cameras and telescopic equipment even before the story hit the media. Some testified they saw blood actually appear on the statue. Others dismissed the whole thing as mass hallucination. And some were so unruly and disrespectful that Father Roberge closed and locked the church. Then he stated publicly that "there is no evidence of any unusual activity in relation to the crucifix or the surrounding area of the church."

This decidedly unmiraculous proclamation seemed to be corroborated when the samples from Father Roberge's white cloth were analyzed: No trace of blood could be detected. But George Arsenault and the scores of people who saw the mysterious substance stand by their accounts. Some question the validity of the testing: Maybe Father Roberge had rubbed so hard that the sample became polluted by all kinds of matter from the wall. Others suggest that since a miracle can happen very suddenly, it can also "unhappen" just as quickly.

So the jury is still out: Did Berlin, New Hampshire, experience a miracle . . . or a mistake?

Shocking Tales

The Girl Who Stopped Time

Back in the Dark Ages, when a member of the *Weird New England* team was still in college, he dated a young New Hampshire woman who never wore a watch. It wasn't an issue of poverty. More likely it was an expression of her irrepressible bohemian spirit . . . or so he thought.

It all came clear on her birthday when, in a rare demonstration of generosity, he presented her with a brand-new Timex right off Woolworth's rack.

"I can't wear a watch," she said, just as matter-of-factly as a vegetarian might say, "I can't eat pepperoni."

Figuring she meant such concessions to temporal conformity were contrary to her principles, he prepared for intellectual debate. Cleverly, he shot back, "Jeez, why not?"

"I just can't," she said. However, she dutifully placed the timepiece on her wrist, and within a few minutes, it had stopped. Stopped dead. But a few moments after she removed it, just like any good Timex, it kept on ticking.

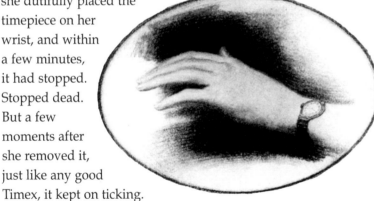

On this girl's wrist or in her hand, time stopped. The same proved true for pocket watches and battery-powered timepieces. There was something about her metabolism, or something, that was just contrary to the concept of personalized time. She speculated that it was something electrical—possibly electromagnetic—that kept her and time at a distance.

Since then, we have heard of similar cases, some far more dramatic.

Magnetic Cons in the Can

Flash back to February 1920 and the Clinton Correctional Facility in Dannemora, New York. Something weird was happening at the prison. Thirty-four inmates contracted botulism after eating canned salmon. Luckily there were no fatalities, but during their well-monitored recovery the men exhibited some pretty bizarre symptoms.

It began when one inmate tried to flick away a crumpled piece of paper—but the paper refused to leave his hand. Other men found they were similarly magnetized.

The prison doctor, Julius B. Ransom, discovered that all thirty-four botulism sufferers displayed peculiar phenomena: Papers would dance around them or jump up and cling to their bodies. Compass needles spun crazily in their presence. Watches stopped. And steel tapes suspended nearby undulated like snakes for no observable reason. Unbelievably, some of the men seemed to glow in the dark.

Dr. Ransom found that an individual's capacity to produce electricity varied with the severity of his illness. As the men's health improved, the charge diminished. When fully recovered, their power switched off.

We can only speculate about what all this means. We know, of course, that human beings generate electricity. Tiny electrical charges produce signals from cell to cell. These impulses can be measured scientifically. Perhaps certain people, either spontaneously or amplified by specific contagions such as botulism, can generate low-amperage current that can affect the environment. Or maybe it's more complicated than that.

Orford's Electrifying Lady

A truly shocking series of events occurred in tiny Orford, New Hampshire, in the 1800s. The tale involves a physician, Dr. Willard Hosford, and what he deemed the strangest medical situation he'd ever encountered.

In January 1837 he was summoned to the home of what he describes as "a lady of great respectability." But her complaint was so odd that it seems to have compelled Dr. Hosford to conceal her true identity.

This unnamed lady—let's call her Electra—was his longtime patient. He describes her as a woman of "nervous temperament and sedentary habits." Overall, she suffered "a weakened constitution" and recurring bouts of rheumatism and neuralgia. But nothing in her medical history prepared the doctor for what he was about to encounter: something he had never seen before; something he'd never even heard of.

His thirty-year-old patient, the wife of a prominent Orford man, had suddenly, and for no apparent reason, become charged with electricity. Somehow she was able to send brilliant sparks shooting from her fingertips.

She had first noticed her singular affliction when she happened to pass her hand over her brother's face. As she did so, vivid sparks shot from her fingers, giving her surprised sibling a substantial jolt. Even Dr. Hosford was not immune to her electrical powers. He wrote, "A spark, three fourths of an inch long, passed from the lady's knuckle to my nose causing an involuntary recoil."

Though the electrical energy caused the woman no discomfort, she found she could deliver an unforgettable jolt to anyone nearby. To the doctor's astonishment she was able to produce sparks up to about one and one-half inches long. These spontaneous electrical discharges came at the unbelievable rate of four per minute.

At first, Dr. Hosford thought that static electricity was somehow generating the charges, so he had the woman wear all cotton. As a control, her sister dressed in silk. The woman remained highly charged; her sister remained normal.

Having thus eliminated that possibility, Dr. Hosford concluded that the source of the power was within the lady herself. It was as if she were a human electrical generator. Whenever her finger was brought close to any metallic surface, a spark could be heard, seen, and felt. In fact, she caused sparks in every conducting body she came near, including the cast-iron stove and her everyday household tools, like needles, scissors, knives, and so on.

It is hard to imagine how this lady of delicate temperament must have felt; perhaps the poor woman suffered severe mental discomfort. At any rate, her nervous agitation increased to the point that Dr. Hosford sometimes had to give her morphine to help her

sleep. But no medicine relieved her symptoms.

Over time, the doctor noticed that atmospheric temperature had some effect: the higher the temperature, the greater the charge. However, changes in barometric pressure had no influence at all.

The Orford woman's eerie electrical power steadily increased from January 25 until the last of February, when it began to decline. By the end of May, it was gone entirely, vanishing as mysteriously as it had begun. During its active period, many corroborating witnesses observed the phenomenon, including scientists from nearby Dartmouth College. Everyone remained absolutely baffled and perhaps a little terrified. Neither science nor religion could explain where the charges were coming from, why, or how they were generated.

Later that year Dr. Hosford submitted his findings to the *American Journal of Science*. The editor, Benjamin Silliman, M.D., LL.D., was unable to shed even hazy light on the mystery, but he validated everything before reporting the bizarre events in his journal.

That was back in 1837. Today we still have no reason for the strange electrical charges. But perhaps somewhere in this account there's a partial explanation as to why some young women cannot wear watches. And for some of the Unexplained Phenomena that follow.

Valentine's Night Massacre

Who knows what was behind the strange events that took place within the dark confines of an innocent-looking barn on Route 5 in Dummerston, Vermont? In the early hours of Valentine's Day, 1984, farmer Robert Ranney headed through the rain and fog to begin the morning's milking. But when he entered the barn, Mr. Ranney discovered a scene of utter horror. Twenty-three of his twenty-nine heifers were dead. One account claims they were lying in a perfect circle with feed still in their mouths. The surviving six cows were fine.

Immediately Mr. Ranney phoned his vet. Upon examination, the doctor determined the animals had been electrocuted. However, there were no signs of a struggle or indication that they had tried to escape. Whatever happened had happened very rapidly.

Since the livestock were extremely valuable, an insurance investigation was required. An inspector agreed that all twenty-three cows had died instantly, probably by electrocution. Although he ruled out foul play, neither he nor anyone else could determine the source of the lethal electricity. Several more investigators, including electricians, checked the scene, but everyone went away equally baffled.

Mr. Ranney suggested lightning but just as quickly dismissed his own theory. The barn had been tightly secured, there were no holes or scorch marks anywhere, and none of the hay had ignited. Perhaps most telling, none of the dead cows had split hoofs, a sure sign of a lightning strike.

The most bizarre suggestion was voiced by ex-policeman and MUFON (Mutual UFO Network) investigator William Chapleau. He went over everything with a Geiger counter and found high radiation in the center of the barn and in the cornfield where the cows were buried. Could the cows have been killed by some freak radioactive discharge from the nearby Vermont Yankee nuclear power plant in Vernon? No, Mr. Chapleau concluded, because Yankee had been shut down at the fatal time.

Having eliminated other possibilities to his own satisfaction, Mr. Chapleau decided that the heifers had been killed by a UFO. During the night in question, four people had contacted him about a "torpedo shaped" UFO over the nuclear plant in Vernon. Also, a strange ball of light had been seen that same night in nearby Hinsdale, New Hampshire.

While a diagnosis of "murder by UFO" might not fly, no better explanation for the eerie electrical deaths has ever emerged.

Spontaneous Combustion, Human Style

On May 12, 1890, Doctor B. H. Hartwell was making a house call in Ayer, Massachusetts. While passing a wooded area, he heard the terrified screams of a woman and saw people signaling to him for help. When he rushed to assist, he got the shock of his life. He and a helpless cluster of witnesses watched a crouching woman screech and contort as blue flames blasted from her back. By the time Dr. Hartwell reached her, most of her clothing was consumed. She died as he watched, her back arched, her muscles rigid from contractions. Still, she continued to blaze as flames twelve to fifteen inches long shot from her.

The doctor and some witnesses eventually extinguished the fire by smothering it with dirt.

Then they noticed something odd: Despite the enormous heat, dry leaves near the corpse, a straw hat, and a shovel's wooden handle were untouched. Only the body of the unfortunate woman had been burned. Were the mysterious flames the result of suicide, murder, or something called spontaneous human combustion (SHC)? This weird phenomenon is a scientific uncertainty.

In 1959, at a Massachusetts Medico-Legal Society lecture, many doctors said they'd had experience with what appeared to be SHC. The group decided the puzzling phenomenon was not as uncommon as one might think. One doctor even admitted that he'd come across such cases as frequently as once every four years.

In the case of many burn victims, no other explanation will fit. A person, generally an adult, will suddenly and for no apparent reason burst into flame. People who claim to have observed this phenomenon say it's a blue flame that burns with the intensity of a blowtorch. It can reduce a victim to ashes in a matter of minutes.

The Small Conflagration

In their book Spontaneous Human Combustion, authors Jenny Randles and Peter Hough discuss the strange affair of Allen M. Small, a fifty-two-year-old man from Deer Isle, Maine. On January 13, 1943, Mr. Small was discovered in his home, his body completely burned. The carpet beneath his corpse was scorched, but there were no other signs of a fire. Apparently, the blaze had started on, or in, Mr. Small, then consumed him totally. How could such intense heat rage without doing any damage to the surrounding environment? Even Mr. Small's pipe was found, intact and unlit near the body, suggesting that his personal conflagration was not a smoking accident.

Although the bed and its occupant were burned beyond recognition, nothing else had caught fire. Even a book of matches nearby had failed to ignite.

All Burned Up!

Some of these cases imply that our old nemesis the sinister Cosmic Joker may be at work, adding a whole new level of malevolence to already bizarre events. A perfect example happened not far from Burlington, Vermont. The scene of the crime: Crown Point, New York, just across the bridge from Vermont (and a little too close for comfort).

On March 24, 1968, a fifty-eight-year-old retiree named George Irving Mott and a lady friend were watching an episode of *The Twilight Zone*. Mr. Mott remarked, "Nothing weird like that ever happens to me. I wish it would."

The Joker must have been listening, because three days later when Mr. Mott's son Kendall stopped by, the first thing he noticed was that the doorknob was warm. Not expecting that variety of warm welcome, Kendall entered cautiously to find the walls of his father's house half covered with an oily black ash. In the bedroom, he witnessed a horrifying sight. His father's single bed had been destroyed. The mattress was burned through; so was the floor beneath.

When the state police arrived, they discovered Mr. Mott's gruesome remains; all that was left of him was three and one-half pounds of ash and a few fragments of bone.

The State Police Bureau of Criminal Investigation summoned Essex County senior fire investigator Anthony Morette. He'd never seen anything like it. Although the bed and its occupant were burned beyond recognition, nothing else had caught fire. Even a book of matches nearby had failed to ignite. Mr. Mott was known to be a nonsmoker who was extraordinarily cautious of fire. In fact, he'd even posted a NO SMOKING sign in his house.

Eventually, Mr. Morette concluded that nothing in the home could have caused the fatal fire. There was simply no external ignition source. Once he had ruled out everything else, only spontaneous human combustion remained.

So where is our elusive friend the Cosmic Joker hiding in all this? Ironically, Mr. Mott was a retired fireman.

Windsor's Wet Wonder

Rocks falling from clear blue skies, weird music in the air, spontaneous bursts of flame. Maybe it's not Cosmic Jokers we're dealing with. Maybe it's elementals. If so, another element remains—water.

In the 1950s, a Windsor, Vermont, physician, his wife, and their two daughters lived in a modest two-story home on Cherry Street, not far from the Connecticut River. Everything was 1950s' normal . . . until the strangeness started.

Beginning on the morning of September 20, 1955, one of the daughters discovered a puddle of water in the concave seat of a wooden chair in her bedroom. Not far away, on the floor, she saw a second pool. Where had they come from? Nothing had spilled. Nothing was dripping. It wasn't raining outside, so a leaky roof wasn't the problem.

Soon other family members began noticing pools of water all over the house, but no one could discover the source. This water from nowhere soaked everything. Bureau drawers filled up. Clothing dripped in the closets. Within closed kitchen cabinets, bowls, cups, and glasses filled with water. Continual mopping and sponging did no good; the water kept coming.

Various experts were called in, including a dowser, but no one could discern the source of the rising tide. Yet water continued to appear. The *Claremont* [N.H.] *Daily Eagle* reported that occasionally it rained inside the house!

By late September, the saturated family had finally had enough. They moved into a trailer in their yard, where, inexplicably, the watery phenomenon did not follow.

When the Associated Press picked up the story, the worldwide attention attracted curiosity-seekers, who paraded by the house. Mysteriously, about a month after the phenomenon started, it stopped. No reason, it just stopped. To shut off the flow of the curious, the doctor issued a press release saying they'd solved the problem. But it hadn't been solved. It just stopped.

Pesky poltergeists? Mischievous elementals? Or that Cosmic Joker again? Who can say? But perhaps we should mention the family name: It was Waterman.

This water from nowhere soaked everything. . . . Within closed kitchen cabinets, bowls, cups, and glasses filled with water. Continual mopping and sponging did no good; the water kept coming.

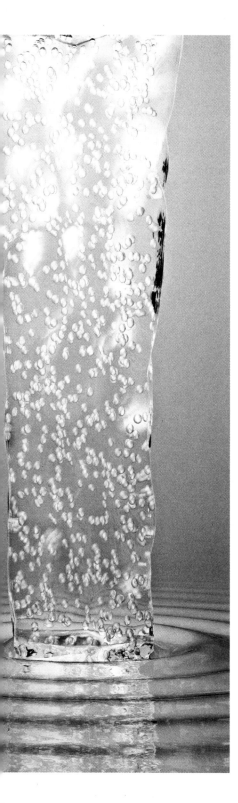

More Weird Water

About a decade later Windsor's watery whatsit reemerged in Methuen, Massachusetts.

The splashdown was on October 25, 1963. Mr. and Mrs. Francis Martin and their eleven-year-old daughter noticed a wet spot on their TV-room wall. Then they heard a loud pop, like someone uncorking champagne. A jet of water spurted from the wall as if a pipe had burst. The fountain flowed for a good two hours as the terrified family watched similar geysers erupting all over the house. Each lasted about twenty seconds, recurring at fifteen-minute intervals. No holes could be discovered from which the water had gushed forth. No water pipes ran behind the walls.

When the Martins called for help, the usual experts slogged through, examining the building for leaks and other moisture problems. Everything proved shipshape and tight as a drum. Yet one witness saw water cascading down the staircase, and another measured a one-inch accumulation on the floor.

The family shut off the house water supply and drained all the pipes. They turned off the heat and opened all the windows to encourage ventilation. They even raised the shades to admit maximum sunlight. All to no avail.

By Friday, persistent wetness, unexpected geysers, and an overall creepy feeling finally forced them to leave. They went to stay with Mrs. Martin's parents at their apartment in nearby Lawrence. When the Martins moved in, the water sprite tagged along with them. The popping and splashing scenario resumed at the new location.

Increasingly baffled investigators examined every nook, cranny, and crawl-space as the unrelenting water splashed around them. Oddly, it affected only the apartment where the Martins were staying—the middle floor of a three-story apartment house.

Just as in Windsor, word leaked out, and local papers had their 1963 Halloween story. Tides of curiosity-seekers made life miserable for everyone. Eventually, however, the mysterious springs ceased to flow.

In certain ways, the Massachusetts case was different from the Vermont episode: Here, a sudden rise in humidity and a popping sound preceded the water's appearance. And when the water came, it didn't simply materialize; it poured, as if from a spigot. Then, after the jet of water ceased, the source spot on the wall would be warm, sometimes hot, to the touch. Last, and perhaps strangest of all, when the Martins moved from Methuen to Lawrence, the water came with them.

Natural or supernatural? Who can say? All we know is that none of the explanations we've heard so far seem to hold water.

Bizarre Beasts

For many people, New England has become a sort of national symbol for the way things used to be.

New Englanders are perceived as somehow outside the mainstream, outside time itself, a group of laconic but likeable farmers living in small, friendly villages surrounded by white picket fences with bright church steeples pointing the way to heaven.

The Norman Rockwell imagery is good for tourism, sure, but too often we lose sight of the "other" New Englanders. The ones who lived in Salem Village. The ones who populate Shirley Jackson's unsettling stories. The village idiots, local sociopaths, and Saturday night sadists.

But even they are not the true New England weirdos. There is another group. They live outside the picket fences—way outside. They hide deep in the forests. They crouch in the shadows of the church steeples. We don't need Stephen King to create them, because they are real, and they are everywhere.

The Pigman of the Devil's Washbowl

In the spring of 1971, a blond teenage boy vanished from a remote farm on Darby Hill in Northfield, Vermont. Worried parents and townspeople joined to conduct a thorough search for the boy, but not a trace could be found. His disappearance remained a mystery.

About six months later more odd events began to occur at other remote farms. About two miles away, on Turkey Hill, other creatures were going missing. Not children, but other living things—dogs, cats, and small farm animals—disappeared without a trace. Suddenly the people of Northfield found themselves searching again. But it seemed like the farmer's son and the farm animals two miles away had just blinked out of existence.

Then another alarming event left the community in a spin. Back on Turkey Hill, a man living on a farm heard strange noises in his yard. It sounded as if something was rummaging through his trash. Was it dogs, coons, porcupines? The man raced to the window and flicked on the outside lights. There, in the bright glow of a floodlight, he saw a solitary figure rooting around in his garbage. It was standing upright and was the size of a man. But, somehow, it didn't look exactly human.

The farmer threw open his door and shouted, "Get the hell out of there!" For a brief moment, the figure looked directly at him. The farmer couldn't believe his eyes. The creature standing before him was as tall as a man, stark naked, and covered head to foot with long, light hair. But the most frightening aspect of the intruder was his face. There was nothing human about it; it had the loathsome features of a pig. Before the farmer could react, the alien creature turned, raced down the driveway, and crossed into the woods.

"It was definitely naked," the man said. "And it ran on two feet." And that is how the Pigman came to Northfield.

Close Encounters of the Pigman Kind

Other encounters followed, each more bizarre than the last. One night a group of terrified teenagers staggered into a high school dance. Some of them were crying. They described what had happened behind the school, where they'd been having a few drinks in the sandpit by the cemetery. There they had seen "a monster." It had come out of the woods, tentatively, approaching them. Again, the description was the same: It walked like a man but had the horrible face of a pig. The teenagers abandoned their beer and raced back to the school.

No one laughed when they told their story. In fact, several students went out to investigate, including a

young man named Jeff Hatch. It was obvious that something had come out of the woods. In a recent interview, Jeff told us, "The grass was beat down. Something had been there." But whatever it was had vanished again. Someone referred to it as Pigman, and the name stuck.

On the Trail of the Pigman

Jeff Hatch and his friends decided they wanted to be the ones to solve the Northfield mystery. They knew there was an old pig farm up near Union Brook, not far from a mysterious area known as the Devil's Washbowl. It was the only such farm around. If there was a pigman on the loose, they reasoned, it must have something to do with the pig farm.

Even today the pig farm has a weird atmosphere. Back then, Jeff recalls, it was a dilapidated place, a big barn surrounded by a scattering of outbuildings, but no farmhouse. The absence of a house somehow made Jeff uneasy as he and his companions approached to explore the old place. Even in our recent interview, Jeff shuddered a bit as he talked about what they found. "There were giant pigs there," he said. "Five and six hundred-pounders—they were gigantic!"

The boys found animal bones in the barn and an area of flattened hay on the floor as if someone had fashioned a makeshift bed. "Something seemed to be sleeping there in the same room as the dead animals."

Just down the road from the pig farm is the Devil's Washbowl, a geological anomaly long recognized for its shiver-producing properties. A dirt road passes through it, making a U-turn at its center. There you'll find yourself in the middle of a deep natural depression. It is always shaded, even on sunny days. Its damp atmosphere never changes. Yet, regardless of the season, the Devil's Washbowl always seems hotter than any of the surrounding areas.

It was along this stretch of deserted road between the

pig farm and the Devil's Washbowl that a number of motorists had curious encounters with an odd, oversized "animal." It was always described as "ghostly white" as it passed unexpectedly in front of a moving vehicle. Such encounters became known as Pigman Sightings; one was made by a lone driver who was startled when a figure raced from the roadside bushes and leaped onto the hood of his car. For a terrifying second, their eyes met; then the creature vaulted off the car and back into the undergrowth. It looked like a man, the driver reported, but it was stark naked, with light hair, and a hideous piglike face.

Pigman Goes Hog Wild

One high school couple decided to brave the Washbowl for some steamy time alone. All went well until the boy got out of the car to answer nature's call. Something seized him, smashed him about, and hurled him up against the side of his vehicle. His girlfriend heard his shouts and felt the impact of his body against the car.

He was the first to be attacked by the Pigman.

Luckily, the young man lived to tell the story, and it was more dramatic than any Northfielders had heard before: This terrified witness had gotten a vivid, close-up look. Pigman stood a good five eight to five ten. His body was completely covered with white hair, and his face was unmistakably that of a pig. But the young man was able to add one new detail to the description of the porcine phantom: Its hands were like neither those of a pig nor those of a man. Pigman had long nails, like claws. To prove it, the young man displayed deep gashes on his chest and arms.

After the assault, town police finally decided to investigate. But Jeff suspects their search was unsuccessful and probably not too thorough.

Jeff and his fellow investigators stayed on the case.

They guessed Pigman might be living in one of the caves near the Devil's Washbowl. The boys examined a number of caverns. In the biggest one, they discovered several piles of bones. "There was no sign of a fire," Jeff told us, "but there was bedding in the cave—hay, probably from the pig farm."

Jeff also discovered footprints in the Washbowl's moist soil. While admitting he is not a skilled tracker, he claims the footprints appeared to be hoofed, or "cloven."

Pigman May Still Be at Large

The Pigman may still lurk by night in the wild hills of Northfield, somewhere in the narrow confines between this reality and the next. To some, his origins are obvious: He evolved from that blond farmer's son who vanished from Northfield's Darby Hill back in 1971. Perhaps he took to the woods and there, living a bestial life, suffered multiple physical deformities. Or perhaps his birth itself was the result of a farmer's coupling with a particularly promiscuous pig. Stranger things have happened in the hills of old Vermont.

Anyway, reduced to a feral state, the neo-savage hunted at night, surviving on pets and trash-picking. Eventually, so the story goes, he moved into a cave, from which he stalked small game.

Perhaps he died of malnutrition, suicide, or a hunter's bullet. Or perhaps he's still there, now in middle age, skilled at concealment and too shy or embarrassed to show himself. Jeff Hatch, who knows the Pigman saga better than anyone, has collected testimony and has told the story many times. He suspects there is a kernel of truth somewhere in this whole mysterious business. Admittedly, he hasn't heard of any new sightings for several years. But it's possible, he says, that people simply aren't squealing.

Pig Hunting at the Devil's Washbowl

I remember the fear I felt all those years ago. I remember the wide eyes, the sweaty palms, the nervous laughter. I remember waking up in the dead of the night, thinking that he was on my trail.

I was a teenager in the 1970s and lived in a rural town south of Montpelier, Vermont, near a town called Northfield. We had heard the tales of this ferocious monster called the Pigman and his many attacks on unsuspecting local people and animals. Naturally, my friends and I decided that we had to see him for ourselves. To a bunch of bored high school kids, the idea of a maniac with the head of a pig presents adventure, excitement, and danger. We quickly gathered as much information as we could on the Pigman and set out on our quest to see him.

So it was that I and three of my closest friends came to drive down a dirt road into the heart of what was known as the Devil's Washbowl one cold fall evening almost thirty years ago. Driving into the Washbowl was like driving down a one-way road into the heart of darkness itself. The area was surrounded by hills, and there was only one road in and out.

It seemed quieter than it should have been. Upon exiting the car, the four of us explored a bit, hoping to find the Pigman in slumber somewhere nearby. We had no such luck. We wound up leaning against the vehicle as a few of my friends smoked cigarettes before we made our way back to the less creepy parts of civilization.

"You know, he could be watching us right now," I told the fellas.

"Yeah. He could be perched up on any of these hills," Jesse said nonchalantly, "just trying to figure out a way to take us down one by one."

"Screw that, we'd take him down and make bacon out of him!" Mark, ever the arrogant one, claimed.

"I don't know about that," Jesse spat back. "They say he's faster than any man."

"Why don't you all shut up?" We turned to see Pete, who had been silent up until this point, getting back in the car. We had succeeded in spooking him. Now that he broke, we proceeded to begin doing what any teenage boy would do to a comrade who admitted fear; we mocked him as thoroughly as our rather uncreative brains could manage. I remember there was a fair share of questioning Pete's masculinity and a lot of him telling us to shut the *%#$ up.

Then, just when we had let our guards down, we heard a high-pitched howl (or was it a squeal?) that shattered the stillness of the Devil's Washbowl.

It wasn't three seconds later that we were tearing back down that dirt road. I remember looking at my knuckles on the steering wheel and they were completely white, just like the other guys' faces were.

I had nightmares on and off for the next few weeks. My friends and I discussed that unearthly noise and that ungodly place. We never trifled with the Pigman again. Best to let sleeping pigs lie, we decided.

—*Chad Clarke*

Pilgrim Parrots, Ghost Squirrels, and the Black Dog of Doom

No doubt Northfield's Pigman would win if there were ever a Most Bizarre Beast in New England contest. But we can't ignore the runners-up. They range from the mildly odd to the unutterably outrageous. For example, on the more benign end of the critter continuum, we have Connecticut's out-of-place parrots.

Most ornithologists would agree that parrots are not native to New England. (Then again, neither are most New Englanders.) But these Pilgrim Parrots live all along the Connecticut coastline, with conspicuous settlements in Bridgeport, Fairfield, Stamford, and Milford. Their population is about two thousand and growing. They reside year-round in huge, globelike condominiums that they construct from sticks in many species of trees. Some prefer less rustic nesting places, like electric poles and the huge spotlights of baseball fields.

Human neighbors are likely to say, "There goes the neighborhood," because Connecticut's parrots are a messy lot. Also they screech and squawk as they sit or fly, vocalizing nonstop. At the same time, though, they are quite lovely. Each is about a foot long, bright apple green in color, with gray, hooded heads. When they are in flight, you can see the bright blue underside of their wings and the yellow-green of their lower chests.

These out-of-place squatters are in fact parrots, but they're called monk parakeets because of their gray hoods. They're native to Argentina, Bolivia, Paraguay, Uruguay, and other parts of South America. Some think that they were imported as pets in the late 1960s and early '70s, and that some escaped, reproduced, and adapted to Connecticut's chillier climate. Then again, maybe the Pilgrim Parrots migrated on their own for the culinary equivalent of religious freedom. In their native countries, they are considered an agricultural pest because they tend to decimate certain crops.

You can see them on Beacon Street off Grover's Avenue in Bridgeport, on Beach Road off Route 1 in Fairfield, or in the Woodmont section of Milford, where they have nested in the pines along Beach Avenue. Also check Stamford near the museum at Sound Waters on Cove Island Park. The best time to spot them is at sunrise as they leave their nests to hunt for food. At sunset, they return home and hang around socializing full blast till bedtime.

Ghost Squirrels

Ever wonder what happens to all the squirrels you see flattened along the roadside? Their ghosts rise from the pavement and move on to the fields and forests of heavenly Connecticut. There, if conditions are right, they frequently manifest in the area around Derby, Milford, Shelton, and Stratford. People who've seen the Ghost Squirrels often think they're hallucinating. I mean, they look exactly like their gray or red counterparts, but they're white. Solid white.

Sad to say, there is really nothing supernatural about these strange white, arboreal rodents. They are in fact real squirrels but of the albino variety.

Interestingly, a similar genetic abnormality is also occurring in the same area. Melanistic, a.k.a. black, squirrels also abound. In reality (which we all know can be confusing) white squirrels and black squirrels are all gray squirrels. They all exhibit identical behaviors and are visible year round, since they don't migrate or hibernate.

We have every confidence that a genetics scientist could explain why all this is so. Our question is, Why here? Why are albino squirrels and melanistic squirrels more prevalent here than elsewhere? Guess it's just another of Connecticut's myriad minor mysteries.

The Black Dog of West Peak

Just when you're feeling safe after an afternoon of squirrel watching, something really weird comes along and snaps you out of your complacency. In this case, it's a cute little dog. And he's lethal.

Like its better-known counterpart, the Hound of the Baskervilles, Connecticut's preternatural pooch has picked topography as alien as Grimpen Mire for its lair: the volcanic hills around Meriden, Connecticut. This craggy, surreal landscape is full of dense forests, deep gorges, grotesque rock formations, and clear, beautiful pools and rivers.

West Peak, the westernmost of the three so-called Hanging Hills, is said to harbor a wide variety of supernatural creatures. But the one that interests us is a tiny black dog of some unknown pedigree. While he apparently brings good luck to some, this appealing pooch brings misfortune and death to an equal number.

Sightings of the Black Dog of West Peak have given rise to a saying that history has proven true: If you meet the Black Dog once, it shall be for joy; if twice, it shall be for sorrow; and the third time shall bring death. Those who have lived to describe it say it is small, black, and looks something like a short-haired spaniel. Everyone comments on its strange, sad eyes. It pops out of nowhere and seems delighted to meet a human companion.

Though there is nothing to tip you off that this is an odd animal, you might check its feet. Regardless of the season or surface—mud, sand, or snow—the little dog leaves no footprints. And it's absolutely silent. Though it may tip back its head and appear to howl, no sound issues from its throat.

The best account of the Black Dog of West Peak comes from W. H. C. Pynchon, a New York City geologist. Around the turn of the twentieth century, Mr. Pynchon visited the Hanging Hills to study their unusual rock formations. One beautiful spring morning he set out by horse and buggy, heading for West Peak. At some point near Lake Merimere, he stopped to study some rocks. There he noticed a little dog standing on a boulder nearby. Tongue hanging out, tail wagging, the friendly little beast just stood watching the geologist at his work.

When Mr. Pynchon moved on, the little dog trotted eagerly along beside his wagon, accompanying him all the way up West Peak and later down into Southington, where Mr. Pynchon entered a restaurant for lunch. The dog waited for him to return to his wagon and then tagged along as the geologist began the return trip to his hotel.

But when they arrived at the spot where they had originally met, Mr. Pynchon looked around and the little animal was gone. By then, the scientist had become quite fond of his newfound sidekick. He whistled and called, but the little dog did not respond.

After a number of years, circumstances brought W. H. C. Pynchon back to Meriden, Connecticut. This time a friend and colleague accompanied him. Mr. Pynchon told his friend about the little black dog from his last visit. Surprised, the friend explained that he too had once experienced a similar encounter with a similar animal. Both men knew of the warning about sighting the dog more than once, but they prided themselves on being men of reason. No such legend would faze them.

On a cold, bright February morning the two made their way toward West Peak. From their buggy, they alternately looked at the scenery and watched for their friend, but he was nowhere to be found. After hitching their horse, they began the rugged climb up steep cliffs toward the summit of West Peak. Then one of them chanced to look up and was surprised at what he saw.

"Look up there!" he exclaimed.

Both men saw the little dog waiting for them near the summit, his tail wagging enthusiastically. His mouth moved up and down as he silently barked hello. A sudden gasp from Mr. Pynchon's companion turned the geologist's blood to ice. He witnessed a frenzy of waving arms and peddling feet as his friend tried to recover his footing on the slippery volcanic rock. Mr. Pynchon grabbed for him but too late. Beyond help, his friend slid down the steep slope, all the while screaming for help. His cries intensified while he was airborne, then ended abruptly as he smashed against the frozen earth below.

This was the third time Mr. Pynchon's friend had seen the dog. And it's my second time, Mr. Pynchon realized. But he was simply not prepared to believe the legend of the Black Dog of West Peak.

So some years later Mr. Pynchon returned to Connecticut's Hanging Hills, lured by the rough beauty of the landscape. He retraced the fatal route he had climbed with his friend. But he was never to write the last chapter of this story. At almost the same place his friend had fallen to his death, W. H. C. Pynchon slipped and fell and died.

Did he see the little black dog before he plunged to his death? He was climbing alone, so there's no way to tell. Not for sure. But those who know the story will swear that he did.

Dover's Fragile Phantom—The Dover Demon

"The Dover Demon is a true enigma, an animate anomaly that intersected the lives of four, credible young people that lonely week in April, 1977."
—Loren Coleman, *Mysterious America*

It was cryptozoologist Loren Coleman who christened it the Dover Demon, but in reality there was nothing demonic about it. It was a frail, friendless thing that seemed more like a lost and frightened kitten on a busy interstate than a malevolent emissary from the unknown. Yet it was unique, a thing unto itself. Investigator Walter Webb, Assistant Director of the Hayden Planetarium at Boston's Science Museum, called the sighting "one of the most baffling creature episodes ever reported." To this day, a quarter century later, it remains unexplained and perhaps unexplainable.

A Wild Ride

Date: **April 21, 1977**
Time: **Approximately ten thirty p.m.**
 Eastern Standard Time
Place: **Farm Street, a narrow, winding road between woods and pastures on the outskirts of Dover, Massachusetts, just fifteen miles from Boston.**
Weather: **Dark but clear.**
Temperature: **55° F; chilly, not cold.**

Teenager Bill Bartlett was driving his VW along Farm Street with Mike Mazzacca beside him and Andy Brodie in the back seat; the boys were just cruising, laughing, and talking. Andy and Mike were so wrapped up in the hilarity of the moment that they missed whatever it was that caused Bill to cry out, "Did you see that!" His voice was pitched an octave too high.

"See what?" asked Andy.

Bill hesitated; he didn't know what he had seen. His headlights had swept a stone wall where something moved, something alive. But it was as if his eyes refused to focus properly, for what he saw was like nothing he had ever seen before.

Whatever it was seemed to be struggling over the piled rocks. Bill's mind ticked off possibilities: a dog, a cat, a raccoon, or an opossum. . . . But it was none of these familiar things. It was walking upright, as unsteady as a toddler, tentatively clutching the rocks with long fingers and toes. Its most conspicuous feature was its head— huge, bulbous, way out of proportion to the body. Its eyes, large orbs glowing orange, stared directly into the VW's headlights. No nose, mouth, or ears were visible.

Bill shook his head, trying to make sense of the alien image. All the proportions were wrong; its spindly neck didn't seem big enough to support its watermelon-sized head. Its limbs were way too long and strangely fragile. It used surrealistically snakelike fingers and toes to somehow grip the stones—flexing, bending, and molding its elongated digits to the contours of the rocks.

It couldn't have been more than four feet tall. It was naked and hairless; its odd peach-colored skin looked rough in the headlights' glow. But most disturbing of all was that the thing, however alien, looked vaguely human.

More than ten years later Bill Bartlett recalled the unforgettable moment and the bizarre creature. "I must confess," he told writer Robert Cahill, a retired law-enforcement officer, "at seeing it, I panicked, screamed, and sped off down the road." That's what happened to Bill Bartlett. But that weird night was far from over.

Midnight Companion

At around midnight, another Dover boy, fifteen-year-old John Baxter, would encounter the Demon. John was walking home after visiting his girlfriend, Cathy Cronin. On Farm Street, where he planned to hitch a ride, he was surprised to see another pedestrian coming toward him. Assuming it was an as-yet-unrecognized friend, John called out. But no one answered. Yet the tiny figure continued to advance.

John called again, "Who is that?" Nothing.

When John stopped, the other figure stopped too. It stood absolutely still some twenty feet away. As he tried to identify his midnight companion, John gradually became aware that two enormous orange eyes were staring back at him. A kind of terror seized him as he stood paralyzed, trying to make sense of what he was seeing. Was it an animal walking on its hind legs, or a horribly deformed child? Just what manner of beast was studying him with those unearthly orange eyes?

When its long fingers reached for a rock by the roadside, John feared that the thing might attack him. Instead, the creature used the rock to propel itself off the roadway and into the nearby woods. John listened to the crunch of its footfalls in the dry leaves. And soon he found himself running. Blindly, madly, he raced down Farm Street, trying to escape an impossible vision that would haunt him the rest of his life.

Other Witnesses

On April 22, the evening after the Bartlett-Baxter sightings, there were more confrontations with the spindly, peachy-colored gnome. Eighteen-year-old William Taintor was driving with Abby Brabham, fifteen, on Springdale Avenue, near downtown Dover. Suddenly Abby noticed the awkward little phantom on top of a culvert over Trout Brook. It hunkered on all fours facing their oncoming car. Shocked by the alien vision, Abby cried for Will to get them out of there. As he sped away, Will passed within eight feet of where the thing crouched, but got only a quick glimpse of it. The otherworldly experience left both teenagers trembling and terrified.

Although Abby was unaware of the previous reports, her description of the Demon tallied with Bill Bartlett's and John Baxter's as to size, large head, hairless body, and absence of nose, ears, mouth, and tail. The only conflict had to do with its eyes: She perceived them as green, not orange.

Investigations and Theories

Since that mysterious twenty-five-hour period, there have been no more sightings of Dover's frail phantom. To us, the real interest of the Dover Demon is not so much what it was—we'll probably never know—but the proliferation of theories about what it wasn't.

First we're certain it wasn't a hoax by, or on, the reporting participants. Everyone who knows them agrees that the young people were honest and forthright, not known for pranks, hoaxes, and other mischief.

In a follow-up investigation twelve years after the fact, writer Robert Cahill interviewed former Dover police chief Carl Sheridan, cop to cop.

"Did it really happen, or was it a hoax?" Mr. Cahill asked.

"It was real," Chief Sheridan replied. "Those boys really did see something out there."

So we are left to contemplate what it was that they saw. To some, the Demon fits the popular description of a large-eyed, bulbous-headed UFO occupant. While we can't rule out this possibility, it must be noted that investigators checked for UFO activity around the time of the Demon sighting; no UFOs were reported on the nights in question.

There is little hope of finding a concrete answer, and speculation gets farther and farther out. Some have suggested sick dogs and shaved monkeys. Others guess ghosts or even fairies. Perhaps the most absurd explanation came from Martin S. Kottmeyer in an article called "Demon Moose" published in *The Anomalist* in 1998. In effect, he suggested that the young people were seeing a baby moose, but Loren Coleman destroyed that theory so thoroughly in his 2001 edition of *Mysterious America* that we feel no need to refute it further.

So, although the saga of the Dover Demon violates the comfort level of everyone who encounters it, we're left with a real mystery.

The Plug-Uglies

New England is home to all manner of trolls, gnomes, and sprites. We can lump them all together and designate them the Plug-Uglies.

In Maine, for example, the Passamaquoddy share their reservations with two races of grotesque little people known as the Nagumwasuck and the Mekumwasuck. They all get along well, like one big functional family, until someone makes the mistake of laughing at any of the weird little people. Then the wee ones turn mean, flashing an evil eye that can sicken or kill its human target. They have been spotted as recently as 1970, so if you see something big and ugly in the woods, run! If it's small and ugly, whatever you do, don't laugh.

Littlefoot?

We're not sure what it was that J. W. McHenry of Waldoboro, Maine, crossed paths with in January 1855. He was busily chopping wood near his home when he heard a series of high-pitched screams coming from the woods.

When Mr. McHenry, axe firmly in hand, went to investigate, he discovered a tiny creature, no more than eighteen inches tall and covered with long black hair. It took one look at Mr. McHenry—who must have appeared to be a giant—about-faced, and dashed off into the protection of the trees. Mr. McHenry lit out after it. Following a rigorous, but not too lengthy chase, the man caught the monster. It wriggled and screeched as it tried to get away, but Mr. McHenry held on tight, and eventually the little critter became tired. Not knowing what else to do with it, Mr. McHenry brought the ugly little hairball home and made a pet of it.

What was it? We don't know. Any records seem to have disappeared. All we have for evidence is this story, and many more like it.

The Derry Fairy

Perhaps the crowned king of ugliness was a bewildering little gargoyle spotted in Derry, New Hampshire, on December 15, 1956. A man was harvesting Christmas trees in the woods when suddenly he looked up and saw something looking back at him silently. Whatever it was stood about two feet tall, and seemed neither human nor animal. Its green skin was wrinkled and looked like folds of elephant hide. The high dome of its head supported floppy ears comparable to those of a bloodhound. Tiny holes bored into the skull where the nose should be, and its eyes were covered with what appeared to be a protective film. Its arms and legs were short, ending with stumpy hands and toeless feet.

The witness says he watched the miniature mystery for a good twenty minutes. Then, realizing no one would believe his odd tale, he decided to capture it as proof. When he lunged at the creature, it let out such a terrified screeching that the witness, rather than the beast, ran away in fear.

Bigfoot in New England

Reports of Bigfoot sightings—and Bigfoot sightings that are not officially reported—are too numerous to recount in this short chapter. No doubt examples worldwide and over the centuries number in the billions. But these few samples will demonstrate that some sort of gigantic, hairy, apelike, manlike being seems to be sharing our space and time, not only all over the world but right here in New England.

The Bennington Monster

One day in September 2003, Ray Dufresne dropped his daughter off at Southern Vermont College in Bennington and was driving north on Route 7, heading back to his home in Winooski, Vermont. At the highest elevation between Bennington and Winooski, in a mysterious area near Glastenbury Mountain, Mr. Dufresne took his "One Step Beyond." Directly beside the road he spotted a "big black thing," over six feet tall, with extremely long arms. It weighed, he guessed, some 270 pounds. He said, "It was hairy from the top of his head to the bottom of his feet." Walking rapidly on two legs, it vanished into the woods.

An experienced hunter, Mr. Dufresne was positive he wasn't seeing a bear or moose. At first he thought someone might be playing a joke on him—someone in a gorilla suit. But that just didn't compute. Why there, in the middle of nowhere? Nothing was around: no houses, no empty cars—nothing. He continued his drive, regretting all the way that he hadn't stopped to investigate.

The mystery deepened as other people began reporting seeing the creature. On September 16 at seven forty-five p.m., writer Doug Dorst was driving along Route 7 toward Bennington College. Approaching the same spot, he said he saw what looked like a "homeless dude . . . in a snowsuit." As Mr. Dorst got closer, the thing turned around, looking directly at him. This was no homeless dude. The creature's face was light brown, its body black. It was over six feet tall and stocky. Of course the possibility of trickery crossed the writer's mind, but there was no obvious evidence of a hoax.

When the story came out in the *Bennington Banner,* two women admitted to having seen the beast the same night as Mr. Dufresne had. They'd been closer, just ten or twenty feet away. Neither saw its face, but they thought it had a tail. They concluded the only thing it could be was a big person in a costume.

Soon suspicion shifted to a known practical joker, a local man named Michael Greene. But Mr. Greene denied any involvement in any trickery. A hunter himself, he knew the dangers of hoaxing. Armed men in pickup trucks routinely drive around in that isolated area. Any jolly jokester romping through the woods in a gorilla suit would be taking his life in his hands.

So the mystery continues.

But it is not a new mystery: It has existed for hundreds of years. The area that includes Glastenbury Mountain has long been known for the odd stuff that goes on there. It was the scene of multiple vanishings during the 1940s and '50s, but long before that, many of the earliest settlers reported spook lights, formless phantoms, unidentifiable sounds, and mysterious odors. This was, and apparently still is, the stomping grounds for the Bennington Monster.

In the first half of the twentieth century, Francis Pitkin of Bennington collected many of the Bennington Monster stories. Among them is an especially frightening account of an early–nineteenth-century stagecoach trip along the ridges of Woodford and Glastenbury mountains. A heavy rainstorm suddenly let loose, forcing the driver to slow down to nearly a crawl. His four terrified passengers cringed with every blast of thunder as jagged bolts of lightning ripped the black sky. Soon the rain was washing so rapidly down the mountainside that large sections of the road were swept away.

The driver had no choice but to bring his stagecoach to a stop in the middle of the wet mountain wilderness. They were surrounded by rain and darkness, and the driver's nerves grew tense as his horses became restless. Fearing the presence of some unseen bear or wildcat, he took his rifle and lantern and stepped down to examine the rutted roadway. The pool of orange lantern light revealed unfamiliar footprints in the damp roadbed. They must have been fresh, because the rain had not yet washed them away. And they were widely spaced, suggesting that the animal that made them was of tremendous size.

Something was nearby — something gigantic. It was spooking the horses, and now it was beginning to spook the driver. He summoned the male passengers, hoping to get their opinion about what might have made the tracks. As the men stepped out, something slammed against the side of the carriage. As the savage blows continued, the women jumped out too. It wasn't long before the wooden coach toppled and fell on its side. The terrified passengers huddled with the driver, quaking in fear as the cold rain continued to beat down on them.

Then someone looked up. His horrified expression caused the others to look where he was gazing. Everyone was staring at two large glowing eyes that watched them

Something was nearby—something gigantic. It was spooking the horses, and now it was beginning to spook the driver.

from the nearby wood. They could tell it was huge even though it was obscured by darkness and tree branches. The creature then roared and tromped off into the night. The silent travelers, now stricken with horror, had met the Bennington Monster. And he, or his descendants, was still around to meet Ray Dufresne, Doug Dorst, and others in September 2003.

Stalked by the Monster on Glastenbury Mountain

Hiking has always been my favorite way to waste away an afternoon. Growing up, nothing made me happier than meeting a group of friends and taking off into the woods. As I got older, I loved to hike alone. A few years back I had an experience that led me to the conclusion that I would never hike alone again.

I lived in Vermont from 1994 to 1997, near Glastenbury Mountain. People told me that it was mysterious, and had a reputation for disappearances and monster sightings. I laughed off their warnings. To me the mystery of the mountain made it intriguing and beautiful. So I often found myself exploring the area alone.

On one notable afternoon in 1996, I had been exploring the mountain's deep forest for a couple of hours when I realized that I was in a pretty desolate stretch. Something about the place began to make me uneasy, and I became overwhelmed with a desire to get out of the woods. I began backtracking toward my car, and after a few minutes, I got the feeling that something was following me. I also noticed a faint but distinct musky smell. My gut told me that whatever the thing was, it was not in my immediate proximity, but it was getting closer.

Everything I had ever been told about the Bennington Monster came flooding back — all the stories about it attacking people, frightening them, stretching back hundreds of years. I know it sounds like my mind was just playing tricks on me, but the panic that I began feeling was very real and intense. I actually felt like I had become a hunted animal. I knew I had to get out of those woods fast!

When I reached a familiar area, I felt a bit safer, so I stopped to rest. This happened twice. Both times, I heard something approximately twenty-five yards behind me moving around in the brush. It had heavy footsteps. I thought I heard faint grunts, though with my heart pounding in my ears like a drum, it is hard to say for sure. I could sense movement in the shadows but never saw anything definitive. I began to feel as though the beast (or whatever it was) was toying with me. It was getting close enough to make me run from it but would then halt within feet of me when I stopped. I felt completely at its mercy.

Finally I ran into two hunters on their way up the mountain. I must have been quite a sight, sweating and gasping for breath, and they immediately asked me what was wrong. Shaking, I told them of my situation, and they escorted me back to my car. They headed back up the mountain with their shotguns. I later ran into one of them, and he told me that, while they never saw the monster, they did see where it had flattened brush in its path and that they detected that same stench I had.

I'll never enter those woods again. Be warned, it is a place not to be trifled with, and as far as I am concerned, its monster is very very real. *–Donna Schneider*

Maine's Pomoola

The so-called Bennington Monster is not unique to the Vermont wilderness. Some version of the big hairy monster seems to have its tradition wherever there are spooky woods and people wandering around in them. For example, take Maine, New England's largest state. Its area is over 33,000 square miles. With the exception of the tourist-crowded coastline, much of the state is wild and undeveloped. What manner of unknown creatures could wander those endless tracts of woods?

In the early part of the nineteenth century, Hugh Watson was at his camp on the shore of Telos Lake, about twenty miles northwest of Mount Katahdin. A longtime woodsman, he was comfortable in the wilds, so he was surprised to be suddenly overcome with a sensation of dread. It was as if he were being watched.

Mr. Watson edged back toward camp, all the while thinking of bears, mountain lions, robbers, and even Indians. With his eyes trained on every shadow and moving branch, he froze when he saw that his campsite was surrounded by unfamiliar skulking creatures. They were poking into things, apparently looking for something. Watson ducked into some bushes and hid most of the night.

When his visitors had wandered off, Mr. Watson returned to a campsite that had been trashed. After the incident, when he told some other locals about it, he learned who the intruders had been and how fortunate he was not to have challenged them. But it wouldn't be the last time they came into his life.

In 1866, Watson was still leading hunting parties into what is now Baxter State Park. Though he had become an old man, his charges, the youthful Zeke and Cluey Robbins, were having a hard time keeping up with him. As the trio penetrated deeper into the Maine wilderness, Hugh Watson began to have a nearly forgotten sensation; he once again felt he was being watched.

That night, around the campfire, one of the Robbins boys asked the old man what was wrong. Hugh told them what had happened long ago. Of course Zeke and Cluey suspected the old man was just telling scary campfire tales, so they tossed it off with a grin.

A few days passed. One evening just before dark Cluey went to the brook to get a bucket of water. As he glanced at the far side of the stream, he saw what he at first thought was another hunter. The individual was gigantic, a mountain of a man, dressed in fur on the hot night. As Cluey watched, the stranger thrust his big hand like a spear into the water and pulled out a fish. He then consumed the wriggling animal.

Before the bizarre fisherman could spot him, Cluey raced back to camp, where he, like Hugh Watson before him, passed a tense and sleepless night. From time to time, he heard footsteps in the darkness outside. Sometimes they seemed to approach the campsite and then back off. Cluey quickly realized that the sounds were being made by a number of creatures. He grabbed his rifle, sat up, and looked around. In the distance, silhouetted against the sky, he again saw the hairy giant. Next morning, he told his brother Zeke and Hugh Watson about the experience.

"That's the Pomoola you seen," Mr. Watson told him. "That's the Indian Devil."

Like Glastenbury has the Bennington Monster, Maine's Mount Katahdin has Pomoola. These furtive hirsute giants are supposedly half man and half beast. Though peaceful by nature, they can instantly turn savage if provoked.

More than a century later, in September 1988, a troop of Boy Scouts had hiked halfway up Katahdin. There they saw one of the mysterious creatures sitting at the edge of the forest, pulling up roots. It had a dark, triangular-shaped face, broad shoulders, and reddish brown hair or fur. One of the scouts said, "It made frightening sounds." Another boy added, "It stunk like rotten eggs."

Woods Devils of New Hampshire

In Coos, New Hampshire's northernmost, largest, and least settled county, they have their own variety of the "devil." For years old-time woodsmen have known about mysterious woodland intruders collectively referred to as Woods Devils. They are said to be tall, hairy, and humanlike in shape, but unlike their Maine cousins, they are extremely thin and grayish in color. They are exceptionally adept at not being seen. A person could almost bump into one before noticing it. If spotted, they can run away at high velocity while producing a scream capable of freezing pursuers in their tracks. Old-timers say there used to be a lot more Woods Devils. Perhaps they are dying out or moving to other locations. Or perhaps people just won't talk about them. It is easy to see why many stories of confrontations with these hairy enigmas might never be told at all. But occasionally some become very public.

A well-documented case from New Hampshire is a good example of what can be accomplished when the press takes such a tale seriously.

Walter Bowers Sr. had lived in Webster for all of his fifty-five years. During bird-hunting season in September 1987, the recent retiree was tromping across a field near Mill Brook in Salisbury. Suddenly he experienced the sensation that he was not alone. He looked around for another hunter or some sign of an animal, but nothing was nearby. Still, he couldn't shake the uncomfortable feeling. Then he saw it, standing in plain sight, in the middle of a nearby field.

"This thing was BIG," Mr. Bowers told Scot French of the *Concord* [NH] *Monitor.* "I would say at least nine feet. Maybe more, maybe less; I didn't stick around to do any measuring."

Questioning by Mr. French brought forth additional details.

"The whole body was covered with hair," Mr. Bowers told the reporter, "kind of grayish color. The hands were like yours or mine, only three times bigger, with pads on the front paws like a dog. Long legs, long arms, like a gorilla. But this here wasn't a gorilla. I'm tellin' ya it

. . . And in Massachusetts

There are several regions in Massachusetts that seem to produce an extraordinary number of Bigfoot sightings. One favorite haunt seems to be a place called the Meadows, an agricultural area situated south of Springfield between the town of Longmeadow and the Connecticut River.

Some people hypothesize that the river is used as a means of travel by the great hairy ones. In fact, a few people say they have seen Bigfoot swimming in the Connecticut. But while people watch Bigfoot, Bigfoot sometimes watches people. A number of individuals in the vicinity of the Meadows have been startled to see big

hairy faces staring in their windows at them. In most cases, police find footprints to corroborate the activities of these unique Peeping Toms. They even found trails of prints, about five feet apart, leading from the river, up a steep bank, then on to the windows of houses, garages, and cars.

A persistent rumor in the area is that a bit farther north there is a system of man-made tunnels that connect to the river. Bigfoot, some speculate, may make his home there. Supposedly, animals have been found near the tunnel mouths, mutilated almost beyond recognition. One recurring tale is of a German shepherd that was would make your hair stand up."

Mr. Bowers told his story to Salisbury police chief Jody Heath, who took no action. He got the same reaction from the local game warden. "He just laughed at me," Mr. Bowers said. "He said it was probably a bear or a moose."

Walt Bowers had been hunting those woods all his life. He'd killed four bears and knew damn well what a moose looked like. "If a man can't tell the difference between a moose and a thing like that," he said, "he hadn't ought to be hunting."

But reporter French believed the woodsman. He visited the site with Mr. Bowers, and his time with the man as they tramped through the forest convinced Mr. French that Walt Bowers was sincere.

"I believe him," the reporter wrote in his column. And then he posed a couple of questions worth considering: "Why would Bowers, a retired caretaker at the New Hampshire Veterans Home, make up such a story?" And, "Why would he subject himself to such ridicule?"

Why, indeed?

found with all its bones pulverized.

A man named Joe used to have a car crushing business in the area. His equipment and trailer office were not far from the river. One hot summer night Joe and some friends were having a few beers outside the trailer. Suddenly they heard noise coming from the river. It was as if something was snapping branches and crashing through the undergrowth. Moments later an eight-foot-tall Bigfoot stepped into view. It seemed fascinated by the piled-up chassis of crushed cars on Joe's lot. After a moment of apparent contemplation, it bent over, picked up one of the crushed cars, and began to walk off with it.

Joe and his friends couldn't believe their eyes. That metal must have weighed a ton and a half!

After walking about thirty feet, the creature threw down his souvenir, scratched his head, walked back to the river, and swam off. When the police came, they made casts of the footprints, and took a statement from the men. Joe insisted the creature had hair. Not fur, but hair—just like a person. But it covered the whole body. And the face looked human, with long hair and a beard!

Before the week was over, Joe had closed his business and bought a gas station in a crowded section of town a good safe distance from the river.

One rainy Monday night, August 23, 1982, John Fuller and David Buckley were working at a dairy farm in Ellington, Connecticut. The clock was approaching midnight, the hour when they routinely went to the barn to check the cows. Dashing inside to escape the rain, they discovered something else had beaten them to it—and it nearly scared them to death. There they stood, face-to-face with a nightmare.

The impression—as is so often the case—was alien and human at the same time.

The alien part was that the creature was gigantic and completely covered with hair. The men guessed it was about seven feet tall and weighed over three hundred pounds. The human components were its face, which looked more like a man than an animal, and its seemingly casual, humanlike posture. It sat on the edge of a feed bin, watching the cows, nonchalantly dangling one of its hirsute hands in the silage bin, perhaps stirring it or reaching for a handful to eat.

When the creature saw David and John, it stood up and took a tentative step toward them. With that, both men screamed and ran back out into the rain. They crossed the yard to the office, from which they immediately phoned the police. When Sergeant Fred Bird of the Connecticut State Police arrived on the scene, he made an earnest effort to locate evidence of their mysterious visitor. The barn was empty, except for the dairy cows. The creature—whatever it was—had vanished completely. The wet yard outside made footprints impossible to identify.

In the absence of proof, it was tempting to dismiss the whole thing as a prank. But John Fuller and David Buckley had never been known as jokesters. The fact is that they were terribly shaken by the mysterious midnight confrontation.

So if the men weren't joking, could someone have been joking with them? Very unlikely. As Sergeant Bird put it, "You play a practical joke like that around a farm, and you're liable to wind up dead. People out in the country have guns, and they don't like to see their animals spooked."

Rhode Island's Rogues

Most books about Bigfoot say that he, she, or it has been spotted in every country of the world and in each of the United States with the exception (for some reason) of the tiny state of Rhode Island. However, the Bigfoot Field Researchers Organization (www.bfro.net) is not so sure about that. It collects Bigfoot sightings from all over the country, and its data indicate that the swampy areas of Rhode Island might indeed conceal a furtive population of the critters, identifiable by their unique coloration. The Rhode Island Bigfoot is ghostly white.

For example, just after a thunderstorm in the summer of 1978, a Charlestown resident who lived near Indian Cedar Swamp was driving around on back roads with her eight-year-old son, looking for deer. Rain was still falling as they rounded a corner to discover that a lightning-blasted tree had fallen across the road. Since the tree was too heavy to move, they had to turn back.

As the woman jockeyed the car around, her headlights flashed on the tree stump. There, twelve to fifteen feet away, she and her son both saw what looked like a white ape, standing next to the stump. The creature was six to seven feet tall, with long hair and long, powerful arms. Its head and flat face seemed to rest on top of its massive chest, making it appear neckless. The woman slammed the car into reverse and peeled out of there.

The young man—now an adult—recalls on the BFRO website, "I'm not a fan of ghosts, UFO's or even big foot. I'm not sure to this day what I saw wasn't a man in a costume, dressed up, out in a rainstorm, a half mile or more from any home, waiting for my mother and me to drive down the road to give us a scare. The only thing I can say is it was a damn' good costume and a damn' good plan. We saw what we saw and this is something I would sware [sic] to on any polygraph test as I'm sure my mother would."

Another peculiar but perhaps more menacing phantom appeared near Wakefield, Rhode Island, in the vicinity of Great Swamp. It was in September 1974—a Sunday night. At about ten p.m., a solitary cyclist was heading back to the University of Rhode Island after spending the weekend with his girlfriend.

When he noticed that his brake needed adjustment, he pulled his bike up under a street lamp on Perry Avenue. As he worked, he became aware of heavy footfalls coming toward him from across the road. Whoever it was remained invisible because of the darkness. Somehow, the footsteps seemed unnaturally loud, like heavy falling rocks rhythmically smacking the ground. And they were getting closer.

The witness wrote, "All of a sudden this dog starts barking like crazy; I can hear the chain snap as it either tries to attack or get away from something."

At that point, he abandoned his repair work, preparing to pedal away. Just then, a "white-looking gorilla" stepped out of the darkness and into the lamplight. For a moment, the two stood eye to eye at a distance of about twenty-five feet. The thing was approximately six feet tall and weighed maybe four hundred pounds. Its wide nose and mouth were humanlike, surrounded with long hair. The eyes were deep set and close together. Animal or human, it was hard to tell. But there was something primal and primitive in its manner as it repositioned itself, now resting on its knuckles as if poised for a sprint.

The cyclist sped away as, briefly, the "white gorilla" gave chase. "I was never so scared in my life. My heart was pounding out of my chest, my eyes had tears in them, and with all my might I pedaled as it ran on two legs, then down on its knuckles, then back up again."

The chase lasted only about five seconds. The creature halted in the middle of the road, where it briefly swayed back and forth. Then it turned and vanished over a rock wall, leaving nothing but the lasting impression that, yes, Bigfoot lives in Rhode Island.

Lake Champlain's Watery Whatsit

"I hereby offer $50,000 for the hide of the Great Champlain serpent to add to my mammoth World's Fair Show. You are authorized to draw on me for any sum necessary to assist in securing the monster's remains." —P. T. Barnum printed in the *Whitehall* [NY] *Times*

At New England's western border there's a vast body of water: Lake Champlain. It plunges like a silver dagger from Canada, filleting Vermont from the rest of the United States. It's one hundred and twenty miles long. At its widest, near Burlington, it spans twelve miles. And, just like the waters off New England's east coast—the Atlantic Ocean—its depths hold many mysteries.

For centuries, the locals have believed that a monster lurks in Lake Champlain, which lies on a latitude similar to Scotland's infamous Loch Ness. Perhaps this tenuous connection explains why hundreds of witnesses have confronted something inexplicable in its deep waters. That something, whatever it may be, is apparently alive—and big and occasionally terrifying.

To defang the monster, locals have taken to calling it Champ after Samuel de Champlain, who discovered and explored the lake. He sailed down from the Richelieu River in 1609 and began four centuries of recorded sightings. But even before he made the scene, local Indians were telling monster stories. They'd sprinkle offerings—tobacco and such—on the water before crossing, as a sort of toll intended to guarantee safe passage.

Since then there have been hundreds, probably thousands, of sightings on both water and land. In 1973, one woman even spotted Champ from the air while flying over the lake in her father's plane.

Some Exotic Sightings of the Champlain Monster

The *Burlington News* reported, "The Lake Champlain sea serpent" — as Champ was then called — "was seen at the 1892 encampment of the American Canoe Association when, coming to the surface in the neighborhood of a flotilla of cruising canoes, he scattered the occupants in panic."

Another interesting sighting occurred in September 1894. The *Essex County Republican* reported that four men saw "the Champlain Sea Serpent" at Cumberland Head, Plattsburgh, New York. "It caused a great commotion in the water . . . and came toward the shore and out of the water six feet or more upon the land."

Out of the water?

A New Century

In the twentieth century, the encounters continued. In 1945, people aboard the S.S. *Ticonderoga* observed the monster cavorting somewhere near the middle of the lake. In 1961, Thomas E. Morse of Westport, New York, was driving beside North West Bay at twilight. What he saw was like something out of the Twilight Zone. He reported, "When first seen it appeared as a massive gunmetal gray approximately 18-inches wide cable on the shore and out into the lake. . . . It appeared to be a monstrous eel with white teeth that raked rearward in the mouth." Mr. Morse said that, while on shore, Champ raised its head a full four feet. It might have been reacting to the sound of the car.

This, like the 1894 sighting, was unusual indeed. The creature, whatever it may be, is rarely spied out of the water. Such land sightings are of special interest because they are less ambiguous, not distorted by tossing waves or the harsh glare of sunlight on water.

On July 30, 1984, the largest mass Champ sighting in history occurred aboard a sightseeing boat, the *Spirit of Ethan Allen.* A private party was in progress, celebrating the wedding anniversary of a Massachusetts couple. Some eighty guests were aboard. The hour was six o'clock in the evening. The boat was near Appletree Point, just north of Burlington. Michael Shea, the boat's owner, is a professional airplane pilot. His keen powers of observation may explain why he was the first to spot something unusual.

"It was a perfect, flat calm day," he said later. "Not a ripple on the water. I saw it about two hundred feet away. First I thought it was a stray wake. I stared at it awhile and noticed [whatever it was] was creating its own wake."

The band stopped playing. People raced to the rails to watch the strange humped creature swimming beside the boat. Many party guests came from out of state; they'd never heard of the Lake Champlain Monster. But everyone—natives and visitors alike—all saw something.

Mike Shea watched the creature for about three minutes. He identified three to five humps, each extending about twelve inches out of the water, and estimated the creature was about thirty feet long. He said it was "green-brown [and] slimy-looking, like a frog." It swam parallel with the *Spirit of Ethan Allen* for one thousand yards until a speedboat approached. Then the creature turned ninety degrees and submerged. Several people saw it reappear about fifteen minutes later. Bette Morris of Grand Isle—daughter of the anniversary couple—snapped a picture. Alas, like so many Champ photographs, the image proved inconclusive.

Monster Hunters

Since then, Champ has been spotted hundreds—perhaps thousands—of times. During its first brush with stardom, back in the early 1800s, waves of tourists flooded Lake Champlain in response to showman P. T. Barnum's offer of $50,000 for the creature's remains. As far as we know, the money remains unclaimed.

Since Mr. Barnum's day, a number of monster hunters have ventured to Lake Champlain. Joseph W. Zarzynski of Wilton, New York, spent thirty summers on

the lake, trying to prove Champ's existence. His book, *Champ: Beyond the Legend,* remains the definitive study of Champlain's aquatic phenomenon. Though Mr. Zarzynski experienced a single sighting, he never found the solid proof he was after.

Perhaps the most compelling evidence came in the 1980s when accidental monster hunter Sandra Mansi snapped Champ's picture. The clear color photograph shows what appears to be the long neck and head of some unidentified aquatic creature. Recently *Skeptical Inquirer* magazine insisted Ms. Mansi mistook a piece of driftwood for a lake monster. To us, such a misidentification strains credibility more than does the possibility of a surviving dinosaur in New England's greatest lake.

Dennis Hall of Vergennes, Vermont, is the best known of today's Champ chasers. In 1985, he videotaped a moving, seemingly living form that he believes to be the elusive critter. In fact, Dennis may also hold the record for Champ sightings, claiming more than twenty in all.

From July 21 to September 10, 1993, he participated in the largest and most generously funded monster hunt in the history of Lake Champlain. A film crew from the Tokyo Broadcasting System was on the water shooting a ninety-minute Champ documentary for Japanese television. Fifteen boats equipped with the latest electronic equipment combed the lake. Helicopters patrolled from the air. A certain section of lake, believed to be a Champ hot spot, was under constant videotape surveillance.

As usual, Champ proved camera shy. But thanks to Jim Hotaling of Willsboro, New York, the disappointed crew did not return to Japan empty handed. He used sonar to record underwater images on a paper-graph. Most were unremarkable: a good-sized salmon, a school of perch. But then the sonar sighted something

interesting: a large irregular mass, twenty feet long, moving in sixty feet of water.

Mr. Hotaling was stumped. "I don't know if it's Champ," he said. "It's abnormal in shape—very dense.

I've never seen anything like it before."

If you'd like to follow this and other developments in the riddle of the Lake Champlain Monster, you can visit Dennis Hall's website at: www.champquest.com.

Local Heroes and Villains

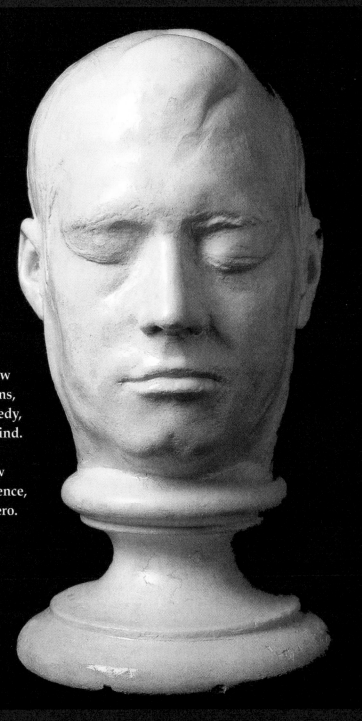

if you were to ask people from "away" (a New England term describing the source of all non-New Englanders) to list the chief Yankee heroes and villains, names like Lizzie Borden, Paul Revere, John F. Kennedy, "Whitey" Bulger, and Ted Williams might come to mind. Well, they've got their own books.

In this chapter, let's meet some lesser known New Englanders who still—due to their heroism, malevolence, or out-and-out peculiarity—are worthy of the title Hero. Or Villain. Or maybe just Nutcase.

The Confounding Fathers of Stotham

Among those people who created the image of historic New England, we have to credit Hubert G. Ripley, who, in April 1920, authored an article called "A New England Village" for the White Pine Series of *Architectural Monographs*. These were scholarly journals, intended for use by historians and architectural students, that documented and preserved information, drawings, and photographs of early American wooden buildings. The titular town, Stotham, Massachusetts, was described as one "which would in later days come to be regarded as a typical example, although perhaps not so well known, of the unspoiled New England Village."

The text was supported by a series of photographs of seventeenth-, eighteenth-, and early-nineteenth-century Stotham structures—homes and farmsteads—some of them designed and built by the town's architect, Ruben Duren. In addition, a detailed town history profiled a selection of Stotham's early settlers and leading citizens, among them Salmon White, Obadiah Witherspoon, Nahum Bodkins, and of course Obijah Podbury of the venerable Podbury family, "who may well be termed the founders of Stotham."

Mr. Ripley's article presented an ideal picture of the quintessential New England village, where "the blighting hand of the real estate promoter, and the withering touch of the speculative builder, are conspicuously lacking."

He writes, "Generations of blushing maidens have

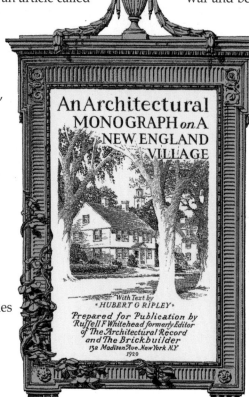

An Architectural
MONOGRAPH on A
NEW ENGLAND
VILLAGE

With Text by
• HUBERT G RIPLEY •

Prepared for Publication by
Ruſſell F Whitehead formerly Editor
of The Architectural Record
and The Brickbuilder
132 Madiſon Ave. New York N.Y.
1920

swung on the old Billings gate, opening on the path leading to the meadows." Some young men went off to war and became heroes. Others, like "Icabod Somes, a wild, untamed, red-headed youth," ran away to sea and became pirates. Cadwallader Simpkins and his partner, Barzillai Plainfield, opened a general store that made them rich and went on to found a profitable and picturesque stone tannery. There is even a haunted house (the Rogers mansion), where treasure was rumored to be buried.

All in all, with photographs and flowery language, Mr. Ripley portrayed the iconic New England small town. Soon after its publication, however, many White Pine Series subscribers were puzzled. They had great difficulty locating the village of Stotham on any Massachusetts map. But it was April, after all. And if there's a Ripley involved, one is well advised to "Believe It or Not!"

Turns out the whole thing was a hoax. Stotham, Massachusetts, never existed. It was the creation of Hubert G. Ripley (if there was a Hubert G. Ripley), a partner in a Boston architectural firm, Ripley & Le Boutillier, Architects (if there ever really was a Ripley & Le Boutillier, Architects). He, or they, had invented the entire town as a way of using up some of the photographs left over from other presumably more legitimate monographs. Like any good New Englander, Mr. Ripley wouldn't let such good pictures (or stories) go to waste. And in so doing, he helped to create a mythical picture of New England.

How John Noyes Beat His Shyness

The Green Mountain State has always nurtured untraditional religious expression. Of the many contenders for Vermonters' souls, one of the most unorthodox was John Humphrey Noyes. Born in Brattleboro in 1811 to wealthy, influential, and especially pious parents, John would eventually challenge—albeit briefly—not only religious, but also social, political, and economic values in America.

Dartmouth educated, John bucked his family's values and became an agnostic for a while. During this time, he practiced law in Brattleboro while he tried to overcome what he called the "family affliction." John, along with his father and uncles, suffered from what they all perceived as a hereditary ailment—a paralyzing shyness around women. How he compensated for that deficit would become obvious as his life continued to change.

In 1831, he experienced a religious awakening that led him to become a graduate of Andover and Yale theology schools. Seeing the light, though, didn't necessarily clear the path before him. He was rejected by the woman he loved, Abigail Merwin, and had his preaching license revoked in 1834. John was propelled into a "dark night of the soul." During this contemplative period, he discarded the time-honored religious notion of eternal damnation. He came to believe that Jesus Christ's second coming had already occurred and that everyone was thus released from sin. (You can see why the church fathers would be a little wary of John.) With no sin to worry about, the remaining task before humankind was to attain perfection. So John contrived his own version of the already existing doctrine of Perfectionism.

Left, John Humphrey Noyes in 1840. Top, the Noyes House at Putney, Vermont. Below, Harriet Holton

In 1838, he married Harriet Holton, perhaps his first convert to Perfectionism. Together they put John's complex and constantly evolving belief system into practice at a commune he founded in Putney, Vermont.

By 1843, his Perfectionist Community included twenty-eight

adults and nine children. They had five hundred acres of land, seven houses, a printing shop, and a store. Hard work and education were two of the commune's more mainstream values.

Soon the group began secretly to practice what John called Complex Marriage. This simply meant that every man was married to every woman, and vice versa. Any pairing of individuals was permitted for sexual intercourse. The only rule was that folks mustn't get attached to each other. Monogamy was considered selfish and idolatrous.

Lucinda J. Lamb

John wrote, "In a holy community there is no more reason why sexual intercourse should be restrained by law, than why eating and drinking should be—and there is as little occasion for shame in one case as in the other."

Still, sexual partners had to gain each other's consent, "not by private conversation and courtship, but through the intervention of some third person or persons." Usually, the Reverend John Noyes himself.

It is not difficult to imagine how well this notion went over with the good people of Putney. But public contempt was temporarily assuaged because at the same time, John was showing some surprising results with his experiments in "magnetic healing." So, people thought, maybe there really was some substance to this odd prophet in their midst.

A Lamb Leads John to the Slaughter

But again, John's path grew bumpy. His attention to, and pursuit of, fifteen-year-old Lucinda J. Lamb, coupled with his apparent disrespect for her parents, began to undermine whatever credibility he'd established. Ultimately, his paradise was lost when a local man, Daniel Hall, who'd almost converted to Perfectionism, decided to pull out in 1847. He turned around and accused John of adultery. An arrest warrant was issued, with ample community outrage to back it up.

"Then," as historian John Parker Lee wrote, "with irreligious haste he fled to New York, and his flight was imitated by many of the Perfectionists." Or, as William Hines somewhat more sympathetically recalled in 1911, "Mr. Noyes and his followers considered it prudent to remove to a place where they were sure of more liberal treatment."

Paradise Regained

The group relocated to New York, where religious eccentricity has always been something of a virtue. There, in the town of Oneida, John founded the now famous Oneida Community. Perfectionists began to build the gigantic brick Mansion House, where they would all live like one great big functional family. At last, John and his growing number of followers were free to continue their practice of Complex Marriage while they resolutely "perfected" other unconventional methods of social harmony.

Within the complex structure of Complex Marriage, the Perfectionists practiced a controversial form of birth control called Male Continence, perhaps best described as knowing when to quit.

What some considered the most misguided of the Perfectionists' beliefs remains controversial to this day: the equality of the sexes. John Humphrey Noyes and his followers believed absolutely that men and women were completely and unarguably equal. Generally, assignments and responsibilities at the community demonstrated this conviction.

As strange as much of this sounds, John Noyes's experiment in communal living was quite successful for a while. In fact, the Oneida Community was the most successful of the many nineteenth-century utopian communities. It supported itself by selling the fruits and vegetables it grew, making animal traps, and creating silverware for America's most elite tables. In general, its people were happy and well educated, and the children produced by Complex Marriage were eager to remain at, or return to, the colony.

As a visiting journalist wrote at the time, "I am bound to say as an honest reporter, that I looked in vain for the visible signs of either the suffering or the sin. The fact that the children of the community hardly ever wish to leave it; that the young men whom they send to Yale College, and the young women whom they send for musical instruction to New York, always returned eagerly and devote their lives to the community—this proves a good deal."

Of course Oneida didn't work its wonders on all prospective members. Charles Guiteau left in 1866 after repeatedly failing to find sexual partners. He then denounced the community, saying that premature sexual experience "dwarfed" community women, making them "small and thin and homely." Mr. Guiteau then went on to bigger things. Fourteen years after leaving, he assassinated James Abram Garfield, leaving the presidency of the United States to Vermonter Chester A. Arthur.

John Humphrey Noyes in 1867. Above, the Oneida Community c. 1865–1875

Ultimately, as is often the case with cults, when the leader steps down, the institution fails. And so it was with John Humphrey Noyes and the Perfectionists. After Noyes passed to his reward, the community abandoned its efforts at spiritual harmony and Complex Marriage and rejoined the mainstream. However, all was not lost. The silverware the community produced evolved into a joint stock company, Oneida, Ltd., that is still in business today.

Some houses where the Perfectionists lived, three and four families in each, remain standing in Putney. No plaques mark these historic spots, and tourists are not encouraged to locate them. To many citizens of Putney, Vermont, John Humphrey Noyes is little more than a colorful if somewhat embarrassing memory.

When Lynn Lost Its Marbles

In the following case, the villain is a long-dead pirate and the hero should win some kind of medal (preferably gold) for sheer Yankee stick-to-itiveness.

The story takes place in one of the strangest places in New England, Dungeon Rock, in Lynn, Massachusetts. It was there, in the early 1600s, that the notorious pirate Thomas Veal is said to have buried a vast treasure, deep in a well-concealed cavern. Mr. Veal himself was guarding his hoard when the great New England earthquake of 1658 sealed up the treasure cave forever, burying the pirate alive with his ill-gotten gains. Almost immediately, treasure seekers began pitting and pocking the earth in fruitless attempts to extract Thomas Veal's gold. But no one succeeded; the earth had gobbled it up and wasn't about to give it back.

Flash forward about two hundred years. America's new interest in spiritualism inspired another get-rich-quick furor. Lynn's treasure pit attracted the attention of Hiram Marble of Charlton, Massachusetts. Believing dead men do tell tales, Mr. Marble—aided by a trusted spiritualist medium—contacted the ghost of the

392 FRANK LESLIE'S ILLUSTRATED NEWSPAPER [AUGUST 10, 1878.

At Work

Entrance to the Cave

Conducting Visitors Through the Cave

MASSACHUSETTS.—THE CAVE IN DUNGEON ROCK, NEAR LYNN, IN WHICH A LARGE QUANTITY OF GOLD AND JEWELS IS SUPPOSED TO HAVE BEEN SECRETED BY PIRATES.—DRAWN BY JOHN HYDE.

dead pirate and learned the precise whereabouts of the treasure.

Confident in his otherworldly contact, Mr. Marble saved up the considerable fortune of $1,500 (about $33,000 today) with which, in 1852, he purchased the land where Dungeon Rock stands. Then he started digging—all by himself. Day after day chipping away at the solid, unyielding stone. Even with drills and blasting powder, the work went slowly, with little encouragement along the way.

An early account describes Mr. Marble as "a man by no means deficient in intelligence . . . [an] energetic and persevering enthusiast—just such a person as often accomplishes great things. . . ."

But, giving the project all his attention, strength, and money, he was able to dig only about one foot every thirty days! So, we wonder, What kept him going? Well, it certainly wasn't his savings. They ran out in 1856, when he was fifty-three years old.

No, it was his unflappable faith in spiritualism and in the ghost of Tom Veal (who communicated regularly

By 1864 — with the spirits still cheering him on — the meandering excavation through solid rock had reached an astounding depth of 135 feet. In time, Hiram's son Edwin joined him in his efforts to reach the pirate's treasure. By this time, Massachusetts's original Big Dig had become a far-reaching curiosity. The penniless Marbles sustained their efforts by charging admission and leading curiosity-seekers by flickering torchlight deep into the bowels of the earth.

In November 1868, when father and son had burrowed to nearly two hundred feet, Hiram Marble died. His son Edwin followed him in January 1880. Edwin's sister remained on the site until the city of Lynn took it over in 1888. She supported herself by selling tickets at twenty-five cents apiece to visitors curious to see her father's lifework, a deep, useless hole in the ground.

The heroic aspects of Hiram Marble's remarkable endeavor are tainted by more than a little sadness. If he was really communicating with the spirit of Thomas Veal, you'd think he'd know better than to trust the word of a pirate.

from the great beyond) that sustained Hiram Marble. Because their dialogues were written, some still survive. In one, Veal earnestly stated, "[D]on't be discouraged: We are going as fast as we can. As to the course, you are in the right direction, at present. You have [but] one more curve to make. . . ."

One more curve! That would be at least twelve feet of digging. Another full year of backbreaking labor in his damp dark cavern. Another twelve full months of suffering the jeers of those who thought him insane.

Man with a Hole in His Head

The morning of September 13, 1848, began like any other in Cavendish, Vermont. But for Phineas Gage, everything was about to change. And, in a way, the world would change along with it.

Phineas was a Lebanon, New Hampshire, man, working in Cavendish as foreman of a construction crew for the Rutland and Burlington Railroad. Then twenty-five years old, he was seen as intelligent, reliable, and well balanced. Some people will tell you that the night before his fateful incident he visited a gypsy fortune teller who made an odd prediction. "You will appear on the stage," she told him, "and you will become famous. But the icy finger of death will touch you before sunset tomorrow."

Phineas put no faith in such tomfoolery. He was a railroad man, not some performer. And if he was going to be on a stage, it would be the one bound for Rutland to see his sweetheart.

The alleged prediction would come true, however, and in the most unpredictable of ways. The actual events unfolded something like this. On that September day, Phineas arrived at the construction site early, as he always did. This morning he was supervising the blasting of some ledge. The process was to drill a hole in the rock, add blasting powder, pack it with sand, then ignite it. A routine job. Phineas had done it a thousand times.

After making sure his men were well clear, Phineas stood over the hole, and like a thousand times before, he inserted a straight iron tamping rod into the opening.

But something went wrong. Maybe the charge was packed incorrectly. Maybe the metal sparked as it scraped against the rock. In any event, the powder ignited, sending the tamping rod into space like a bullet. Smoke momentarily concealed the accident scene as a shower of pebbles clattered down. The explosion roared along the track like a locomotive out of control.

Soon, through the veil of smoke, the men saw their boss on the ground. Unbelievably, he was trying to get up. Could it be that he had survived the blast? They rushed to him and saw that his clothes and hands were burned, his face and head covered with blood. Trying to control the bleeding, they gently carried him away to see Dr. John Harlow.

At first, the doctor thought Phineas had two wounds: one below his left eye, another at the top of his head. But as he examined them, he grew more disbelieving. Phineas Gage had suffered but a single wound. Unless Dr. Harlow was mistaken, a three-foot, seven-inch tamping iron, weighing thirteen and a half pounds, had been blown completely through Mr. Gage's skull! It was impossible; it would have destroyed half the man's brain.

Upon cleaning bone fragments from the openings, Dr. Harlow confirmed his fears: He could touch the fingertips of both hands inside Phineas Gage's head! Yet, impossibly, the man hadn't even lost consciousness. More miraculous still, Phineas would be up and walking within the week. He returned home to Lebanon, New Hampshire, just ten weeks later.

But Phineas had changed. Once steady as rock, he was now fitful, irreverent, boisterous, and unpredictable. He could never follow through on even the simplest plan. His eyesight and balance would be forever impaired. Those who knew him said he was no longer the Phineas Gage

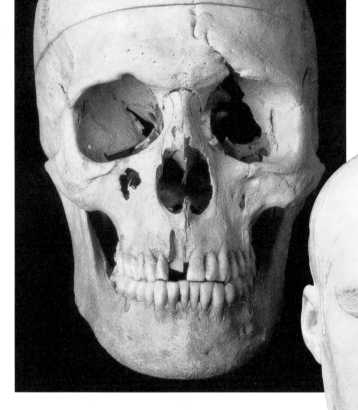

Somehow he survived another twelve years in his degenerating condition. But between 1859 and 1860, his health took a dramatic turn for the worse. Plagued by weakness and frequent epileptic seizures, Phineas went to San Francisco to live with his mother. He died there on May 21, 1860.

Though there is much folklore surrounding the life and death of Phineas Gage, one thing is certain: His tragedy led to important medical discoveries in brain research. At a time when linking emotional activity to the topography of the brain was unheard of, Mr. Gage's accident proved that the connection between brain and behavior is, in fact, physical. The airborne tamping bar actually severed the frontal cortex of his brain, where thinking takes place, from the limbic system—the seat of the emotions. As a result, after the accident Phineas's thoughts could no longer govern his emotions.

Today his case is still studied by medical students and neuroscientists all over the world. You may visit Phineas's skull, death mask, and his engraved tamping rod at the Warren Exhibition Gallery at Harvard Medical School, located on the fifth floor of the Countway Library of Medicine.

they knew. The railroad, in whose service he had sustained his injuries, refused to hire him back.

Although Mr. Gage's miraculous story was almost universally doubted by doctors and scientists, showman P. T. Barnum saw it for what it was: an exploitable oddity with a strong human interest component. Phineas Gage ended up on the stage, after all. He and his tamping bar became a featured attraction at Barnum's New York City Odditorium, where he was billed as the Only Living Man with a Hole in His Head.

Phantom Clowns Accost New England's Kids

Let's face it, deep down inside we've always suspected that clowns were up to no good. Whether it's the frightening wigs, the garish outfits, or the nightmarish face paint, there's just something creepy and disturbing about these so-called happy hobos and harlequins. In 1981, people's deep-rooted fear of clowns seemed to be justified, as a rash of evil-clown sightings swept across the country. In the following report, Loren Coleman, a noted delver into the unknown, tracks the bizarre case of these masquerading menaces.

* * *

In the spring of 1981, Boston, Massachusetts, appears to have been the port of entry for a strange new version of the Pied Piper story. During the first week of May, some individuals in multicolored clothes began trying to entice schoolchildren into coming along with them.

On May 6, 1981, the Boston police, responding to persistent complaints, warned parents and school officials that men in clown suits were harassing elementary schoolchildren. One of the men was seen wearing a clown suit just from the waist up; from the waist down he was naked. According to reports, the clown had driven a black van near the recreational-horseshoe site of Franklin Park in the Roxbury area of Boston. He also appeared in the Jamaica Plain neighborhood of Boston near the Mary F. Curley School.

A day earlier, in the adjoining city of Brookline, two clown men reportedly had tried to lure children into their van with offers of candy. The Brookline police had a good description of the van: older model, black, with ladders on the side, a broken front headlight, and no hubcaps. After the clown men and van had been seen near the Lawrence Elementary School on Longwood Avenue in Brookline, the police told school administrators to be "extra cautious."

By May 8, reports of clown men in vans harassing

children had come in from East Boston, Charlestown, Cambridge, Randolph, and other cities near Boston. Police were stopping vehicles with clowns delivering birthday greetings and "clown-a-grams," but no child molesters were arrested.

Frustrated policemen finally pointed out that virtually all of the reported sightings originated with children age five to seven. The headlines in the May 9 issue of the *Boston Globe* told the story: POLICE DISCOUNT REPORTS OF CLOWNS BOTHERING KIDS. The public had been calmed, and that was the end of the story. Or so the papers would have had us believe.

The focus of activity now shifts a thousand miles west to Kansas City, Kansas, and Kansas City, Missouri. On the afternoon of May 22, police cruisers on the Missouri side crisscrossed the city chasing a knife-wielding clown in a yellow van that had been reported at six different elementary schools. Earlier in the day, at eight thirty, a mother had watched a yellow van approach her children as they walked to a school bus stop. The van stopped, and someone inside spoke to her two girls, who then screamed and fled; the vehicle sped away.

The children told their mother that a man dressed as a clown and carrying a knife had ordered them inside. By noon the police had received dozens of similar reports— of a clown in a yellow van. The calls did not taper off until five o'clock that afternoon.

Residents of the two Kansas cities called it the Killer Clown Affair. Some parents in Kansas were even keeping their children out of school. Before long, "group hysteria" was touted as the explanation for the reports. But incidents continued. The police and volunteers were never able to capture any clowns, but witnesses insisted the costumed figures they had seen were real and not imaginary.

The story of the phantom clowns went unnoticed on a

national scale until I began getting a hint we were in the midst of a major new phenomenon. Slowly, after contacting fellow researchers by phone and mail, I discovered that the phantom clown enigma went beyond Boston and Kansas City. Indeed, the reports filtering in demonstrated that a far-reaching mystery was developing. Local media in the individual cities were not aware they were living through a series of events that were occurring nationwide. The national media was not spreading the word, but something quite unusual happened in America in the spring of 1981.

But what was it that happened? Was it group hysteria, as some newsmen would have us believe? Or more? Phantom clowns in at least six major cities, spanning over a thousand miles of America in the space of one month, is quite a mystery. Were the "clowns in vans" sighted elsewhere in the United States? Are they still being seen? Only time will tell.

Today people kindly try to inform me that the phantom clown sightings of 1981 were just mass hysteria caused by Stephen King's book *It,* which tells a scary story about a clown who tries to abduct children. But the first editions of Mr. King's book were not published until 1986. So much for that theory.

Since those sightings in 1981, the world has become a much different place for children. The very real school violence and satanic scares of the last decades have taken a toll on innocence. Phantom clowns were sinister enough in 1981; in the twenty-first century, they are downright terrifying.

Perhaps the phantom clowns have something to tell us. Certainly the shadowy monklike figures mentioned so often in occult literature have become almost too commonplace and familiar. The Men in Black terrorizing UFO witnesses from their Cadillacs may be too obviously sinister. The denizens of the netherworld have apparently dreamed up a new nightmare to shock us. Leagues of phantom clowns in vans thus have now joined the scores of Fortean, ufological, and flying saucer "people" for a new chapter in the story. The cosmic joker is alive and well, and living in a clown suit. –*Loren Coleman*

Mudgett's House of Corpses

To the surprise of those who rhapsodize about bucolic New England, the Yankee states have produced their fair share of noted murderers. Ted Bundy was born in Burlington, Vermont. Albert DeSalvo, the Boston Strangler, was from Massachusetts. And Lizzie Borden—well, she may have been judged innocent, but somebody gave her father those forty whacks.

For some reason, however, the Granite State of New Hampshire seems to have given us one of the most hard-nosed and heinous of the bunch: the little Mudgett boy from Gilmanton. Born in 1868, he seemed to come into this world missing something essential. Not an arm or a leg or anything visible. In fact, he was considered rather handsome and exceptionally bright. What was missing was empathy, conscience. Despite his hardworking parents and strict Methodist upbringing, Herman Webster Mudgett was the embodiment of pure evil.

We can't be sure what sins he committed on his home turf; those were no doubt done in secret. It would be consistent with his personality type—the sociopath—to presume he de-winged flies, tortured house pets, eviscerated livestock. And if a town lad or lass were to come up missing or dead, no one would have ever suspected little Herman.

Holmes's birthplace in Gilmanton, New Hampshire

Fortunately for Gilmanton, he took his malevolence on the road. He went off to study medicine at the University of Vermont and continued his course work in Ann Arbor, Michigan. At both schools he demonstrated an elevated interest in cadavers, more so those of women than of men.

But Herman had more lucrative, loftier goals than medicine in mind. He intended to go into business. Schools paid good money for cadavers and skeletons. Those were marketable items Herman could produce. And if he did it just right, he could make a lot of additional profit on the side.

So, with the profits he had made from some less glamorous crimes—stealing horses, swindling the innocent, and forgery—Herman headed for Chicago and, in 1892, built a mammoth hotel just in time to accommodate guests for the great World's Fair, the Columbian Exposition of 1893. It was here that Herman came into his own. Conducting business as H. H. Holmes, he supervised the building of his castle, never employing a single group of workers long enough for them to learn its secrets. Though the ground floor was conventional enough, a modest line of storefronts, the second and third floors were reserved for Dr. Holmes's dirty work. Guests—usually single, unattached women—checked into his hotel and never checked out.

During construction, Holmes had created various ingenious methods of offering his victims "a good night's sleep." One room was a lightless "asphyxiation chamber," where Dr. Holmes allowed his guests to suffocate. Or, if he was feeling merciful, he'd turn on a gas jet, hastening their departure. Since the walls were lined with asbestos, he might light a match as well, burning them alive. Some of the bedrooms had trapdoors that would drop victims into airless chambers. The most sinister rooms were plated with iron and had disguised blowtorches directed into them; in effect, they were ovens.

Every death chamber was equipped with an alarm that sounded in Dr. Holmes's quarters if someone tried to break out. He enjoyed keeping certain women as prisoners for several months before finally doing them in. All his victims, we don't know how many, vanished into acid vats in the basement, efficiently delivered there via hidden chutes. Their possessions were stolen, their skeletons sold

to medical schools. It was an efficient, profitable operation, a murder factory.

Fortunately for the single women of the world, Holmes pushed his luck and became involved in an insurance fraud. The ensuing investigation uncovered the horrors of the castle. After his arrest, Herman Webster Mudgett, a.k.a. Dr. H. H. Holmes, admitted to killing from twenty to twenty-seven people. Some had estimated the death toll at over two hundred. What the real figure is, we'll never know.

The monster from New Hampshire was hanged in Philadelphia on May 7, 1896. To reinforce the satanic rumors about his evil nature, legend says a streak of lightning ripped the sky at the moment the rope snapped his neck.

And other odd things continued to happen. Dr. William Matten, a witness for the prosecution at Holmes's trial, suddenly dropped dead from blood poisoning. Additional deaths rapidly followed as if Demon Holmes were on a postmortem murder spree. Dr. Ashbridge, the head coroner, was diagnosed with a deadly illness. So was the judge who had sentenced Holmes to death. The prison superintendent committed suicide for no apparent reason. The priest who gave Holmes last rites on death row died mysteriously; the jury foreman was electrocuted "accidentally," and the list goes on.

Today, in a Philadelphia cemetery, the monster's body is embedded in cement in a coffin buried beneath two additional tons of concrete. It seems he was squeamish about grave robbers and medical dissection. To this day, his grave is unmarked.

His family lies beneath the New England soil of Gilmanton, New Hampshire, where their graves may be seen. They were a good, upstanding people. Then one day the devil dropped by.

Holmes's murder castle

Gustave Whitehead and daughter Rose with plane number 21

Heroes of the Air

When we consider the early heroes of American aviation, Wilbur and Orville Wright immediately soar to mind. American historians keep hammering home the fact that the Wright Brothers invented the airplane and flew it near Kitty Hawk, North Carolina, on December 17, 1903.

But many people—especially people around Bridgeport, Connecticut—are adamant that the first flight occurred in 1901, not 1903. And that it was accomplished by a local German-American named Gustave Whitehead. In fact, he supposedly made four flights in a contraption powered by a motor that, like the aircraft, he had designed and built.

Either story could be true. In the final analysis, it all comes down to record-keeping. The Wright Brothers kept good ones, Mr. Whitehead did not. And neither flight is a real surprise. After all, at the turn of the twentieth century,

the world was poised on the brink of successful manned, heavier-than-air flight. Even in the 1890s, certain pioneers were flying man-carrying gliders and experimenting with unmanned, motor-driven models.

But what are we to make of one little-known inscription that can be found at the Old North Church in Boston? Mounted on the brick wall of the churchyard is documentation of an astounding bit of history and an unsung hero of the early American skies, John Childs.

John Childs?

He's the guy who flew in 1757, about a century and a half before the Wright Brothers or Mr. Whitehead.

The plaque tells it all—almost. It says HERE ON SEPTEMBER 13, 1757, JOHN CHILDS—WHO HAD GIVEN PUBLIC NOTICE OF HIS

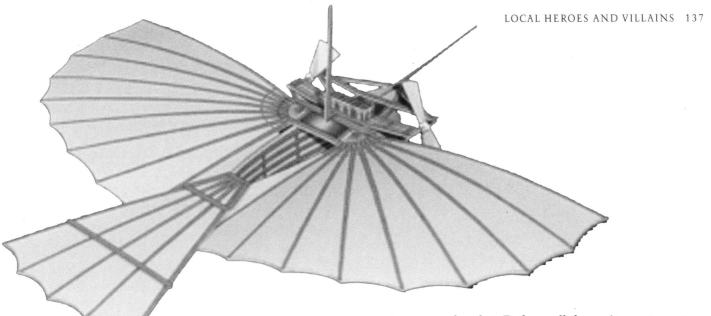

INTENTION TO FLY FROM THE STEEPLE OF DR. CUTLER'S
CHURCH—PERFORMED IT TO THE SATISFACTION OF A GREAT
NUMBER OF SPECTATORS.

The plaque is in full view for anyone who cares to look. What it fails to mention is that the event was so successful and so greatly appreciated by the Boston public that the next day, September 14, Mr. Childs did it again.

On the second day, according to a contemporary newspaper account, before a huge crowd, Mr. Childs "set off with two pistols loaded, one of which he discharged in his descent; the other missing fire, he cocked and snapped again before he reached the Place prepared to receive him."

Mr. Childs's launching pad is well recorded: the steeple of the Old North Church. So is his approximate point of touchdown: a slope about seven hundred feet away from the steeple. Each flight lasted from sixteen to eighteen seconds.

Mr. Childs's aviation exhibitions must have been a wonderful event, but then something happened; we're not sure exactly what. Perhaps all the excitement was too much for our Puritan forefathers. For whatever reason, the authorities stepped in and Mr. John Childs was forbidden to fly "any more in the Town." In effect, the Puritans banned aviation—a law that is still on the books.

After that, John Childs seems to have flown right out of New England history. But he has left us with an interesting puzzle. Assuming he wasn't an angel or a devil, just how in the world did he manage to fly over the skies of Colonial Boston?

On the Orgonon Trail of Wilhelm Reich

Dr. Wilhelm Reich was born in 1897 in Austria, where he earned his medical degree, then studied psychoanalysis under Sigmund Freud. In 1933, he fled the Nazis and came to the United States, eventually settling in out-of-the-way Rangeley, Maine. We can only imagine how surprised he must have been when authorities burned his books and threw him into federal prison. It was that good old New England hospitality; we like making people feel right at home.

So what did Dr. Reich do to get the government so upset?

It all had to do with his experiments with what he called Orgone, his newly discovered energy that influenced human health and behavior, and, he assured anyone who would listen, pretty much everything else. He saw it as some type of primordial cosmic force that is everywhere and is responsible for the color of the sky, gravity, galaxies, political behavior, and, perhaps most important, a good orgasm (from which Dr. Reich derived its name).

Although Dr. Reich is long gone, his hilltop home-cum-laboratory, called Orgonon, still stands in Rangeley exactly as he left it and is now maintained as a museum. Recently, *Weird New England* visited the place to see what we could learn about Wilhelm Reich and his energy source.

The experience was an eerie one, almost like stepping onto a vintage 1950 sci-fi movie set: the mad scientist's laboratory. The house and lab look just as they might if the good doctor had merely stepped out for a little stroll in the woods (fact is, he hasn't gone far; he's buried in a crypt on the grounds). His clothing still hangs in the closet, his papers are strewn around, and his experiments look as if they are awaiting his return.

We paid our $5 to get in, sat through the slide show (no PowerPoint here; this is the 1950s, remember), then wandered

through the museum and house, admiring pictures of Dr. Reich's various wives and girlfriends.

Then we got to the Orgone Box at the museum. These were partly what got Dr. Reich into trouble. Supposedly, a box "accumulated" the Orgone energy, which in concentration would have healthful effects on its occupant. The box, made of wood with a metal-lined interior, was just big enough for one person to sit in. It looked like some sort of one-man sauna or perhaps an overdesigned one-holer outhouse.

According to the brochure, the design theoretically allows Orgone—that's the orgasm energy, which of course is everywhere—to enter, but not escape. Voila! An Orgone Accumulator.

We were curious about another of Dr. Reich's inventions, the Cloud Busters, so we went to take a look. These appear for all the world like antiaircraft guns, which may have gotten the doctor into a bit of trouble all by

themselves. Dr. Reich claimed his Cloud Busters could create rain. Newspaper clippings on the wall said he'd used one to save the Maine blueberry crop during the 1953 drought.

We asked the young lady at the museum why the barrels of the Cloud Busters were plugged with little black stoppers like those you might see in the drain of a bathroom sink. She explained that if they didn't keep them covered, it might rain in the museum. She was kidding, wasn't she?

Dr. Reich saw himself as a persecuted genius. So do his followers. With no proof at all, it seems, the FDA had a federal court label the accumulator bogus, proclaiming Orgone energy nonexistent. Then, in an unprecedented act of bureaucratic bullying, they ordered his books and other publications burned. We've known the government to make mistakes before. They were especially good at them during the '50s, the era of Joseph McCarthy and Dr. Reich.

After years of wrangling with the FDA over the effectiveness of his Orgone Accumulators, Wilhelm Reich was jailed for contempt of court in 1957. He was sent to Lewisburg federal penitentiary in Pennsylvania, where, in November '57, he was found dead in his cell, apparently the victim of a heart attack.

Perhaps the final word on this subject should go to Albert Einstein. In 1941, Professor Einstein had a private five-hour conference with Dr. Reich during which Reich explained his unusual theories. At the end, Dr. Reich said, "You understand now why everyone thinks I'm mad."

Einstein replied, "And how!"

Personalized Properties

Our homes are extensions of ourselves. Whether we live in a castle overlooking the Connecticut River or under a grassy mound of earth, our surroundings speak volumes about us. The construction material might be bricks and mortar, or rolled-up newspaper, but the bottom line is that we are where we live.

From the very beginning, New Englanders have had their own architectural language. And, like New Englanders themselves, some structures are wonderfully individualistic. Even the most eccentric dwelling in the United States, the Winchester Mansion of California, took a New Englander to build. Combine Yankee ingenuity with home design, and the result can be magic. It is so today. It has always been so.

NO TRESPASSING

VIOLATORS WILL BE EATEN

Lord Dexter's "Mouseum"

All his life Timothy Dexter longed not for riches, but for the adoration that inevitably accompanied them. Luckily, he had a knack for making money.

Dexter was born into modest circumstances in Malden, Massachusetts, in 1747. He later moved to Newburyport—then, as now, a haven of art, refinement, and culture. Clever in an offbeat sort of way, he made his fortune through almost preternatural twists of fate and outrageously eccentric business dealings. He actually shipped coal to Newcastle. Because he did it during a

The Original Lord Timothy Dexter House in 1810. Newburyport, Mass.

miners' strike, Dexter's coal was worth its weight in gold. Against common sense and sound advice, he shipped 42,000 bed-warming pans to the tropical West Indies. With them, he shipped a slew of cats. The pans sold rapidly as molasses ladles. The cats arrived just in time to end a plague of mice.

But growing wealth failed to earn him the adulation he sought. So he purchased a grand mansion in Newburyport's "best" neighborhood and insisted everyone address him as Lord, an obsolete and inappropriate title in the newly formed American democracy.

Immediately, and at great expense, he began to modify his home, determined to turn it into the newest wonder of the world. He called it Lord Dexter's Mouseum (the Lord preferred his own spelling of museum), had it topped with a giant eagle, and decorated it with forty bigger-than-life garishly painted wooden statues of famous people. Among the giants were Adam, Eve, Napoleon, King George, Venus, and of course the one he deemed "the first in the East, the first in the West and the greatest philosopher in the Western World," Lord Timothy Dexter himself.

People arrived in record numbers to witness this new wonder. And wonder they did. Then they laughed. The mansion was just too over the top, even for that entertainment-starved time.

Lord Dexter's remaining life was punctuated with eccentricities ranging from grotesque to endearing. For example, he flaunted his sense of self-importance by employing a colorful retinue including an African servant, a dwarf, several cooks, kitchen maids, laundresses, gardeners, and—perhaps his most inspired hire—Jonathan Plummer as his personal poet laureate. It was Plummer who penned the following tribute to his patron:

> *Lord Dexter is a man of fame,*
> *Most celebrated is his name,*
> *More precious far than gold that's pure:*
> *Lord Dexter shine forever more!*

As a permanent record of his greatness, Lord Dexter published his opinions on politics, religion, and his contemporaries in a short autobiographical tome aptly titled *A Pickle for the Knowing Ones* (subtitled "Plain Truths in a Homespun Dress"). The entire book was a single run-on sentence unfettered by punctuation or recognizable spelling.

Pickle was met with unanimous critical disapproval. Lord Dexter responded by adding two pages to the second printing. They contained nothing but an assortment of punctuation marks with the instruction: "Mister pinter the Nowing ones complane of my book the fust edition had no stops I put in A nuf here and they may solt and peper it as they please."

Today *Pickle* remains one of the great curiosities of American letters. Lord Dexter's Mouseum still stands on Newburyport's High Street. Though the eagle survives, the grounds have been stripped of their colorful wooden entourage. "The first Lord in the younited States of Amercary" now resides in the town's Old Burying Ground, gone but definitely not forgotten.

The Passion of Pepperell

This personalized property in Pepperell, Massachusetts, was inspired by motives more noble than vanity. In fact, Mr. Noel Dube was divinely inspired. It began with one of those inexplicable things, one of those unanswerable questions: Why does the Virgin Mary come-a-calling? And when she does, why does she call upon the most unlikely people?

When she spoke to Mr. Dube around 1990, she asked him to build her a community shrine. He agreed, of course. Who could refuse? But, like the rest of us, he was inexperienced at shrine-building. Also, due to age and a World War II disability, he was not wealthy. Still, he decided to give it his best shot.

The only property he owned was his house at 47 Heald Street, so it was there that he'd build the shrine. First he commissioned an artist who went to work on a series of

devotional paintings. By 1991, tucked away behind a hedgerow, giant vibrantly colored scenes began to appear. The most conspicuous may be the twenty-two-by-sixty-foot mural reproducing the miraculous visions of Fàtima, Portugal, in 1917. There, witnessed by thousands of people, the sun—or possibly a UFO—went streaking across the sky. This alleged miracle gives Mr. Dube's shrine its name: The Our Lady of Fàtima Community Shrine.

Visitors will find an assortment of religious statues, walkways, benches, grottoes, and gardens. On the far side of the yard there is a twelve-by-thirty-foot, gold-framed portrait of Jesus. That's as tall as a three-story house. And in between, in lurid comic book colors, are the fourteen stations of the cross in which the gory events at Calvary are graphically depicted. Although none of this can be described as subtle, there is a certain visionary quality about it. After all, Mr. Dube did anticipate Mel Gibson's *Passion* by over a decade.

Today a twenty-four-foot blue cross also adorns the property. It is brightly illuminated by lamps comparable to those used on motion picture sets. Why a twenty-four-foot blue, illuminated cross? Mr. Dube, who was born on Christmas Day in 1919, explains, "Jesus asked for it."

Our Lady of Fàtima Community Shrine receives about 4,000 visitors a year. We hope Jesus and his mother are as happy with Mr. Dube's work as we are.

The Sanctuary of Love

When Salvatore Verdirome was visited by the Virgin Mary, his experience with the apparition did not go smoothly. "It appeared to me and said something," the Norwich, Connecticut, man told *The New York Times* in December 2000. "I couldn't quite catch it." So, unsure of his intended message, he did what any true visionary would do. "I just started building."

Verdirome began building an elaborate shrine to the Mother of Jesus and spread it out over his entire small property. He took forty-seven bathtubs, up-ended them, and painted them sky blue. He placed a statue of the Virgin Mary inside each one and spread piles of green glass in between them. He constructed three large wooden crosses, a fence, and a stone wall with the Ten Commandments chiseled into it to go along with the bathing Blessed Mothers. His goal in constructing all this was to enlighten others about their own faith. "Some people really don't know what religion is," he said.

Soon people began visiting his strange roadside shrine and dubbed it the Sanctuary of Love. Busloads of people visited the odd site each day, beckoned by the wooden sign Verdirome has posted on the road in front of his house. WELCOME TO THE SANCTUARY OF LOVE, it read. YOUR FAITH BROUGHT YOU HERE.

Unfortunately, Verdirome would have needed a whole lot of faith or some sort of miracle to keep the sanctuary thriving. He owed over $60,000 in overdue property taxes and $40,000 in overdue electric bills. The city took his land away from him and put him in an old folks home. While various groups attempted to raise funds for him, none came through with the cash.

The eighty-four-year-old still managed to build on his

A Hill Full of Statues, but No Tax Exemption

By PAUL ZIELBAUER

NORWICH, Conn., Dec. 7 — In what must be this town's only residentially zoned Sanctuary of Love, there are many bathtubs. Forty-seven, to be exact.

They do not hold water or naked people; rather, with their hulls painted sky blue, turned on end and half buried into Salvatore Verdirome's backyard, the rows upon rows of secondhand tubs serve as sturdy shelter to an equal number of plaster statuettes of the Virgin Mary.

Mr. Verdirome, 80, a retired carpenter, began building the sanctuary on his small hillside property about 30 years ago, by hand, alone, with his own money and with the goal of capturing a vision of Mary that he said he had in the late 1960's.

But now there is trouble in Mr. Verdirome's paradise, tax trouble. City officials say that unless someone can come up with about $100,000 that Mr. Verdirome owes, the Sanctuary of Love may soon become the property of the Norwich Finance Department.

Taxes were the last thing on Mr. Verdirome's mind when he began creating his shrine.

"It was a vision of the Virgin Mary," he explained. "It appeared to me and said something, but I couldn't quite catch it." Hardly deterred, he said, "I just started building."

Now the hill topped off with three large wooden crosses has become something of an oddball tourist destination.

"I can't really pin down where they come from," Mr. Verdirome said today about the busloads of visitors who pull up onto the shoulder of North Main Street, which winds past his house. "I guess there's something about this sanctuary that draws them here. Don't have the slightest idea."

Maybe it's the large hand-painted wooden sign, posted at eye level along the road, that says: "Welcome to the Sanctuary of Love."

provocative sobriquet for his steep garden of tubs and Virgin Marys, Mr. Verdirome gave a simple answer: "A friend here, a Jewish man, started calling it a sanctuary, and once this fellow started it, someone else added 'of Love,' and it's been that way ever since."

Mr. Verdirome, the son of Sicilian parents, has lived in southeastern Connecticut since 1941, when he left his boyhood home on the Lower East Side of Manhattan to join the merchant marine in New London.

He later became a rigger at Electric Boat, the once-vast company that built fleets of nuclear-powered submarines for the United States Navy. Since retiring sometime in the 1970's (he is not sure of the exact year), Mr. Verdirome has

cials to have him either start paying down his $100,000 debt — $60,000 in property taxes and about $40,000

Salvatore Verdirome enshrined 47 statuettes of the Virgin Mary in upended bathtubs in his backyard in Norwich, Conn. City officials say Mr. Verdirome's unpaid taxes may threaten his ownership of the hill, called the Sanctuary of Love.

Mr. Verdirome, who admitted spending much of his days by himself, sitting in a small room.

Photographs by C. M. Glover for The New York Times

former property despite all this, with a down-to-earth belief that the government does not really want his land. "If they take it over, what are they going to do with it?" he asked.

Sadly, Mr. Verdirome and his sanctuary are no longer with us. He passed away in 2004, but not without notice.

–Chris Gethard

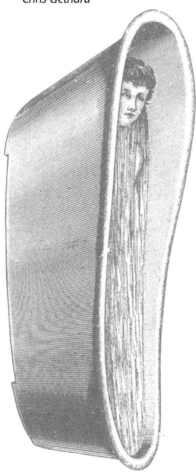

Say So Long to Sanctuary

Salvatore Verdirome, 84, Builder of Backyard Connecticut Shrine, Dies

By THE ASSOCIATED PRESS
May 29, 2004

Salvatore Verdirome, a carpenter whose singular religious vision transformed his backyard into a terraced shrine of bathtub Madonnas and became a place of solace for people who lost money at the Foxwoods Resort Casino, died in Norwich, Conn., on May 15. He was 84. The cause was a stroke, *The Norwich Bulletin* reported. He had lived at a nursing home since he was forced by illness and pressure from tax collectors to leave his home in Norwich.

He was working as a carpenter at the Electric Boat submarine yard in 1971 when he said he was struck by a religious vision: the steep-hilled yard behind his three-family house should be terraced with statues of Jesus, the saints and the Virgin Mary. The place became the Sanctuary of Love. . . .

Mr. Verdirome, with his long gray hair and beard, became a distinctive figure around eastern Connecticut as he scrounged junk shops for old tubs. Some people would drop old bathtubs off in front of his house; only the old-fashioned kind, with an oval shape and claw feet, would do.

All together, he assembled about 50 bathtub statue shelters, and then worked on other parts of his vision: the Ten Commandments, the Stations of the Cross, and the Sea of Glass from the Book of Revelations. The sea was made of chunks of aqua glass Mr. Verdirome got from a Thermos factory.

Visitors could travel through the shrine on marble and concrete walkways, decorated with mosaics and religious sayings. The shrine became increasingly popular after the Foxwoods casino opened nearby in Mashantucket, Conn. Gamblers would stop to pray at a favored statue. Mr. Verdirome never charged admission, but some people left coins and other donations in a bucket by the entrance.

Money troubles ended up being the sanctuary's undoing. City leaders in Norwich foreclosed on the home after it accumulated $100,000 in unpaid taxes and utility bills. Foreclosure proceedings started in 2000, and a social worker found Mr. Verdirome a place in a nursing home. In 2002, Norwich auctioned off the statues and any other items of value on the property.

The Black Church of Salem

One particular tourist draw that's not supposed to be a tourist draw (as opposed to the town's many wacky museums) in Salem, Massachusetts, is the former church that was bought a few years ago, painted black, and turned into some sort of home base for the black arts in Salem. All I know is that the owner drives a hearse, has placed two very large gargoyles in front of the door, burns red candles on the steps at Halloween, and has a plaque that says NOT A CHURCH, GET OVER IT near the front door.

This in a town with avowed satanists (watch your

cats every Halloween folks—there have been some nasty cat sacrifices in the not too distant past). This could be a total joke or real, who knows? It was actually for sale for a while, but unfortunately they had taken down the for sale sign by the time I got there to take a picture. I'm not sure if they sold the place or else got so sick of prospective buyers actually being just curiosity-seekers. What can I say? It's Salem.—*Caroline Angel*

Boston's Skinny House

Folks making their home in New England's greatest city can live in some pretty disparate conditions. Some dwell in cardboard boxes above subway vents, others in cramped studio apartments. But there is only one skinny house. This anorexic anomaly at 44 Hull Street is just thirty feet long and ten feet wide, tapering to a mere thirty-six inches in the back (what they call the back yard). Yet it is four stories high, the floors connected by steep, narrow stairs.

Looking at it from the street, you might be puzzled about how to enter. That's because you're looking at the side. The front, which is typical of an eighteenth-century home, is in the alleyway to the left.

But we must ask, Why was it built? And why would anyone move into it?

Legend says that in Colonial times Joseph Eustus and his brother inherited the land the house sits on from their father. But while Joseph was away, his brother built a grand house for himself, leaving only a thin strip of land—surely not enough to accommodate another dwelling. Joseph fooled everyone, however, and erected the skinny house. And at four stories it was tall enough to cut off his brother's view of the harbor.

Over the years, the skinny house has sheltered many people. Its newest occupants, Jennifer Simonic and Spencer Welton, squeezed in but found doing so a bit of a chore. Their queen-sized bed was too big to haul up the narrow stairs, so they had to cut its frame in half and hoist it through a window.

And why would they move into such a place? Well, with Boston real estate prices being what they are, it's better to have a skinny house than a skinny wallet.

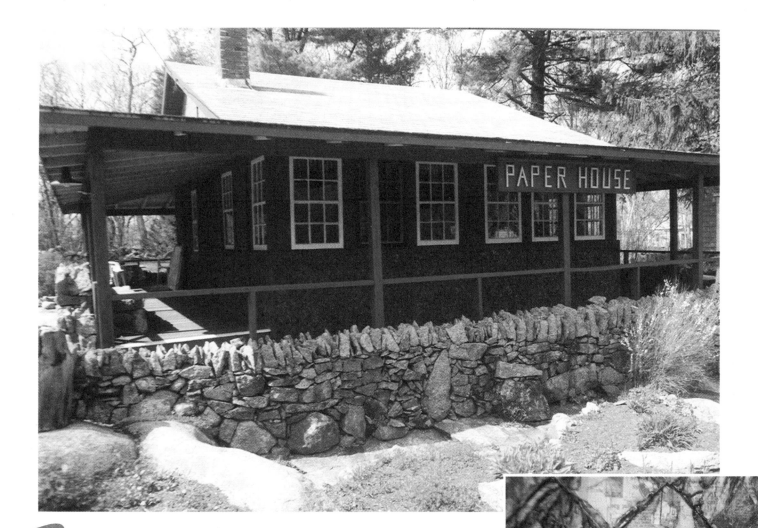

Pigeon Cove's Paper Palace—Rockport, MA

In the days before recycling, a man like Elis F. Stenman might have been flummoxed about how to get rid of all the newspapers he read—six or more per day. He was quoted as saying, "I always resented the daily waste of newspapers after people read them for a few minutes."

Being thrifty and also an inventive sort, the Swedish immigrant came up with an imaginative solution. He'd build his pad . . . of paper!

Work began in 1922 and required a lot of reading and rolling. Mr. Stenman would wrap sheets of newspaper, thousands of them, over thin wires,

producing cane-sized logs. Once pasted and dried, they became building material. Twenty years later the project was complete. The house itself was finished in two years—the contents took eighteen more to complete. Everything under his roof was made of paper. Exterior walls consisted of 215 individual sheets under two tons of pressure.

When furniture was required, he hauled in more paper. Chairs, tables, cots, bookshelves, lamps, a writing desk, a grandfather clock, even a piano—everything is made of paper. His wife, Esther, turned strips of magazine covers into draperies for the windows.

The place is a veritable newspaper museum. You can read about Lucky Lindbergh's trans-Atlantic flight in the grain of the desk. Hoover's 1928 presidential campaign is recalled on the radio cabinet. If you know where to look,

THE PIANO IS COVERED WITH ROLLS OF PAPER

you can brush up on zeppelins or the disappearance of Amelia Earhart. For linguists, the bookcase is made of foreign newspapers.

What motivated Mr. Stenman's singular obsession, and what kept him going, remain a bit of a mystery. Not only did he preserve twenty years' worth of newspapers, but he created a historical record as well. He may also have given us a clue about how to solve the housing shortage, if only people keep reading.

Nowadays the Paper House is open as a museum and is run by Mr. Stenman's family. Upon entering Rockport, follow Route 127 to Pigeon Cove. Take a left onto Curtis Street, then another onto Pigeon Hill Street. It costs $1.50 to get in. They accept paper, not plastic.

READ ALL ABOUT IT!

Amazing house built out of 100,000 newspapers

...And so is the furniture

When it comes to recycling, no one can top Elis Stenman — he built a house almost entirely out of 100,000 used newspapers!

What's more, every piece of furniture in the amazing house in Rockport, Mass., is also made of newspapers, including chairs, tables, a cot, lamps — even a grandfather clock.

One desk is built entirely of papers with headlines trumpeting Charles Lindbergh's historic first flight across the Atlantic.

A bookshelf is constructed only with foreign newspapers, sent to Stenman from embassies around the world. The grandfather clock is made with newspapers from capital cities of 48 states.

Stenman, who died in 1942, used to read five newspapers a day, and the thrifty Swedish immigrant hated to throw them away.

"I always resented the daily waste of newspapers after people read them for a few minutes," he once said.

In 1922, Stenman began saving papers for his project.

"He'd wrap the sheets of paper around a piece of fine wire, tightly rolling them until he had a stiff piece, like a thin cane, about three-fourths of an inch in diameter," said Stenman's niece Vivian Curtis, who now lives next door to the Paper House. "The rods were as strong and sturdy as wood."

In 1924, Stenman hired a carpenter to erect a frame of a house, with a wood floor and a brick fireplace — then sent him home. Stenman began filling in the frame with his handmade rods and wallboards, which he made by gluing 215 sheets of paper together. Similarly, he fashioned hundreds of shingles with triangle-shaped sheets of paper, var... make them weatherproof.

Using the rolled-up papers, Stenman began constructing furni... for the next 20 years he co... work on his masterpiece. Esther even made drape... strips of magazine covers. Paper House is a tourist ... captivating visitors from ... world.

WHAT A PAD — OF PAPER! House is built entirely of news... except for frame, floor and chimney. Vivian Curtis, late... niece, plays on paper piano in living room. At left is gran... clock, made up of tightly rolled papers.

The Doomed Dolls of Dummer

Maybe they're gone; maybe they're still there—rumors have it both ways. But at some point the accompanying photographs may be the sole record of what could only be described as the Invasion of Lawn Figures from Hell.

Around 1990, Mildred Smith began to personalize her property by creating a terrifying tableau to adorn the grounds of her mobile home, situated at the intersection of Routes 16 and 110A in Dummer, New Hampshire. In fact, this "outsider artist" constructed what could easily be the set of a zero-budget horror film. A parade of appalling apparitions, like a procession of the damned, litters the lawn of this otherwise conservative-appearing dwelling. Ghostly, mysterious, even monstrous, these effigies will make you scratch your head until it bleeds. No virgins in a bathtub here, but rather a phantasma-goria of terrifying toddlers in hardhats, adult-sized demonic dummies bent under invisible burdens, maske[d] malevolent scarecrows, and other things too horrible to contemplate—all silent, unmoving, and sinister.

What is it all about? What could the owner be thinking? Only Mildred Smith knows for sure. She may not see her handiwork as strange, but for the rest of us, it's not only weird but somehow subtly disturbing.

Alien Art

If you drive north along US 95 in Maine and go just as far as you can, you'll discover the town of Houlton, perhaps best known for its German POW camp during World War II. It is a small place, rural, full of farmers, tradespeople, and kind folks.

But keep going. Find Military Street and drive to its end. There you'll encounter an exhibit of outsider art that can't get much farther out. It's a gathering spot for mystical denizens of alternate realities. You'll see Bigfoot, space aliens (and the UFOs they arrived in), and, oh yes, there's Santa, arriving in his sleigh. Even a stray dinosaur or two.

The place is quite literally out-of-the-way. Almost out of this country, and maybe out of this world. Yet this is no clandestine military installation; the Alien Art Outdoor Museum is an even bigger secret.

The owner of the property—whose name is classified information (but let's call him Jerry)—is perhaps as mysterious as his eclectic and eccentric creations. His private museum is also his home, and, strictly speaking, neither is really open to the public. This odd environment is more for the personal enjoyment of its creator and his dog. But if someone from this world or any other should happen by, there's a lot to see. And if Jerry's there and in a talking mood, you'll get more than you bargained for.

The artwork, fashioned from wood and less readily identifiable odds and ends, ranges from totem poles to rooftop flying saucers to an anatomically correct Bigfoot. There's a frontier-style fort, out-of-place palm trees, and . . . and . . . jeez, we really don't know what they are.

But we're sure Houlton's Alien Art Outdoor Museum is a unique site, although not easy to find. Hidden on the northern border of the U.S.A., right on the edge of this reality, secluded, unadvertised, unique, and not-for-profit. It is outsider art for outsider art's sake. Don't forget to bring your camera; without pictures, no one will believe you.

Holmes at Home

Actor William Gillette didn't really build a house; he designed and constructed a giant theatrical stage on which he could act out all of his fantasies, eccentricities, and idiosyncrasies. His imposing medieval fortress, which looms above the Connecticut River in Hadlyme, Connecticut, was built between 1913 and 1919 at a cost of around $1 million (roughly $18 million in today's dollars). This elaborate fantasy was made possible by another fantasy, Mr. Gillette's definitive stage portrayal of Sherlock Holmes. It was he who forever imprinted Conan Doyle's character with distinctive embellishments such as the calabash pipe, the deerstalker cap, and the Inverness cape. The immortal phrase "Elementary, my dear Watson" was Mr. Gillette's, not Sir Arthur's.

But there was nothing elementary about my dear William. A New Englander by birth (Hartford, Connecticut, 1853), he went on to make his fortune in the theater, writing, producing, and starring in plays. A man of myriad talents and a curious vision, he designed his home with an eye toward magic and mystery, filling it with a sorcerer's array of quirky gadgets and gizmos.

The actor's bedroom was positioned on a balcony overlooking a great hall reminiscent of a Bavarian hunting lodge, with a massive fireplace and oak beams. It was here guests like Charlie Chaplin and Helen Hayes would gather. Using a system of cleverly placed mirrors, Mr. Gillette could covertly observe activity in the hall—in effect spying on his guests. Other "stage effects" and mechanical marvels include secret staircases, twisting passageways, trapdoors, and hidden panels for improbable entrances and exits. He designed forty-seven hand-carved oak doors, each with a different, ingeniously perplexing puzzle lock. If a guest was clever enough to open one and pass through, the door might unexpectedly double-lock behind him. And of course Gillette's Castle includes a room designed to replicate Sherlock Holmes's famous flat at 221B Baker Street in London.

Of all his clever accoutrements, perhaps the most ingenious is a vanishing bar. It would instantly disappear if police or Prohibition agents happened by.

William Gillette died in 1937. He was farsighted enough to stipulate in his will that his enchanting creation must not be taken over by "some blithering saphead who has no conception of where he is or with what surrounded." He got his wish, maybe. For better or worse, the state of Connecticut bought the estate in 1943 and has run it as a public park ever since.

A Castle in the Kingdom

There are a fair number of castles scattered throughout New England—every state has an offering or two. But as far as we know, only one is actually located in a kingdom. In Irasburg, within Vermont's fabled Northeast Kingdom, motorists are often flabbergasted to see the stone turrets of a fifteenth-century palace poking through the treetops. Count them: There are seven cylindrical towers of varying heights rising under conical roofs.

This is not a time-slip, nor some teleported Camelot fortress. Despite its ancient appearance, it is the relatively new home of Harv and Sara Gregoire, who one day decided they wanted to live in a stone castle. So they built one. All by themselves. Starting around 1990.

Why Vermont? Well for one thing, there is an excellent supply of stones. And there is a kingdom.

The couple erected their regal residence mostly unassisted, a two-person construction company. They quickly discovered there were no available do-it-yourself guides for the home castle builder, and experienced castle craftsmen were long dead. Luckily, Yankee ingenuity came to their aid. The entire building process took about six years. If some of their techniques were a bit unorthodox, that just contributes to the place's charm, or weirdness, depending on your orientation.

The interior living space is complete with kitchen, library (one volume is the book they wrote about their castle-building experience, *Seasons of Choice*), and about eight other modestly sized rooms. Medieval prints cover the walls, along with mounted heads of wild boar, goats, and deer.

Maybe it is a time-slip after all. A slide back to an era of self-sufficiency, when people realized their dreams all by themselves, through trial and error, working outside the shackles of convention and social norms. Making their own choices . . . doing their own thing. Whatever you want to call it, King Harv and Queen Sara created their own kingdom.

Can You Dig This?

During the nineteenth century, the wealthiest American egomaniacs built their architecturally magnificent and aesthetically competitive "cottages" along the waterfront in Newport, Rhode Island. But nearby Portsmouth offers a groundbreaking option to opulence: the mound house, a human anthill designed and constructed by a local carpenter with a unique back-to-the-land vision. This little hole in the earth could be mistaken for a tomb, but that would be a grave error. It is alternative housing at its most dramatic. In summer, it's cool and covered with grass. In winter, it's insulated with snow. And if world events get any worse, it's already a bomb shelter. The environmental benefits are probably self-evident, but the aesthetics may take a little getting used to: Last time we visited, there was a goat grazing on the roof.

Maine Man Captures Bigfoot!

New England is dotted with dotty museums. There's the guy in Conway, New Hampshire, with the world's biggest cufflink collection. Onset, Massachusetts, is where Richard T. Porter filled his house with thermometers and called himself the Thermometer Man. And on Peak's Island, Maine, Nancy 3. Hoffman (yes, 3. is really her middle name) resides with a seemingly infinite number of umbrella covers.

Odd, yes, but one of the most legitimately weird museums we've stumbled upon recently is in the heart of historic Portland, Maine. There's nothing about the building itself that will tip you off. It's an unassuming two-story house on a quiet residential street. No signs, no banners, nothing to suggest monsters dwell within.

But wait till you meet the doorman!

Walk up the steps, open the porch door, and . . . what's that? A giant, hairy, eight-and-a-half-foot, five-hundred-pound Bigfoot towering above you. Its enormous size is almost enough to make anyone flee in terror. But hold your ground; it's only a replica. And the

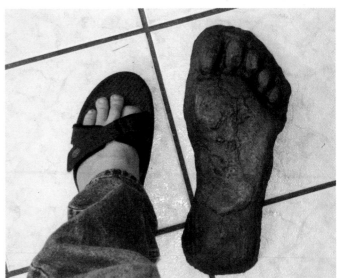

curiosities multiply as you step inside.

What you had mistakenly perceived as a modest family dwelling is in reality the International Museum of Cryptozoology. It's also a family home, occupied by one of the world's most respected cryptozoologists, Loren Coleman, author of twenty-seven books, over five hundred articles, and technical consultant on many TV shows and movies. Mr. Coleman, whom we've met earlier in

this book, is a man who lives with monsters. Such strange arrangements are an occupational hazard for cryptozoologists, those dedicated people who study unexplained animals in an attempt to either prove or disprove the existence of such creatures. Mr. Coleman's roommates include a full-sized, anatomically correct coelacanth (a six-foot fish presumed extinct for 65 million years, found alive in 1938, and still swimming around). There are replicas of the many oddities he has investigated over the years, like the Dover Demon, Mothman, and various aquatic anomalies such as the Loch Ness Monster and his American cousin, Champ from Lake Champlain.

And of course there's Bigfoot, that large hairy hominid that has been seen, fleetingly, in all fifty states and almost every country of the world. Mr. Coleman displays Bigfoot hair samples, Bigfoot fecal matter, and enough authentic casts of Bigfoot tracks to lead any cryptozoologist on a merry chase.

So why is this renowned scientist living in a cryptozoo? Because in over forty-five years of investigations, Mr. Coleman has accumulated a large number of souvenirs, research materials, assorted oddities, and books. In time, storage became a problem; cohabitation was the only solution.

Evidence of the planet's hidden population of crypto-creatures fills five rooms. After visitors safely pass the Bigfoot bouncer on the porch, Mr. Coleman guides them through his house of horrors—er, make that cabinet of curiosities—starting in the living room and continuing through the dining room, hallway, kitchen, and then upstairs to a bedroom that holds the world's largest cryptozoological archive, some 20,000 volumes.

Keep an eye open for the dreaded blood-sucking Chupacabras, various mystery cats, and a specially sculpted one-of-a-kind model of the puzzling Dover Demon.

You can use the other eye for winking as you examine

specimens of horned bunny rabbits called Jackalopes, a glass-encased "Feejee mermaid," and a stuffed specimen of the infamous fur-bearing trout that once flourished in the frigid waters of the north country, all of which Mr. Coleman displays with tongue firmly in cheek to demonstrate the zoological pranks that can be pulled on naïve naturalists.

There are also museum-quality skulls of various known bipeds: Gigantopithecus, Paranthropus, and Australopithecus. And there are prehistoric skulls: Peking man, Rhodesian man, Heidelberg man. There are also skulls of gorillas, chimpanzees, rhesus monkeys, and more. All these are offered so you can speculate on exactly where Bigfoot might fit into your family tree.

While everything is curated with Mr. Coleman's unwavering good humor, he is deadly serious about what he is doing. As he says, "My purpose is to share, educate, and give a feeling for the passion of this field. The place is about researcher, fan, colleague, and student exchanges of information and knowledge."

And he puts his money where his mouth is, or rather, he doesn't. There is no charge for visiting the museum. He says, "If people buy a cryptozoology book, read one in their local library, or enter the fields of natural history, anthropology, zoology, or cryptozoology, I will be fully compensated."

Like many of its inhabitants, Director Coleman's museum is a little difficult to find. Of course that's all part of the fun. But a good place to start your crypto-safari would be on the Web at www.lorencoleman.com.

Vermont's Spiderman

At the end of a twisty dirt road in Williamstown, Vermont, is what might be the strangest farm in New England. No, they're not combating the collapse of Vermont's dairy industry by raising llamas or emus. These people farm . . . spiders. And spiders, of course, produce webs. This experiment in arachnid agriculture is the brain-child of Will and Terry Knight. And they have been at it for half a century. Will calls their farm the world's first website.

While many of us associate spiders with horror movies, dark corners, and graveyards, Mr. and Mrs. Knight have an entirely different vision of their eight-legged livestock. They see them as artists and their intricate webs as art.

Mr. Knight stumbled onto this unusual art form quite by chance. Years ago he was spray-painting something in his garage. When he moved the painted surface, he found a spiderweb clinging to it. This accident made him realize how beautiful and intricate the webs actually are. It was then that he went into spider farming.

In the spring, Mr. Knight collects the spiders' sticky egg sacs and sets them out. When the eggs hatch at the end of May, they yield 300 or 400 spiderlings. And the little spinners start their work. Will says each spinner leaves a special sign at the bottom of the web, an artist's signature.

Mr. Knight mounts individual webs on wooden plaques. He has filled the bays of his garage with glassless window frames hanging horizontally. Each contains eight ten- by twelve-inch empty rectangular windowpanes. It is in these frames that the spiders weave their wonders.

Over the years, Mr. Knight has developed a technique for spray-painting the seemingly delicate webs before capturing them on black-painted backgrounds. The result is a unique piece of wall art that is unusual, beautiful, and just a bit mysterious. Like snowflakes, no two are alike.

There is a lot of lore associated with spiders, and Will

Knight knows it all. He says that nineteenth-century doctors believed that arthritis and other diseases could be cured by simply ingesting a few spiders. Some people kept live spiders in amulets around their necks to pop like pills in case of emergency. And practitioners of natural medicine have long known that a spiderweb placed on a wound will stop the bleeding.

These seemingly fragile webs are actually made from the strongest natural fiber known. And, unbeknownst to these tiny creatures, art and industry may be about to collide. Right now, in Montreal, researchers at Nexia Biotechnologies are concocting a sort of magical potion from—of all things—spider silk and goat's milk. Their modern alchemy has produced a fantastic fiber that is tough enough for spacesuits, surgical sutures, and incredible as it seems, bulletproof vests. So the tiny spider, spinning away in Williamstown and all around the world, is finding a place in art, politics, and science.

Perhaps Will and Terry Knight's one-of-a-kind Spider Web Farm will be the first of many websites. Though it seems remote, the simple barn spider may eventually redefine—even revitalize—the dying Vermont farm.

Nash Dino Land

This is definitely not Jurassic Park. Like the dinosaurs themselves, Nash Dino Land seems on the verge of extinction. But somehow it survives, preserving the memory of a self-made, larger-than-life, paleontologist and the giant animals who roamed South Hadley, Massachusetts, long before he did.

In the 1930s, Carlton Nash tripped over a stone and discovered a long-lost footpath covered with ancient tracks—dinosaur tracks. During the Mesozoic era, the huge lizards left their mark in the Connecticut River mud. Around 100 million years later, give or take a few millennia, Carlton bought the land, footprints and all. There he launched a groundbreaking enterprise: mining authentic dinosaur tracks. For a good while, he did a booming business selling his unique fossil footprints to museums, parks, and estates all over the world.

Then he opened his quarry to tourists, initiating a one-of-a-kind attraction. Those who met Carlton Nash will never forget him. Animated, colorful, conspicuously eccentric, he populated his homemade theme park with crude signs, makeshift exhibits, and humorously inept dinosaur mock-ups. He even covered his gift shop with fossils so he could proclaim it the World's Oldest Building.

But living and working in this unorthodox theme park

Cornell Nash, *Carlton's son, does what he can to keep Dino Land alive.*

apparently left Carlton longing for something more. He received no academic recognition for all his digging and displaying. As his quarry began to run low, Carlton tried to reconfigure his two stony acres as an educational institution, but clearly business was on the rocks.

For a time, Carlton seemed to think his future might be in chickens rather than dinosaurs. Perhaps inspired by that age-old remedy for everything, chicken soup, Carlton plastered his property with chicken paintings and signs reading CHICKENS CARRY THE CURE FOR CANCER! FIND OUT WHAT THE MEDIA AND MEDICAL ESTABLISHMENTS DO NOT WANT YOU TO KNOW! He claimed to have made a marvelous discovery, some kind of chicken

extract that could cure cancer. Again he failed to attract the attention of the scientific community.

Carlton Nash died in 1997. Today his life's work, Dino Land, represents a dual loss to science: the depletion of what he claimed was the world's largest dinosaur footprint quarry and the secret of how chickens can cure cancer.

Though past its glory days, Dino Land is still worth a visit, not for what it is, but for what it was—a unique bit of Americana that's now following the trail of the dinosaurs into oblivion.

Roads Less Traveled

The body of New England is crisscrossed with a system of veins and arteries known as roads. Mostly tarmac in these modern times, they evolved from dirt, which evolved from well-traveled footpaths worn into the region's epidermis by generations of Indians. Today we are beginning to learn what the Native Americans knew long ago: Sometimes body systems go wrong. For whatever reason, certain New England roadways are tainted by unknown contagions. In some cases, they seem to be misfiring like malfunctioning nerves.

Strange things happen on these roads.

The consequence is that some thoroughfares are avoided altogether. Others are too essential to be avoided, so weird things are regularly reported. Despite any official signs, we suggest you visualize imaginary caution warnings before entering any of the following roads less traveled. . . .

An Alternate Route

There is an odd stretch of highway paralleling the Connecticut River that may violate certain natural laws other than gravity. It is the segment of Route 5 connecting Brattleboro, Vermont, with Bernardston, Massachusetts.

This is a forlorn and neglected bit of rural road that once served as a main thoroughfare before it was upstaged by I-91. Today businesses are boarded up, houses and trailers are few and far between. And it is dark. Strangely dark.

Weird animal sightings are business as usual here. UFOs fly overhead. Ectoplasmic entities lurk in the bushes along the roadside. A couple of years ago a young couple returning from their honeymoon happened to snap a picture inside their car as they were driving along. Later, examining the developed print, they discovered a passenger reflected in their rearview mirror. A woman's face is clearly visible in the back seat. Neither of the honeymooners recognized her, nor could they explain how

she could have been with them in a moving car.

But one of the strangest occurrences on that road happened to Linda Smith (yes, that is her real name) and her husband back in August 1969. One hot Friday night, the Smiths were heading south on Route 5 at eleven o'clock. They were tired from a long day on the road and eager to get to Northampton, Massachusetts, where they had a hotel reservation. The radio was on: a baseball game. The Red Sox and the White Sox in Chicago.

Suddenly the signal from WBZ-Boston faded. At her husband's urging, Linda fiddled with the dial, finally recovering the game. But the announcer recited the call letters of a Chicago station. Surprised, she made some remark about how radio waves bounce around strangely at night. Then she saw something on the left-hand side of the road: two brilliantly lighted motels, side by side. One had a NO VACANCY sign. The other said VACANCY and had a big, lighted, inviting-looking swimming pool.

It was then that their radio faded a second time. When Linda recovered the signal, it was again coming from nearby Boston.

The rest of the trip was uneventful. They reached Northampton and got a good night's sleep. But the next day things got weird.

After spending an exhausting afternoon looking at

Where they both thought the two motels should be they found only an empty meadow. Odd. Could they both be misremembering?

property, Mr. Smith suggested that on the ride back home they check in to one of the motels they had seen the night before. Linda agreed, lobbying strongly for the one with the swimming pool. About five p.m., with sundown still a few hours away, they reached Bernardston and continued north on Route 5.

Where they both thought the two motels should be they found only an empty meadow. Odd. Could they both be misremembering?

Linda insisted they go all the way to Brattleboro, turn around, then drive slowly back to Bernardston as they had done the night before. They found no motels at all—only the empty meadow.

Finally they gave up and sought out another place to stay. Next morning, still puzzled and a little uncomfortable with the whole situation, they took a final drive along Route 5 in search of the mystery motels. Still nothing. The buildings—both of them—had vanished.

Today, thirty-five years later, Linda continues to puzzle about the odd events of that hot August night. Mundane explanations occur to her: fatigue, misperception, mirages, things like that. But she was there; she recalls the brightly lighted buildings, the signposts, the out-of-place brilliance on a dark, empty highway. She knows what she saw. And then it was gone.

Had the Smiths seen a vision? Or were they in that altered state where lighted buildings can all at once blink out of existence? Do light rays, like their car radio's fickle signal, somehow get . . . misdirected?

Linda just doesn't know. And probably never will. But she still shudders when she speculates about where she and her husband might have ended up if they had been tempted into that brightly lighted motel with the swimming pool and the VACANCY sign.

Richford's Magic Road

Generally we wouldn't encourage *Weird New England* readers to violate the law. But in this case, we're talking about the law of gravity. Apparently, there are a number of places around this world of ours where gravitational forces play by their own rules. And our own New England seems to have its fair share of such anomalies.

The late Dolph Dewing of Franklin, Vermont, said he'd discovered a bit of contrary country, up around the Canadian border. Wristwatches skip a beat. A hunter's bullet will not dependably hold a straight trajectory. And cars, even big ones, are said to roll uphill!

We had our doubts. When it comes to gravity, all experience and learning points toward one indisputable conclusion: Objects tend to fall. Period. Nevertheless, on a bright September morning, we lit out for Vermont's north country in search of Richford's magic spot.

From a small cluster of buildings known as East Richford we followed the five-mile stretch of gravel road that connects with Route 105. This is a road that exemplifies the word "country." Ancient farmsteads, tiny graveyards, sagging fence lines, all surrounded with a green density of pastureland and hills. A bald streak on a nearby mountain defines the U.S.–Canada boundary.

Now here's the thing: Although there are no visible clues to tip you off, the road swings in and out of Canada. Naturally, there is some confusion about which laws apply. Who can say? Maybe the law of gravity is occasionally repealed.

Somewhere around here Dolph Dewing had found his magic no-man's-land. At first, he told a few friends. They may have laughed but were soon convinced. After that, he took a busload of observers from the Franklin Senior Center. Then, on October 11, 1985, he brought the local media to witness the odd phenomenon.

Reporter Nat Worman of the *County Courier* described how Dolph stopped his 1979 Dodge at the bottom of his Magnetic Hill. He stomped the accelerator, racing the engine to demonstrate that the vehicle was in neutral. Then he waited. In less than a minute, his car was moving forward at about ten miles an hour. Thirty seconds later it reached fifteen per. Clearly the two-ton Dodge and its four passengers were moving uphill!

It may have been an optical illusion; it might have been antigravity. But whatever it was—magic or magnetism—Dolph Dewing was convinced it was a real mystery.

The topography hadn't changed much in the twenty years since Nat Worman's article. With his newspaper photo as a guide, we quickly rediscovered the mysterious site, parked the car, and waited. Nothing happened.

Well, maybe that was the wrong hill. We moved ahead to a steeper rise and tried it again. Wrong hill again. After several moves and failures, we finally gave up, ending a budding but inglorious career as lawbreakers.

By now, it was about lunchtime, so we headed back to Richford to find a restaurant. Seated at the counter, we struck up a conversation with a friendly-looking man and asked if he was from the area.

"Lived here all my life," he said, which from the look of him must have been sixty-plus years. After a bit of verbal footsie, we told him about our visit to East Richford's Magnetic Hill and our failures there.

A stiff nod said he knew the place well. "What kind of car you driving?" he asked, peering over the top of his eyeglasses. We told him it was a Honda Civic.

"There's your problem," he said. "Not enough metal in them Christly things to work on any magnet."

We hadn't thought of that. But guess it just goes to show that every successful lawbreaker needs the right tools for the job.

If Leominster is too off the beaten track, why not check out the Greenfield, Massachusetts, version of a magnetic hill? It has the same mysterious effect on vehicles and might be a little easier to find.

Next Stop, Chartierville

There must be something about Canadians and antigravity. It seems that as you get closer to the Canadian border, all hell breaks loose with gravitational forces.

For example, if you're driving north in Pittsburg, New Hampshire, go just as far as you can along Route 3. When you hit the international line you'll have to stop at the Canadian border before entering Chartierville, Quebec. When the officer asks the purpose of your trip, say you want to see the magnetic hill (we dare you!). He (or she) is likely to smile and, without hesitation, point to a small sign. The fact is, you're there. Or almost.

We have experienced this one ourselves, and it is truly amazing. You drive down a hill. Park at the very bottom. Put your car in neutral and be sure your foot's off the brake. In a few minutes, you'll be pulled back uphill toward the United States. For this reason, New Hampshire Route 3 was avoided by draft dodgers during the Vietnam War.

But is it antigravity? An optical illusion? Magic? Or just plain patriotism? Who can say? All we know for sure is that it is fun, strange, and against logic as well as gravity.

As you roll uphill, you'll sense powerful unknown forces moving your car and you. And this one works even on Honda Civics. Bon voyage!

Let's Go to Leominster

For a long while Leominster, Massachusetts, claimed it had the only hill in New England with enough "magnetic" power to pull an unmanned automobile against gravity. Well, perhaps they needed something to brag about in addition to Johnny Appleseed and the world's largest collection of combs.

As we shall see, New England has many magnetic hills. Nonetheless, what they said may be true; you have to read the fine print: "unmanned automobile."

The mystery site is on Lowe Street. Its magnetic attributes were discovered around 1939 by a traveling salesman who had parked his car in a little depression on the road in front of R. W. Hapgood's place. He had turned off the ignition but forgot to leave the car in gear or engage the emergency brake. After his appointment, he returned to discover his car was driving away without him! He said it climbed about fifty feet uphill before it stopped.

The story spread, and soon people were lining up to try it for themselves. Neighboring town folks and out-of-staters got in on the act. People went uphill on bikes without having to pedal. Others tried it with baby carriages, skates, anything that could roll. Enterprising youngsters started charging people for brief bike rentals.

Lowe Street's Magnetic Hill caused quite a stir for a while, but it was quickly forgotten. As usual, the debate was magnetism versus magic versus misperception. All we can say is go and try it for yourself. But don't follow the salesman's example: Stay in your car.

Antigravity in Greenfield

If Leominster is too off the beaten track, why not check out the Greenfield, Massachusetts, version of a magnetic hill? It has the same mysterious effect on vehicles and might be a little easier to find. It is part of Old Shelburne Road, located directly behind the Big Y store on Route 2, just before the overpass on the first curve. Interestingly, this is on the Mohawk Trail at the exact geographic beginning of the Berkshire Mountains and is, perhaps, a preview of the weird things those hills contain.

Anyway, stop your car directly under the Route 2 underpass and orient it so it is facing east. Then go through the ritual: engine off, neutral, no brakes, high expectation, elevated faith. Your car should roll uphill a good two hundred feet or more. If it works, you have mastered the first key to unlocking the secret of levitation.

Perpetual Prom Night

There is a reputedly haunted stretch of Route 4 between Sherburne and Mendon, Vermont, where a ghostly young woman, probably a teenager, is spotted with some regularity. Who she is, or was, and why she patrols this particular bit of highway has never been explained. Presumably, many people have seen her and passed right by, not realizing they were seeing something out of the ordinary.

One of the best sightings was reported by a non-Vermonter named Barry Snell. It happened one spring evening in 1978. Mr. Snell was driving his VW Beetle west along Route 4 toward Rutland. On a four-lane section of road near the Sherburne Pass he saw what looked like a group of people on the right-hand side of the road. "Suddenly," he says, "a girl in a prom dress streaked in front of my car. I slammed on the brakes, narrowly missing her. I immediately pulled over, quite shaken."

As he looked around, he realized the girl had vanished. Visibility was good, and there was no nearby building she could have ducked into. She was just gone. Oddly, the crowd had mysteriously vanished too. Understandably concerned, Mr. Snell wondered why the girl had dashed in front of his car. It was as if she'd had no sense of risk; so, he concluded, she must have been in distress, or drunk, or in danger.

Mr. Snell continued checking and found there was in fact a prom going on in the area that night. He made his way to the rented hall and told a chaperone what had happened. He admitted he had almost killed a girl in a prom dress, and now he was worried about her well-being. Someone, he insisted, had to find her to make sure she was okay. But the chaperone seemed puzzled. No one was missing from the dance hall.

After that, Mr. Snell tried to put the incident out of his mind. It had all been puzzling, but, he assumed, perfectly natural. Then, about two years ago, while taking a drive, he mentioned the odd incident to his wife, Nancy. As he spoke, she turned ashen, saying, "You'll never believe what I saw last week on one of those 'unsolved mystery' type TV shows."

She told him she had watched a program about "a 'vision' of a girl in a prom dress who comes out around prom time in Vermont." She recalled that several people were interviewed, including one woman who said that she actually drove right through the apparition.

Mr. Snell found his wife's revelation most unnerving because it cast his whole experience in a very different light. Could he possibly have seen a ghost? He just doesn't know. And neither do dozens of other people who have seen the terrified fleeing phantom dash across Route 4.

On a four-lane section of road near the Sherburne Pass he saw what looked like a group of people on the right-hand side of the road. "Suddenly," he says, "a girl in a prom dress streaked in front of my car."

Wet Lady in White

At night, a prom dress and a bridal gown could look pretty much the same, but witnesses in Wallingford, Connecticut, are sure their female phantom is decked out for a wedding. The story is that sometime in the 1930s a young woman was left waiting at the altar by her runaway groom. Humiliated and depressed, she wandered off by herself and—perhaps overreacting a bit—threw herself into a nearby pond, where she drowned.

Since then, she has been spotted by numerous motorists on Whirlwind Hill Road, the site of the tragedy. The conditions are invariably the same: It will be a rainy night, and she'll be making her way along the side of the road, dressed in a rain-soaked wedding gown and apparently weeping. Sometimes she'll gesture as if asking for a ride, but when the driver pulls over and looks back, she'll be gone.

This forlorn roadside apparition took on additional credibility recently when she was spotted by two Wallingford police officers. Perhaps she's still out there searching for her long-lost fiancé. Someone should stop and tell her she's better off without him.

Ghost Runner of Manchester

From Manchester, New Hampshire, near the campus of Southern New Hampshire University, comes a story about a ghost runner. It is said that a man was out very late one night jogging on River Road, was hit by a car, and died on the spot. The story continues that every night the ghost runner jogs down the street. Late one January night, at about two a.m., I was leaving a party at SNHU with some friends and saw the ghost runner. It was about ten degrees outside, and he was jogging down the street dressed only in a T-shirt and shorts, and did not make any footprints in the snow. Not only that, but it was very odd that someone would jog at two a.m. I screamed for about a block, scared out of my mind! –*Jenny R*

The Terrors of Tower Road

Tower Hill Road in Cumberland, Rhode Island, is a dark, twisty, east-west stretch that connects Route 114 with West Wrentham Road. It is named, presumably, for the old wooden fire tower at its summit. Sandwiched between Diamond Hill State Park and Ash Swamp, it is a good deal more rural than one might expect in this populated portion of a tiny state.

Tower Road is yet another argument that some sections of New England hint at a fraying of the frontier between this world and some other. A tangible sense of unease prevails here, provoked by dangerous curves and an ominous atmosphere. Cameras seize up. Cell phones conk out. People see red eyes peering from the dark shadowy undergrowth, or glowing orbs floating in the sky and among the trees. Paranormalists flock to the area because of the numerous visions, described as ghosts, that have been reported along the narrow roadway.

But are they ghosts?

Most frequently seen is the apparition of a little girl playing in front of a house. She'll vanish before your eyes as you move closer. A phantom boy riding a phantom tricycle is often spotted as well. What's notable about this apparition is that he is not seen as you approach, but only through your rear window as you drive away. A most disconcerting experience. At twilight, a ghostly boy and his dog are occasionally spotted. Passersby have recognized them both as having been killed some years ago in a car accident.

But the most terrifying claim is that the apparitions seen are not ghosts at all, but mutilated corpses, human and animal, that shamble along the rural roadside.

To say that Tower Hill is a "ghost filled" stretch of road might be to dismiss it too quickly. If we are seeing intangible tricycles and incorporeal canines, we are not seeing ghosts. And corpses do not ambulate in the world of the spirits. Perhaps we should consider alternative explanations for the myriad mysteries of Tower Road. Time-slips. Other dimensions. Total unknowns.

Ambushed on Downs Road

My sister had a run-in with these supposed demon children things on Downs Road in Hamden, Connecticut, and it's pretty scary. Her boyfriend at the time used Downs Road as a shortcut to get to his house many a time, but the night my sister was in the car they were pretty much ambushed by these creatures. She told me they were driving down it when something jumped in front of their truck, so they stopped, not wanting to hit it. The second they did, the truck started getting hit with rocks from all sides and the thing that was in front of them disappeared somewhere.

They started to panic and sped off, but as they started to move, they heard a horrible screeching noise on the side of the truck. They didn't bother looking back or even stopping the whole way back to his house. When they got there, they saw huge scratches and marks all down the side of the truck that fitted the shape of nails perfectly.—*Nick*

Fleeing from the Cabin on Downs Road

In the summer of 2001, a couple of friends and I decided to check out Downs Road in Hamden, Connecticut. It was nine o'clock at night, and we all packed into my Ford Explorer.

Downs Road is literally in the middle of nowhere. It leads nowhere. There is a small development of new houses, and at the very end of the street, there are two stop signs and a narrow dirt road. We parked my car at the dead end and decided to walk down the dirt road. It was pitch-black. We walked huddled together for about a quarter of a mile, and some of my friends wanted to turn back, but we kept on going. We finally saw a small cabinlike house up ahead. We all felt our stomachs drop. We couldn't see too far ahead of us, but we crept up to the house.

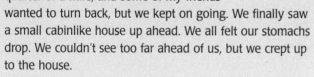

Within about ten feet of the house, we heard scrambling in the woods; then something like a door slammed. We ran for our lives, and to this day, we haven't gone back. Whatever it was that was chasing us was extremely quick. I would like to have a professional examine this cabin, because we were too scared to go back to visit it, even during the day.—*Terence McTague*

Enveloped in Evil on Downs Road

This is about a road called Downs Road in Hamden, Connecticut. Me and my friend Kara heard from this girl that this road was haunted, so one real cold night we decided to go down there. The road is supposed to be home to these inbred people who are exceptionally smart when communicating through telepathy.

As soon as you go down the road, it is like a blanket of darkness and an uncontrollable fear covers you. It's about a mile and a half, and the street is very, very narrow. There are only two streetlights, and there are no houses. I swear you cannot go three minutes down that street without feeling like you can't breathe. I saw what looked like a baby on the side of the road, and when I looked to the side, I saw a bald guy lying in the woods. I couldn't handle it anymore, so I freaked out and told my friend let's get out of there. I was shaking the whole way home. The feeling that you get when you go down there is like no other I have ever felt. It's like evil and darkness is enclosing you and you can't get away and it slowly suffocates you. I don't recommend going down there!—*Angel*

A Tombstone Every Mile

An associate from Maine tells us about a stretch of road on which we never plan to travel. It is the Haynesville Road, the very one Maine native Dick Curless sings about: *If they buried all the truckers lost in them woods / There'd be a tombstone every mile.*

But it is more than lost truckers, blizzards, and black ice you have to worry about as you travel through Haynesville Woods. Apparently, it is one of those "soft spots" in the universe where all manner of oddities occur. Bigfoot seems to lurk in this vicinity, crossing the highway or peering from behind roadside trees. A disproportionate number of UFOs zigzag overhead. The ghosts of car crash victims have sometimes been seen wandering as if lost. Seemingly alive, they linger long after their wrecked vehicles have been towed away and their corporeal selves have been committed to the earth.

Some people still travel the ninety-mile length of the road, though it can be avoided, since Interstate 95 bypassed it in the 1960s. The rerouted traffic just makes it more remote and barren. Ninety miles of nothing: no gas station, no restaurants, no houses, no phones. Just trees and darkness. If a driver broke down or skidded off the road, who knows what kind of hell he could be in for?

As far as we can determine, no one has lived to tell about it, but the rumor is that on occasion an unearthly darkness descends over the road and part of the adjoining forest. It is so dense that car headlights cannot penetrate it. If anyone—trucker or motorist—drives into that preternatural darkness, they vanish forever. Our associate, who teaches at a college in Maine, says, "None of my students are comfortable talking about the place, which makes me curious. . . ."

We're curious too, but not enough to drive up there and check it out.

The Haunts of Hartland

On the back roads of Hartland, Vermont, there is apparently a commune of so-called "Hippie ghosts." (We know the word hippie is passé, but there's no reason to update a term for people forever stuck in another time.) According to local lore, the spirits of five young men and two women will wander forever in the sharp ravine between Garvin and Hartland Hills.

Apparently, the group was made up of wealthy out-of-state students who had rented a house during Christmas break in 1971. Their plan—at least the part they talked about—was a skiing vacation at Woodstock and Ascutney. The locals will tell you a lot of dope smoking was going on in that house. Anyway, something went wrong. Match, candle, woodstove, no one knows. A blaze started, and within moments the whole place was in flames. Too dazed to react, all five young people perished in the blaze.

To this day, locals driving the road between Garvin and Hartland Hills report seeing ghostly long-haired strangers walking on the roadside after dark. A Mr. Sawyer says he saw another phantom with a flaming chair in his arms, running madly from a fire he'll never escape.

Hitchhiker from Hell

Route 44 in Massachusetts can be relatively uneventful until you hit a mysterious five-mile stretch between Seekonk and Rehoboth. Of course Rehoboth makes up one of the corners of the Bridgewater Triangle (*see* Fabled People and Places), so any triangular road signs should signal weird things ahead.

In this case, the menace seems to be a perfectly ordinary New Englander, almost stereotypical in his plaid shirt, blue jeans, bushy beard, and full head of curly red hair. Trouble is, he's kind of a funny-acting fella. He appears and vanishes. And there is something slightly diabolical about him; he has been known to taunt and jeer at motorists who have been unlucky enough to encounter him.

He was first brought to the attention of the uninitiated in Charles Robinson's 1994 book *The New England Ghost Files.* One of the more terrifying tales in the book, the story of the red-headed hitcher leaves an indelible imprint on the reader. The problem is Mr. Robinson puts all the characters into the Witness Protection Program by using pseudonyms throughout. For the serious researcher, this practice is a nuisance because it makes the tales impossible to verify.

Since Mr. Robinson's book hit the stands, sightings of this red-headed phantom have continued, lending the whole thing an elevated credibility. It is uncertain when "Red" made his first appearance, but Mr. Robinson's first report is dated 1969.

Witness 1: At about eleven thirty one winter night, a man was driving on a deserted stretch of Route 44 in rural Seekonk. He says he glanced at the passenger-side window and saw a face pressed up against it. This was odd, because he was traveling at about fifty miles an hour.

The driver could make out the plaid shirt, the red hair, and an unsettling grin on the phantom's face. By the time the man pulled over and stopped, the uninvited rider had vanished. Reportedly, the witness told Mr. Robinson, "That incident has left me shaken-up for the past twenty-five years."

At about ten o'clock on an evening in 1973, Witness 2 picked up a hitchhiker on that same stretch of highway. The hitcher didn't seem unusual in any way, with his plaid shirt, blue jeans, and red hair. But when he got into the cab of the witness's truck, he refused to respond to conversation. He just grinned in a weird sort of way and stared at the increasingly uncomfortable driver. The hitcher's behavior was strange enough to make the driver pull over to let him out. But instead of opening the door and climbing down, the hitcher vanished before the man's disbelieving eyes.

On February 25, 1981, a woman driving to Seekonk hit the red-headed hitchhiker. He just seemed to materialize out of the air, but there was no sensation of impact or sound of a collision. Nonetheless, she stopped her car and got out to check. Although there was no sign of the man, a horrible, evil laughter echoed from the nearby woods.

As she nervously continued on her way, the man appeared in the road a second time. Again, he seemed to just appear before there was time to stop. She passed right through him and kept on going.

Perhaps the most unsettling episode recounted by Mr. Robinson took place about ten p.m.,

October 16, 1984. A couple's station wagon broke down on the evil stretch of Route 44, right near the Seekonk–Rehoboth line. The woman remained in the car while the man went off to look for help.

Soon he came upon the red-headed man sitting beside the road. He approached and asked where he might find a telephone. The man didn't respond, just grinned. After repeating the question several times, the witness concluded something must be wrong with the man. At that point, Red twisted his face into a grotesque expression and began laughing maniacally. Mr. Robinson quotes the witness as saying, "And the laughing kept switching locations. First I heard it in front of me, then behind me, then to the left of me. It was bizarre. I began to run along the highway back toward the car, and, as I did, the laughing followed me for a good two or three hundred feet. It scared the heck out of me. And then it suddenly stopped."

When he got to his stranded vehicle, he discovered his wife in tears and highly agitated. Apparently, she had been having a simultaneous encounter with the same phantom. She had turned on the car radio, and a strange voice had cut in. It addressed her by name, taunting and mocking her before exploding into a fit of menacing laughter. She leaped out of the car and stood frozen until her husband returned.

Charles Robinson has either created or documented what has become a solid piece of New England folklore. An expanding circle of people talk, write about, and investigate the Red-Headed Hitcher of Route 44. First-person encounters multiply, while friend-of-a-friend reports are too numerous to list. This odd, folksy phantom is certainly no passive apparition. But his intention seems to be to frighten rather than to harm. Or is it? This dark stretch of road has been the scene of more than its share of accidents over the years, many of them fatal.

A researcher from the Rehoboth area has interviewed a number of people who've had run-ins with the hitcher. Her efforts have disclosed a possible identity: a local farmer who was killed while changing a tire on Route 44. While the physical descriptions of the two characters match, their behaviors are entirely different. This devilish dichotomy adds another layer of mystery to Rehoboth's unfathomable phantom.

Weird Times on Dracula Drive

There is this place called Dracula Drive, I think it's in Trumball, Connecticut. Supposedly, there was a mental hospital there some time ago, and it was said that Melonhead kids had escaped and were never found. They later grouped up in the woods there. Ever since then, strange things would happen there.

My father told me that he once went down that road, and it was snowing on one side and on the other it wasn't. Of course this is explainable if you think about it, but it's still odd. Some people say that things stop working once you get some ways in, like cell phones, but of course that's explainable too. But cars suddenly not working? Or even cell batteries suddenly dying? I even heard a friend's cousin saying that she went down that road one night with a few friends, and when they were looking around from inside the car, they saw something running really far in the distance, wearing what they thought was white but a very dirty white. They saw it only for a while, but then it was gone. —*Skry*

New England Ghosts

A History of Haunting

New England is a ghost-crowded land. A spectral census of our six states would require a volume the size of an encyclopedia. Some of our venerable haunts have been appearing since Colonial times; others date back even further. Long-dead Native Americans still put in appearances, like the ghost of an Indian girl murdered in the 1600s. And then there are the Yankee ghosts that are relative newcomers—spirits of people who passed on in modern times. The spirit world is being pushed to the point of overcrowding.

For the purposes of this chapter we've picked only a couple of representatives for each state, a sort of ectoplasmic electoral college. It will be up to the reader to decide which state is the most haunted.

A Rain of Rocks

Historically speaking, it is a bit difficult to pinpoint the very first recorded New England ghost. One possible candidate comes from New Hampshire.

This long-forgotten bit of paranormal lore took place in Portsmouth, when New Hampshire was still a British colony. The scene for the "haunting" was a tavern on Great Island, today's New Castle Island. Though it's an old story, from way back in 1682, the strength of its documentation is assurance that something mysterious really happened. Somehow, George and Alice Walton, along with their family, incurred the wrath of one or more supernatural entities. Over the course of three months, paranormal aggression brought the farmer-tavern keepers to the brink of despair.

It started one Sunday evening in June, when a series of taps disturbed the family. The racket escalated fiercely, sounding as if a summer hailstorm was battering the roof and sides of the house. Investigation quickly showed that their home was being pelted by a rain of rocks!

About ten o'clock, when the clattering ended, the Waltons cautiously ventured outside, trying to identify who, or what, was attacking them. In the bright moonlight, they discovered their yard was littered with stones. But they could neither see nor hear the troublemakers.

While they attempted to investigate further, a second volley of stones whistled around their heads. Terrified, they raced to the porch. But the stones found them anyway, striking with uncanny precision. They ran inside and bolted the doors.

When a new bombardment began *inside the house,* the Waltons realized it was not the work of local jokesters. Flying rocks shattered glass, banged within the chimney, and bounded along the floor like cannonballs.

The children retired to their upstairs rooms, but they were chased back downstairs by the sound of snorting and heavy breathing. Everyone stood helplessly as the chaos continued for hours. Then the candles leaped off the table and went out, leaving the family in utter darkness. Admittedly, all this may have been the work of some especially clever mischief-makers, but certain things convinced the Waltons that the stones were hurled by supernatural hands.

First, some were hot, as if they had been taken from a fire. Second, Mr. Walton marked several stones, counted them, and placed them on a table. When he turned his back, the same stones began soaring around the room. Third, the lead crossbars on the windowpanes were bent outward, suggesting impact from inside. And finally, the women in the house were terrified when a hand—or the apparition of a hand—came through a window.

Escalating madness continued day and night. Wherever Mr. Walton went—to the barn, the field, or elsewhere—he was sure to receive a shower of stones. These weird events continued for three months as the entity, whatever it was, wreaked havoc, hurling stones, bricks, and heavy implements such as mauls and crowbars.

If one should doubt the testimony of the Walton family, the full range of these spectral events was carefully recorded by a credible eyewitness: Richard Chamberlain, the secretary for the colony of New Hampshire. Because his status in the community might have been at risk by openly chronicling the unbelievable proceedings, it took the good man a full sixteen years to work up enough courage to tell the story. He published the details in England in 1698 but signed his pamphlet with only his initials.

To this day, we don't know for sure what got into the Waltons' house. Was it an indignant Native American spirit wanting his land back? The shade of some deceased colonist having a little postmortem fun? A clever band of organized tricksters? Or, as we might call it today, a poltergeist?

Predictably, a neighbor suspected of being a witch was immediately blamed for the Waltons' supernatural siege, foreshadowing the horrors of the witch trials that were to come in Salem, Massachusetts, a decade later.

A Mere Mass of Light

If it was something other than a ghost that pestered George Walton and his family, then maybe the honor of being New England's first ghost really goes to Nelly Butler and the tiny seacoast village of Machiasport, Maine. Since her appearance happened *after* the American Revolution, we might even grant her America's first ghost status.

In this dramatic case, people actually got to meet and talk with the spirit. In fact, some were sternly lectured by this loquacious specter.

In the summer of 1799, Captain Abner Blaisdel and his family began to notice odd noises in their house. Though somewhat irritating, the sounds didn't interfere with the family's daily routine. But then, with the beginning of the new year, the Blaisdels began their baffling collision with the paranormal.

On January 2, 1800, Abner and his daughter, Lydia,

heard noises, as if someone was talking in their cellar. When they went down to investigate, they could see no one. Yet they were able to start a conversation with . . . something.

The disembodied entity said her name was Nelly. Further, she claimed she was the deceased wife of a local man—Captain George Butler—and the daughter of David Hooper, who lived nearby.

Nelly's earthbound "husband" was away at sea at the time, but her father was summoned to see if he could validate the spirit's claim. He was a crusty old coot, not one to put up with anyone's shenanigans—whether they were alive or dead. But he traveled six snowy miles to the Blaisdel home and descended into the cellar. There, Mr. Hooper posed questions that no one but his daughter could answer. When the voice responded correctly, the shaken old man became a believer.

But the ghost did not appear to her father. When she finally showed herself, it was to Captain Blaisdel's family, rather than her own. While walking home, Abner's son Paul saw a woman "float over the fields." Startled, the lad raced home in a panic. The next night Nelly was furious because the boy had neglected to greet her properly when he'd seen her outside.

This was typical of Nelly's self-righteousness. Between January and February of 1800, she took to herding people into the Blaisdels' cellar and lecturing them about their moral behavior. Somehow she seemed to know more than a comfortable amount about the private lives of the neighbors.

In May, Nelly materialized to twenty people in the cellar. One witness said, "At first the apparition was a mere mass of light, then it grew into a personal form, about as tall as myself. . . . At last [it] . . . became shapeless, expanded every way and then vanished. . . ." Another time Nelly assembled a group of two hundred people and admonished them with religious harangues and predictions. Surprisingly, many came true.

A local minister, the Reverend Abraham Cummings, grew concerned that folks were getting too preoccupied with Nelly. He was convinced the whole thing was a hoax perpetrated by Captain Blaisdel. The doubting cleric set off to confront the captain, but on his way he had an experience that would change his view of this world and the next. He saw a mysterious globe of white light. As it moved toward him, it took the shape of a woman. He said that she was "glorious, with rays of light shining from her head all about, and reaching to the ground."

Most accounts say this was Nelly Butler's last appearance. Apparently, her mission was complete because she had convinced the skeptical clergyman of her existence. Rev. Cummings spent the rest of his life traveling and preaching, vividly recounting the marvelous things he had witnessed and assuring all who would listen of the heavenly life to come after earthly death. In fact, he even recorded the events and testimony in a book called *Immortality proved by the Testimony of Sense,* published in Bath, Maine, in 1826.

The John York House

Some ghosts who got their start before the American Revolution may still be around.

Quite possibly, one long-lived phantom dwells in an especially haunted part of Connecticut—the town of North Stonington, which borders the Pachaug Forest, a vast and dreadfully haunted place.

North Stonington is a beautiful rural area that appears much as it did two hundred years ago. It is there, at One Clarks Falls Road, that you'll find the John York House, once a tavern and now an occasional B&B. Constructed by John York around 1741, this Revolutionary War–era post-and-beam was run as a tavern on the busy post road between Providence, Rhode Island, and New London, Connecticut. Supposedly, George Washington slept there.

While that may not be true, there are strange tales about the house that are more firmly rooted in fact. A drunken traveler fell down the steep staircase and broke his neck. Two Revolutionary-era soldiers—best friends—fought each other near the bar. No doubt possessed by demon rum, one stabbed the other to death. Afterward—so the story goes—it was impossible to remove the dead man's blood from the wide wooden floor planks. Because the stains couldn't be cleaned or disguised, the only solution was to tear up the floorboards and put them back upside down. The blood is still there.

And so is something else. . . .

During the 1960s and '70s, owners Hugo and Mariam Wilms documented all sorts of ghostly high jinks: heavy footsteps on empty stairs, falling furniture, a levitating mattress, paintings and photographs that mysteriously changed position on the walls. Especially vexing was the brass barometer that repeatedly unbolted itself from the wall and flew across the room, landing on the floor without dents or broken glass. Things got so chaotic that the couple hired professional ghost busters, who supposedly banished the haunt from the premises.

But maybe not. Soon after, it was Mr. and Mrs. Wilms who vacated.

The house sat empty until December 1996, when two young biologists, Leea and David Grote, acquired the property, planning to open a bed and breakfast. During their application hearing, a zoning commissioner asked what they intended to do about the "ghost issue." Well, as trained scientists, they weren't too concerned; they were more interested in historic preservation and accurate restoration.

But soon enough the skeptical young scientists began to experience what anyone else might call "ghostly activity." They cautiously admitted to a couple of occurrences that were . . . ambiguous.

Leea said she clearly heard someone persistently calling her name from the bottom of the stairs. However, she checked and was sure she was alone in the house.

If exorcists actually had evicted ghosts from the John York House, it is no surprise that the Grotes' most frightening episode took place in the yard. For no discernible reason, a sealed window in the back of a guest's van exploded, blasting shards of glass into a five-foot semicircle around the vehicle. Its other windows were already open, so the explosion was not the consequence of heat and pressure. It may have been a defective window or, perhaps, the work of ghosts.

Then again, it may have been the combustion that inevitably results when the scientific world collides with the world of spirits.

The Mystery of Hannah Nute

In 1801, William Farrar, along with Daniel Webster, graduated from Dartmouth College in Hanover, New Hampshire.

William married a Vermont woman, and they settled in Lancaster, New Hampshire. There he became a prosperous lawyer and deacon of the Congregational Church. At some point, the family decided to employ a youthful live-in helper named Hannah Nute. On the day in 1818 when Hannah moved in, the nightmare began.

One evening Hannah began to hear strange noises in her downstairs bedroom. It might have been made by a squirrel or a mouse, except that it wasn't a scuffling sound. It was a distinct, rhythmic rapping. Hannah bolted from her room, screaming for Mrs. Farrar.

At first, the older woman suspected Hannah had been having a bad dream. But when she accompanied the young woman downstairs, Mrs. Farrar got the surprise of her life. Three loud bangs issued from directly beneath Hannah's feet. The girl began screaming again.

Moments later an irritated William Farrar appeared at the door, demanding an explanation. Before his wife could speak, the rapping began anew. "I'll get to the bottom of this," he said, grabbing a fireplace poker and heading for the basement. His fruitless search of the empty cellar only convinced Mr. Farrar that he needed an outside opinion. He summoned his minister, the Reverend Joseph Willard. With Willard in the room, three loud knocks again sounded.

In the following days, every inch of the house was thoroughly investigated. When nothing was found, talk turned to omens, signs, and hauntings. Again suspicion fell on the young servant girl. As someone pointed out, the rapping occurred only when Hannah was in the room.

Four skeptical town fathers gathered to investigate. Ignoring her protests, they tied Hannah's hands and feet and placed her on her bed. Then they scrutinized her every move. Impossibly—even with Hannah thoroughly restrained and under constant observation for an entire night and day— the rapping persisted, taunting the self-appointed "experts." Defeated, the men left the house.

Though she was exonerated, Hannah's grueling ordeal had left her exhausted, weak, and sickly. She begged to be dismissed from her position. Reluctantly the Farrars agreed.

While Hannah prepared to leave, the rapping became more active than ever. As she walked down the hall with her belongings, loud thumping followed her, thundering like the footsteps of an invisible giant.

Did the mysterious presence leave with the departing maid? Or did it remain to torment future occupants? In the early 1850s, after William Farrar's death, the Norris family purchased what had locally become known as the Haunted House. Soon eerie manifestations began to pester them. Doors opened and banged shut as if under their own power. Shrieks echoed in the night. A "log rolling" sound and a "loud thumping" pounded from the attic. One of the Norris daughters experienced a terrible fright in the basement. In all her remaining years, she refused to reveal exactly what horror she had seen.

Interestingly, in the late 1850s the Catholic Church bought the house and tore it down, replacing it with the rectory that now stands at 163 Main Street. One wonders why. Could it be that they know something the rest of us do not?

Holy Spirits?

Haunted churches are rare in ghost lore, not because there are so few of them, but because churches like to keep a lid on their hauntings. It's okay if the Holy Spirit resides there, but any other kind is another matter.

This story unfolds in Crompton, Rhode Island, part of today's West Warwick. The town got its start in 1807 when space to build a cotton mill on the Pawtuxet River was carved out of the primeval forest. Business grew, and demand for employees quickly exhausted local supply.

In the 1840s, groups of Irish immigrants, fleeing the potato famine, flocked to Crompton because they were skilled in textile trades. These were Irish Catholics—papists—so friction quickly ignited between them and the intolerant Anglo-Protestants already there.

To attend mass, Catholics had to walk all the way to Providence, a good ten miles from home. As their population grew, the Catholics wanted a church of their own. But the local Protestants conspired to stop them from bringing papist worship into town. No one would sell them the land on which to build a church.

But the Catholics were not without resources. Sympathizers Paul and Mary Doran conspired right back and acquired a one-acre lot under the pretense of expanding their own holdings. Then they deeded it to the Roman Catholic bishop of Hartford. In 1844, work was begun on the church.

Mary Doran died shortly after ground was broken. Some say her early death was the result of a retaliatory curse; others argue against supernatural causes. But the work she did to establish St. Mary's Catholic Church will never be forgotten.

Apparently, she is still there to remind us.

For decades, church members have been aware of a vaguely eerie air pervading the tiny church. In the old days, people—especially children—avoided the place because it made them feel "uncomfortable." Even today some members of the congregation will not go into St. Mary's alone at night. The consensus is that a ghostly presence haunts the church.

Over the years, many people have had run-ins with the mysterious shade. Father Edmund H. Fitzgerald, pastor of St. Mary's from 1984 to 1992, is convinced the church is haunted by Mary Doran's spirit. Time and again, alone in the church, he would hear footsteps on the hard cedar floor. They sounded as if they were right behind him, but when he turned around, no one was there. However, Father Fitzgerald says he never found his otherworldly encounters to be frightening.

In a written affidavit, he states, "One Christmas eve [in 1989 or '90] following the Mass of the Christ Child, the tower bell rang of its own accord after the congregation left the church grounds." This occurred around five p.m. as Father Fitzgerald was locking the

door to leave. He immediately went back in to investigate. "The bell rope was moving up and down all by itself," he says, "but there was nobody in the church. That bell can only ring from someone pulling the rope." To emphasize the point, he adds, "Even recent hurricanes did not cause the bell to ring in this way."

But to Father Fitzgerald the bell wasn't alarming. "What better time for it to ring," he said, "than to celebrate the birth of the Christ Child?"

Another sonic mystery is that the church organ will occasionally play without the aid of an organist, even, as Father Fitzgerald has said, when "the instrument was closed, locked, and covered with its cloth. And the loft lights were extinguished."

Only once does Father Fitzgerald believe he actually saw the ghost. He was inside the church looking through a window at the parking lot. He is positive a figure was standing next to him; he saw it out of the corner of his eye. But when he looked directly at it, it was gone.

The question remains, Does Mary Doran linger as a caretaker spirit, forever watching over the church she helped to establish? If not, then what's in there?

Ghosts and Misdeeds at Searles Castle

In Great Barrington, Massachusetts, is a place called Searles Castle. It's a real stone castle right in the middle of town, complete with secret passages and its own lake. It was originally built as a house for the Searle family.

The story goes something like this: There was a husband and wife living in the house with a small staff. The wife was terminally ill but not very close to death. The husband, without the traditional company of his wife, looked toward one of the maids for relief (I think you know what I mean) and he would sneak through a hidden staircase next to the master bedroom closet and right up to the maid's quarters at night.

After some time they fell in love, and wished to marry, but the wife was still hanging on. So, of course, they killed the wife so they could be together.

After his wife's death, the husband wore black in public and during the day, but at night when the staff retired for the evening, he and the maid would carry on like teenagers. Although the wife was gone, the secret staircase was still in use, but in the opposite direction. The maid would enter the master bedroom and play lady of the house every night. That is, until one night when on her way to meet her lover she suspiciously fell down the stairs to her death. A few days later the husband was coming down the main staircase of the house, when the great chandelier fell on him and killed him as well.

The story continues that all three ghosts—the wife, the husband, and the maid—still chase each other around the house. They have been spotted many times by numbers of tourists. The husband has been seen standing in the middle of audiences during performances while I was there, and I had a candelabra blow out on me mysteriously on a perfectly calm night, indoors, while trying to investigate the second floor alone.

And there's more. On the other side of the lake behind the house was a small gazebo. This was one of the wife's favorite features of the house, but she hated to have to walk through the marsh to reach it. So the husband had an underground tunnel built under the lake. Fast forward to the 1970s. The castle was a school at the time, and one day a young boy found the underground tunnel while exploring the basement. As the boy made his way through the long, and no longer lighted, tunnel, the roof gave way, crushing the little boy and flooding the basement. After the cleanup, the tunnel was concreted shut and the basement declared off-limits. The school was closed down shortly after that, and rumors of the boy's ghost haunting the grounds and the basement have persisted ever since.—*Ever Curious, NYC*

The Bloody Tower

In 1887, an innovative project was going on in Brattleboro, Vermont. On a hilltop overlooking the vast grounds of the Vermont Asylum for the Insane (today's Brattleboro Retreat), conventional therapy had stopped when the building of a grand, medieval-looking tower was completed.

At the time, doctors believed that hard, purposeful labor would help mental patients regain their stability. So a group of inmates was put to work creating one of those scenic overlooks that dot so many New England hillsides.

However, the doctors failed to consider one thing. Certain mental patients envisioned another use for the tower. In the years immediately following its construction, a fair number of individuals climbed to the top and hurled themselves off it. The rock outcropping that supports the edifice offered instant death to anyone meeting it head-on. Although the actual number of suicides is a closely guarded secret, the tower was quickly sealed off.

Today, the double-locked tower is a little difficult to find, but once they locate it, a growing group of people have reported seeing a unique form of ghost—one that is airborne. A hazy humanlike form will appear at the tower's summit, remain there a moment, and suddenly hurl itself into space, remaining briefly visible until it vanishes before impact.

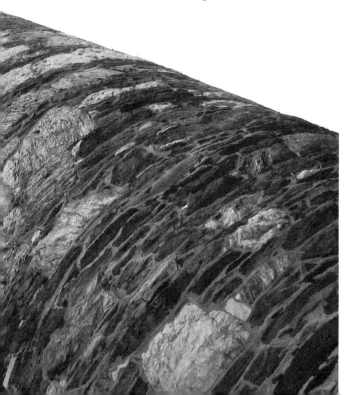

Rhode Island's Official Haunt

In Foster, Rhode Island, there is an "official" haunted spot. The state deemed it so in 1885, but the fact is the haunting began long before that.

Early in the nineteenth century, Rams Tail Factory was an active industrial complex consisting of several houses, a warehouse, and offices, all surrounding a mill for spinning and weaving cloth. William Potter managed the factory by day, and his partner, Peleg Walker, served as the night watchman. He'd walk the grounds, checking building after building by lantern light. Then, at daybreak, he'd end his shift by ringing the factory bell to summon the workers. For some reason a falling out—presumably having to do with money—put an end to the partnership.

On the morning of May 19, 1822, Peleg Walker was discovered hanging from the bell rope. It looked like suicide, but it might have been murder. In any event, he was buried in the nearby cemetery under a tombstone that reads LIFE HOW SHORT/ETERNITY HOW LONG.

But it seems that death did not put an end to Peleg's work, for Mr. Walker still walks the grounds.

The haunting commenced almost immediately after his death. With no human hand to guide it, the factory bell would ring every morning. Workers removed the bell rope, but the bell continued to sound. Then they removed the bell itself, yet its ring remained.

After that, things escalated. For several nights, workers were awakened by the noises of the mill running all by itself. When they examined the giant mill wheel, powered by the Ponaganset River, they found it was running against the current.

With that, many employees decided to leave. The few who remained began experiencing an odd phenomenon by night: They witnessed the dimly glowing ghost of Peleg Walker, lantern in hand, moving from building to building just as he had in life.

By the middle of the nineteenth century, the factory closed. The town's historical records attribute Rams Tail Factory's failure to Peleg Walker's ghost. By the end of the century, the whole place had burned down. But the ghost still walks the ruins, making his eternal rounds.

Fire and Ice

Often disasters seem to create ghosts. Look for the site of a major calamity, and chances are you'll find a ghost there.

A perfect example can be found in White River Junction, Vermont. It was there, more than a hundred years ago, that Vermont's worst railroad disaster occurred on a vast wooden trestle spanning the White River.

It was two o'clock in the morning on Saturday, the fifth of February, 1887. The Montreal Express, heading north from Boston, pulled into the station at White River Junction, then quickly headed out again. Seventy-nine passengers were aboard with a crew of six trainmen. The train was behind schedule, over an hour late. Quite possibly, it was moving a bit too fast as it approached the Woodstock Bridge, about four miles outside town. The temperature was an arctic 18 degrees below zero.

Conductor Sturtevant of St. Albans walked along slowly, taking tickets from sleepy passengers. In the cars, woodstoves unsuccessfully fought the freezing weather.

As the train came onto the bridge, Mr. Sturtevant stopped his collecting. Something was wrong. He could feel it. An unfamiliar grinding. A disturbing sound in uncomfortable contrast with the rhythmic rumble of the wheels.

The conductor pulled the bell cord. Reflexively, Engineer Pierce hit the brakes. But several tons of train could not stop at once.

As the chain of cars slowed, the last in line, a sleeping car, hit a defective section of track. The car jumped the rails, dragged along the railroad bed and onto the bridge. There, almost at rest now, the sleeper tipped, tottered, and eventually tumbled over the side of the bridge.

Its weight pulled the next three cars over the side along with it. When the coupling snapped, all four cars—two sleepers and two passenger cars—broke away from the rest of the train, plunging off the bridge. They descended forty-three feet until they smashed against the solid ice surface of the river.

Stoves and oil lamps inside the train flared. A dry wind fanned the flames, quickly igniting the crashed cars. Instantly, lethal spears of flame stabbed at the wooden bridge. Tons of blazing timber collapsed around and on top of the cars. Within minutes, everything was ablaze!

Trainmen and those who'd escaped the fall worked atop the slippery ice, blindly fighting their way through flames and suffocating smoke, hoping to save anyone they could. But there was little they could do; the conflagration's intense heat forced them away from the trapped passengers. Despairingly, they watched the inferno, deafening themselves to the tortured screams of the dying.

Luckily, Brakeman Parker had leaped to safety, and he ran the four miles back to town for help. A rescue train was quickly outfitted with physicians, volunteers, railway men, and wrecking equipment. When the rescuers arrived, the most severely injured were carried some four hundred feet to the nearest building, ironically known as the Paine House, for its owner, Oscar Paine.

Thirty-one passengers died that night. Some drowned as the fire melted through the ice. Some were crushed; others were cremated or mangled beyond recognition. Five railroad men also perished.

Today there is little to remind us of the Woodstock Bridge disaster. Granite abutments still stand, modified now to support a new, 650-foot bridge. The Paine House and barn remain nearby. It is said that victims' blood from the upstairs rooms soaked through the floor, and it can still be seen on the kitchen ceiling below.

Locals will tell you that animals will not stay in the barn; something inside frightens them. People passing

FRANK LESLIE'S ILLUSTRATED NEWSPAPER

Entered according to Act of Congress, in the year 1887, by Mrs. Frank Leslie, in the Office of the Librarian of Congress at Washington.— Entered at the Post Office, New York, N.Y., as Second-class Matter.

No. 1,639.—Vol. LXIII.] NEW YORK—FOR THE WEEK ENDING FEBRUARY 12, 1887. [Price, 10 Cents.

there at night sometimes report distant cries or hopeless sobbing from the building's dark, empty interior. And near the river, over one hundred years after the tragedy, passersby continue to report the sharp aroma of burning wood—occasionally tinged with a more unpleasant odor.

But most mysterious of all, certain individuals have witnessed a ghostly uniformed man believed to be the shade of Conductor Sturtevant. He's only seen by moonlight, apparently patrolling the empty tracks, an eternal caretaker forever guarding against another disaster.

But here's the most disturbing detail: There are frequent reports of a ghostly child dressed in nineteenth-century clothing. This diminutive phantom is always spotted at dusk, suspended just a bit above the water as if standing atop an ice mass that long ago melted.

There is much speculation about the identity of this ghostly youngster. Some witnesses believe he is the spectral image of a small boy who escaped the tragedy but watched his father burn to death, trapped in the wreckage. Though the boy survived the 1887 crash, he returns to the fatal spot, night after night, waiting for a parent who will never find his way to safety.

TERRIBLE RAILWAY DISASTER IN VERMONT.—A TRAIN ON THE VERMONT CENTRAL ROAD PLUNGES INTO WHITE RIVER, TAKES FIRE AND IS CONSUMED—BETWEEN FIFTY AND SIXTY LIVES LOST.

SEE PAGE 159.

The Hoosac Tunnel: Hell's Mouth

"This ride into the tunnel is far from being a cheerful one. The fitful glare of the lamps upon the walls of the dripping cavern—the frightful noises that echo from the low roof, and the ghoul-like voices of the miners coming out of the gloom ahead, are not what would be called enlivening." *–Scribner's,* December 1870

If Mother Earth had a mouth, it would probably resemble the gaping orifice known as the Hoosac Tunnel in North Adams, Massachusetts. It seemed that cold breath belched from the dark opening on the raw spring day that *Weird New England* ventured there. Groundwater dripped from the ceiling like saliva. Toothlike chunks of ice and bricks crashed lethally to the floor as if the tunnel were biting at us. Sounds echoed deep inside like gastrointestinal distress. Truly, the place sounded hungry. There was no doubt we were looking at a monster, a man-made leviathan that, in its birth throes, took the lives of nearly two hundred people.

Today the Hoosac Tunnel is considered one of the most haunted spots in New England. Think about it: A tunnel nearly five miles long. A sinister nineteenth-century precursor to Massachusetts's "Big Dig."

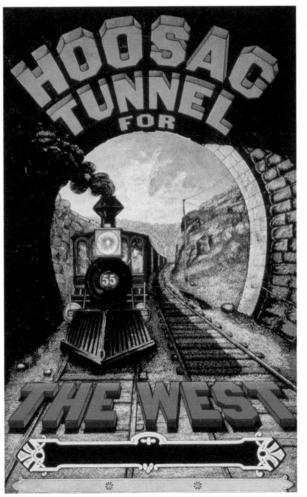

Before it was built, you really couldn't get there—wherever your destination—from here. The mountains proved an unyielding obstacle to commerce. A railroad tunnel seemed just the solution, a direct route through the earth itself.

But almost from the moment construction commenced in the early 1850s, bad luck prevailed. The digging started with an innovative boring machine that immediately got stuck in the rock. No one could extricate it. The crew had to start over in a different spot. Meanwhile, another team commenced digging five miles away on the other side of the Hoosac Mountains.

It's hard to imagine how they could dig from both ends at once, bore a horizontal shaft through mountains almost two thousand feet high, and meet in the middle. Somehow, using plumb bobs, piano wire, and pencils, they managed, creating what was then America's longest tunnel—almost five miles long, twenty-four feet wide, twenty feet tall. The two headings, as they were called, met almost perfectly; they were less than an inch off!

The tunnel is slightly inclined in both directions from the elevated middle. This is so water will run out, but it also prevents a clear view straight through the mountain. Looking

trace. Had he run away or somehow vanished? Either could have been the case as fellow workers became convinced that the angry ghosts of Misters Brinkman and Nash were wandering the dark pit.

Exactly one year later to the day, Ringo Kelley's body turned up in the tunnel—precisely where the men had died. He'd been strangled. Deputy Sheriff Charles E. Gibson investigated, determining that death had occurred between midnight and three a.m. of the day Mr. Kelley had been discovered. But no clues, not even footprints, were ever found. No suspect was ever identified.

Perhaps the tunnel's worst calamity took place on October 17, 1867. Crews had half completed digging the central shaft, a thousand-foot vertical conduit that was intended to mark the halfway point and eventually to provide tunnel ventilation. This opening would also become the fastest way of introducing laborers into the center of the tunnel, by dropping them in a giant bucket rather than trucking them in almost two and one-half miles from either end.

But thirteen men would never see the hole completed. Fumes from a naphtha-fueled lamp somehow escaped and exploded, setting fire to the hoist house above. A deadly hail of three hundred newly sharpened drill bits rained down on the men below. The winching machinery and flaming fragments of the hoist house followed. Air pumps

in, you can see only black—the tunnel seems to go on forever.

The whole project took twenty-four years and cost over $21 million (about $300 million today). Predictably, problems continued throughout the construction, so many, in fact, that numerous laborers decided the tunnel was cursed. Some walked off the job and never came back. Deaths and desertion made the required eight hundred to nine hundred jobs difficult to keep filled.

And then there was the notion that the tunnel was haunted. . . .

Dark Deaths Under the Ground

On March 20, 1865, explosives expert Ringo Kelley, working on the Hoosac Tunnel project, prematurely touched off a blast that killed his two companions, Ned Brinkman and Billy Nash, crushing them under untold tons of rock. Soon after, Mr. Kelley disappeared without a ceased to function, leaving the miners stranded and without oxygen as the pit began to fill with water. Helpless onlookers realized that nothing could be done except to speculate whether the men would suffocate or drown.

Over the next few months and all through the winter, people in the vicinity reported indistinct shapes near the water-filled pit. Some even heard muffled cries that seemed to be coming from the earth itself. Whenever it snowed or the mountaintop was engulfed in heavy fog, laborers swore they saw miners carrying axes and shovels—who appear for a moment, then vanish. Upon investigation, no footprints could be seen in the undisturbed snow.

These eerie visitations subsided a year later, after workers made a grisly discovery. After the flooded shaft was finally emptied of water, the last of the bodies was recovered. Though some had been killed by falling drill bits and debris, others had apparently survived the initial assault. Somehow, they had managed to construct a crude raft to keep from drowning, but their efforts had proved fruitless. They perished miserably, victims of asphyxiation or, worse, starvation.

When at long last they were buried, their specters seemed to be at rest.

Following these and other similar reports, a Dr. Clifford J. Owens decided to act as an early ghost buster. His account of his expedition into the tunnel is reported in Carl R. Byron's book *A Pinprick of Light:* "On the night of June 25, 1872, [Drilling Superintendent] James McKinstrey and I entered the great excavation at precisely 11:30 p.m. We had traveled about two miles into the shaft when we halted to rest. Except for the dim, smoky light cast by our lamps, the place was as cold and dark as a tomb. . . . Suddenly I heard a strange mournful sound. The next thing I saw was a dim light coming from . . . a westerly direction. At first, I believed it was a workman with a lantern. Yet, as the light drew closer, it took on a strange blue color and . . . the form of a human being without a head. The light seemed to be floating along about a foot or two above the tunnel floor. . . . The headless form came so close that I could have reached out and touched it, but I was too terrified to move.

"For what seemed like an eternity, McKinstrey and I stood there gaping at the headless thing like two wooden Indians. The blue light remained motionless for a few seconds as if it were actually looking us over, then floated off toward the east end of the shaft and vanished. . . ."

They Went In, But They Never Came Out

Ghosts vanish in the Hoosac Tunnel, but so do people. And they don't always reappear in the manner of Ringo Kelley.

Take Frank Webster, for example. In October 1874, he vanished. When searchers found him days later, he was in shock. Finally he explained that weird voices had called him into the tunnel. Once inside, he saw ghostly figures milling about. They took his hunting rifle away from him and beat him with it. He had the scars to prove it—but no rifle.

The next year Harlan Mulvaney, an employee of the Boston & Maine Railroad, fled the tunnel in an unexplained panic and subsequently vanished. He was never seen or heard from again.

A century later, in 1973, Bernard Hastaba set out to walk through the tunnel. He entered at the North Adams portal but, strange as it seems, he never emerged. And he couldn't be found inside. He has apparently vanished entirely. Perhaps he wandered into a secret room that's supposedly hidden near the center. It's bricked up, they say, and it's said to conceal horrors best not disturbed.

Hoosac's Unspeakable Horrors

In 1984, while in the tunnel with a railroad official, a professor and part-time ghost hunter named Ali Allmaker had the uncomfortable sensation of someone standing close to her. She reports, "I can attest to the claim that it is an eerie place. I had the uncomfortable feeling that someone was walking closely behind me and would tap me on the shoulder at any moment or, worse, pull me into some unknown and unspeakable horror."

In 1994, Kevin from Boston reported that while in the old control room opposite the ventilation shaft, he heard "whisperings" and saw a "shape" about three feet tall and completely black. "It always stayed just outside the beam of my flashlight, about twenty feet distant. I have to conclude it was the light that kept it away from me. What I saw was real and moved with deliberation, and I didn't have reason to believe it was friendly."

Locals in the area still claim that strange winds, ghostly apparitions, and eerie voices are experienced around and in the daunting tunnel. Some researchers have left tape recorders in the tunnel and have reported hearing what seems to be muffled voices when they play back the tape. There is also rumor of a "hidden room" in the tunnel. The room is said to be bricked up and house unspeakable horror. Balls of bluish light and "ghost lanterns" are also said to haunt the tunnel, and legends abound of "ghost hands" both pushing people in front of oncoming trains, as well as pulling them to safety.

—Dan Boudillion

Faces of Fire

Some people contend that islands are especially haunted places because of the old notion that ghosts—for whatever reason—cannot cross water. Therefore, resident spirits are stuck, making islands little containment areas for supernatural entities. In her book *Peripheral Visions,* Judith W. Monroe records a highly unusual haunting on Swans Island, Maine. It is so bizarre that it is well worth examining.

Swans Island is eight miles long and six miles across. It's separated from the mainland by a forty-minute ferry ride south from Bass Harbor. Made up of three small villages, its total living population hovers around 327 souls. The number of summer visitors is unpredictable, and the total ghost population is yet to be determined. Apparently there are a fair number—three are unique in New England ghost lore.

Ethel, for many years the island's postmistress, and her brother John recalled for Ms. Monroe an episode that happened to them around 1930 when they were children. One windy and starless night they were walking home, taking a shortcut near a cliff above the harbor. The night was bitterly cold, but luckily Johnny was wearing their father's oversized coat, which they discovered was big enough for both of them. Ethel put her right arm into the right sleeve; Johnny did the same with the left. Warmed by the coat and their proximity to each other, the children awkwardly made their way along the cliff path like some kind of two-headed, four-footed beast.

Johnny reminded Ethel that their shortcut would bring them near a cave with a dark reputation. In the old days, it was reputed to be a pirate hideout where booty was stashed. More recently, the cave had been used by bootleggers, since Swans Island has always been "dry." Illegal liquor and pirate treasure might have made the cave a tantalizing destination for two youngsters, but not that night. It was too cold, too dark.

As weird as the two children must have looked struggling along in a single overcoat, they were soon to witness something far stranger. It began with an unfamiliar noise coming approximately from the spot where they believed the cave to be located. As they stood staring into the darkness, shivering more from fear than from the cold, something began to emerge from the blackness—something bright, like fire.

Then, between them and the ocean, an explosion of light reared up from beyond the edge of the cliff. At first, it was a shapeless mass, a fireball, but then it began to separate into three distinct flaming spheres—one large and two smaller. To the

bulky overcoat made rapid motion impossible. After floundering and falling, they finally freed themselves from the confining fabric. Now using it as a shield, they fled in the direction they had come, never daring to look back to see if the blazing demonic faces were pursuing them along the dangerous cliffside path.

Somehow, pulses pounding, they made it back to safety. Only then did they dare to look behind them. The fiery phantoms had vanished. The terrified children took the long way home.

When they dared to tell their parents about their strange adventure, the details were not met with the dismissive derision they expected. Their mother simply said, "It would be better, I think, if you didn't go up that way again at night." Their father added, "Once, years ago, a man died up there on that hill. Maybe it was him."

children's amazement, each fiery ball had the unmistakable features of a face: eyes, ears, nose, mouth. The flaming heads spouted gusts of fire as they hovered there against the black backdrop of night.

Seized by terror, the children tried to run, but the

Nothing more was ever said about their strange adventure, but the image of those three flaming heads was burned into their memories for the rest of their lives.

Green and White and Dead All Over

Be alert while traveling through Burlington, Connecticut. Many travelers have encountered a strange green mist that forms before their eyes into the shape of a beautiful woman. The apparition, fittingly enough, has come to be known as the Green Lady of Burlington. This gentle ghost will appear without warning, glow green for a while, smile at you, then just fade away.

Legends say that her grave is located in a small cemetery tucked away in the woods down a back road near her former home. In the Green Lady's time, this area was rather remote, with not much around except a garbage dump. It is said that her life ended when she drowned in a nearby swamp. Some say that she glows green because she is covered in muck and slime as she rises from the swampy ground in which she is buried.

Curious locals still visit the cemetery in hopes of encountering the Green Lady. Those who believe that they have discovered her former residence report that they have seen a portrait of her through an open window. The picture hangs in a dimly lit room in the otherwise dark and spooky old house.

Easton, Connecticut, is the home of Union Cemetery, regarded as one of the most haunted locations in the entire United States. Many have reported supernatural encounters occurring within the borders of this burial ground. Most common are reports of the infamous White Lady.

The White Lady has been seen by hundreds of people, most often walking among the graves of the cemetery in the dead of the night. She also occasionally walks the roads in the surrounding area. She wears a white nightgown and a bonnet.

—Chris Gethard

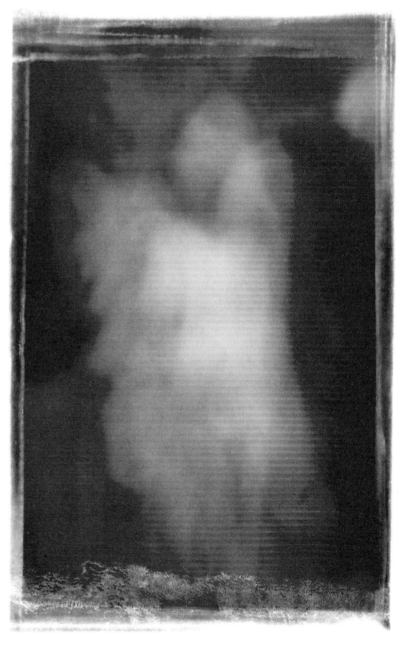

Old Stagecoach Inn

The biggest trouble with ghost stories is that most of them are the same. We hear about minor disturbances: footsteps in empty rooms, lights switching off and on, and myriad things that go bump in the night. For a ghost to really hit the big time, it has to do something remarkable.

In Waterbury, Vermont, the Old Stagecoach Inn has a long-standing reputation for being haunted. Supposedly, the spirit of former owner Nettie Spencer lingers there. She died at age ninety-nine, suggesting her reluctance to leave.

When Jack Barwick and his son John bought the inn in 1993, they dismissed the legends. Jack, a former scientist with several patents in his name, said, "We started out as confirmed skeptics . . . but after we'd been here a while, we began to reexamine this—because things were happening!"

Room cleaners saw chairs rocking by themselves. Freshly made beds became mysteriously disheveled. A bottle of Irish whiskey vanished under the nose of a bartender.

But the Oscar—or should I say Caspar—winning performance was a little stunt the ghost pulled off in the fall of 1995.

It was a Sunday morning, and the inn was busy and full. Suddenly, Jack saw three people coming down the stairs for breakfast—people he didn't recognize. He had personally checked everybody in, so he knew all the guests.

He approached them politely and asked, "Which room are you staying in?"

They replied, "Room three."

Now the peculiar thing about room 3 was there'd been a last-minute cancellation the night before. And Jack was the only one who knew about it. "When did you arrive?"

he asked, his curiosity mounting.

"Around two this morning."

More puzzled than ever, Jack asked who had checked them in.

"An elderly woman," one of them explained, "wearing a long dress. She took us up to the room."

To this day Jack and John are puzzled by the incident. As Jack told us in a recent interview, "Now this thing really began to look weird." None of Jack's employees stay on the premises overnight. And none of the other guests fitted the old woman's description.

Locked door. Closed room. Cancellation that nobody knew about. Even if someone had wandered in off the street, how could they find the only vacant room in the place?

The description of the woman who let them in—elderly, long dress, with a bun in her gray hair—didn't fit anyone at the inn. The description fit Nettie Spencer, who's been lying in her grave since 1947.

The Haunting of Baerstead

In 1998, I moved to Ashby, Massachusetts. The house that I moved into was a great century-old Victorian and was very large. I was extremely excited to move into this house for it was unique in two ways: First, it had a name—Baerstead, which is from the last name of the original owner. Second, it was supposedly haunted. I got the large house for only $100,000 because of this second fact, and, my God, was it haunted.

The house had a very bizarre history. It was built in 1902 as a wedding gift by a Mr. Baer for his fiancée. But his fiancée would not live with him in it, for she wished to live in Boston. So he built a tower onto the house so that she might view Boston, and she agreed to marry him. They prospered in the house at first, but Mrs. Baer soon became depressed and ultimately killed herself. Some say her grave is located in the basement. (I have found an unmarked headstone, but have not probed for a grave.)

After Mr. Baer died, the house became the property of the town, which later sold it to an elderly man during WW II. This man was a Nazi. He was also insane. He went as far as to write a letter to the town counsel requesting that he be able to use the gas chamber he had created in his basement. He was sent to an asylum for obvious reasons, and the house then became a boarding home and a hippie commune.

The hauntings were first reported around this time. First, while removing the gas chamber from the basement, the house's then owner spotted a female specter. Then for many days the house was haunted by what seemed to be a poltergeist. Furniture was moved around with no explanation, and on the second and third floors, an odd fog was sighted, which materialized and dematerialized with no cause. Many a person was baffled by the eerie lights that emanated from the tower.

These hauntings continued after I bought the house. My dogs would bark at nothing, and would be hypnotized by walls. I'd see people in mirrors who were not in the room. Objects would go missing in rooms, and sounds would become distorted. The house has now been exorcised, and only once since have I spotted something that may have been a ghost. There is one anomaly, though, a section of my lawn leading to a path in the woods beyond my back door is always discolored and grows sickly in a set path, a very straight and very organized-looking path. I have found no reason for this.—*Webster*

Imprisoned Spirits

As recently as 2002, Maine newspapers were reporting strange goings-on at the new $76 million prison in Warren.

At night, while inmates slept, cell doors would unexpectedly swing open. The prisoners—at least those who were visible—made no attempt to escape, but it was as if something unseen were on its way out, or in.

The doors are made of steel and weigh about four hundred pounds each. Since they are operated by pneumatic locks and compressed air, the spontaneous openings may be nothing more than a mechanical glitch. Or something supernatural could be at work. Either way, phantom door openings are not what you want in a prison.

While no one is quick to holler "Ghosts!," the whispering goes on. After all, such liberating antics are familiar in Maine jails. The same thing happened at the Androscoggin County Jail in Auburn and the Cumberland County Jail in Portland.

In fact, one might conclude that jailhouse ghosts are something of a tradition in the Pine Tree State. They are in the newest jails and in the oldest.

In York, which was settled about 1623, is a creepy barnlike structure known as the Old Gaol. It is the oldest prison in the country. Today it is preserved by the local historical society, so it is exactly as it was in the 1700s. It's always dark, frigid, or stifling, depending on the season, and hopelessly secure. Some ingenious gaolkeeper even installed sharpened saw blades as window frames. If an escapee somehow managed to sever the inner iron bars, they'd flay their hide wriggling through the narrow opening.

One memorable woman prisoner was an Indian slave named Patience Boston, accused of drowning her master's baby. Patience was pregnant when she was incarcerated and gave birth to a son. She was hanged when he was still a baby.

Today the jail has an eerie exhibit. You can sit outside the window where long ago the Reverend Moody heard Patience's confession. If you push a button, you'll hear a reenacted recording of that same confession—a ghostly experience in a spooky environment.

But stranger still is that the electronic ghost is apparently understudied by a real one. An odd spirit has been seen wafting around the old jail. Though, strictly speaking, the specter's identity is unknown, Patience is the prime suspect.

Over the years, many spirit confrontations have occurred in the Old Gaol. Today some modern museum workers refuse to remain in the building alone—especially as it begins to get dark.

If the oldest and newest of Maine's jails are haunted, their ghostly antics seem to suggest some kind of elusive metaphor: Ghosts are trapped here, yes, but something more powerful than prisons must be holding them.

Cemetery Safari

Each of the United States likes to boast about something. Some state may claim it has the most scenic views, or the tastiest maple syrup, or the longest seacoast, or the shortest seacoast, whatever. Superlatives are essential to pride of place, not to mention successful tourism. One of New England's bragging rights might very well be that its cemeteries, and the tombs within them, are the weirdest in the nation!

Hell's Eighth Gate?

Step into the lush green grounds behind the so-called Spider Gates Cemetery in Leicester, Massachusetts, at your peril. More than one person has run screaming from the place, pursued by . . . who can say? For some reason, this lovely spot has picked up a tarnished reputation. Some people even assert it's the eighth gate to hell!

On his informative website, Daniel V. Boudillion (www.boudillion.com) chronicles some of the horror stories that have come out of the spider's web: Folks say that the place is haunted, that disembodied voices can be heard there while unknown things rustle in the shadows on windless nights. There's a patch of ground where no grass will grow and another where a mysterious white substance oozes from the earth. Supposedly, the cemetery contains a raised area, known

as the Altar, where satanists have permission to conduct their diabolical rituals. As if to confirm this, some people swear they have heard terrifying roaring sounds in the woodland around the cemetery. Outside the stone wall that surrounds the cemetery are a random scattering of sizeable rocks. If you turn them over, you'll discover indecipherable runes etched by unknown hands.

Directly across from the gate, there is allegedly a second cemetery. And, not far from that, there's said to be a cave where a girl was killed and mutilated, and a tree where, during the 1980s, a young man hanged himself. Somewhere close by, a haunted house waits for an unwary victim, and there's a swamp in the vicinity that all would be well advised never to enter.

What can it all mean?

It is difficult to determine why this peaceful Quaker burial spot—with graves dating back to the 1700s—should have picked up such an unsavory reputation. The only real explanation is the provocative effect the unusual design of the gates may have on the dark side of the imagination. The wrought-iron sunburstlike patterns do

in fact look like spiderwebs. Hence the name. In truth, Spider Gates Cemetery is actually called Friends Cemetery, though it doesn't always seem to be friendly.

We can't guarantee anything supernatural will happen if you venture there by night, but we can promise you an unpleasant experience. Friends Cemetery is private property and is heavily patrolled, closely guarded, and peppered with motion detectors. Goblins and ghouls may or may not be waiting to grab you, but the police sure are.

To Hell's Gate and Back

I initially investigated Spider Gates with a friend on November 17, 2001, a crisp, clear autumn morning. First, the cemetery was hard to find and we did quite a bit of driving around, feeling puzzled. The road maps and topographical maps show its location, Earle Street, to be a public throughway, not a narrow gated private dirt road. It took a while to sort all this out. The cemetery is in the woods between the Worcester Airport and the Leicester Landfill. Earle Street is several hundred feet up Manville Street from the landfill entrance.

We parked near the landfill and proceeded to bushwhack our

way through the woods. This was a mistake because it necessitated having to cross Kettle Brook, a rather vigorous small river. In any event, we did indeed find Spider Gates.

Spider Gates is a beautiful cemetery in a sylvan setting. It is on a small rise, surrounded by trees. Its walls are aligned to the cardinal compass points, the gate being in the north wall. We thoroughly explored the cemetery and the surrounding countryside for anything to substantiate its reputation as a magnet for unholy powers.

First—and this needs to be made clear—there is only ONE gate, not eight. There is just one entrance—the main one with the wrought-iron spiderweb pattern. Whether this truly is the Eighth Gate to Hell, I can't say. Certainly, I did not experience anything untoward upon entering the cemetery through it.

The gates themselves are of interest. Although the pattern of the wrought-iron gates is said to be a spiderweb pattern, it is actually more of a sunburst pattern with radiating wavy rays. They have a distinct Art Deco look to them.

Immediately to the left upon entering the cemetery is a large oak tree. Attached to a fork about fifteen feet up is a short length of thick weathered twine that hangs down about a foot or so. I would speculate that this is the "hanging tree." There is no official record of anyone ever hanging themselves here, however, and I would guess it is the twine that gave rise to the rumor.

Some visitors report hearing a roaring from the woods. Others speak of leaves rustling when there is no wind, and still others claim to have heard voices. All I can say to this is that the cemetery is literally under the landing approach for Worcester Airport, and certainly there is the occasional roar, but from above.

Our investigation of the immediate grounds complete, we looked for the cave where the girl was said to have been killed. We did not find any obvious caves, but did find on the southern slope behind the cemetery a small overhang of rock. Also, not far away the old path of Earle Street crosses a once marshy area over a Shaker-style laid-stone culvert. The culvert was conceivably large enough to stuff a body in, but again there is the problem that there is no official record of a girl being murdered in this area.

Further along, the old path of Earle Street runs through a swamp and up a steep hill to Mulberry Road. Interestingly, it is the base of the hill on Earle Street, and not the cemetery, that is the site where most of the reports of frightening encounters and eerie feelings have actually originated. Grown men have been known to run from this spot in terror and for no known or obvious reason. I, however, did not run from this spot in terror, and I can only hope this is not a derogatory reflection on my manhood.

We searched high and low for the second cemetery, the one that can only be found once. We did locate a cemetery close by at a Catholic home for orphaned boys. It was a sad melancholy little place. On the way home we drove by it on Mulberry Road, thus finding it for a second time. I would imagine this disqualifies it to be the one indicated in the rumor.

Is Spider Gates haunted? Is it a home of Unholy Powers, perhaps a gate of hell? My visit did not reveal anything to confirm this reputation. I found it to be a quiet, pleasant, woodland place. But perhaps the true test is a nighttime visit, and it has been noted that supernatural events tend to find those who aren't actually looking for them.—*Daniel V. Boudillion*

Demons Can Go to Hell at Spider Gates

There is a small town on the outskirts of Boston, and on one side there is a huge forest. If you walk far enough into them you see there are eight gates that look like steel spiderwebs with locks. If you walk through all of them, I heard there is a clearing. Legend has it if you enter the clearing at night and attempt to walk out back through the gates, you will be killed by some spirit.

They say that a bunch of devil worshippers practiced there and were one night conjuring a demon, but they called up the wrong demon and were all killed. So now the demon protects the clearing and will kill anyone who enters it and tries to leave. I heard this is because the devil worshippers would sacrifice a person before leaving so the demon they called up for the night would be satisfied and would go back to hell willingly.—*Nate*

Hope Cemetery

To Vermonters, Hope Cemetery on Route 14 in Barre is the crown jewel of all cemeteries, the Uffizi of necropolises. Situated in the proximity of Vermont's famous marble and granite quarries, it is where many talented stone carvers left their mark, themselves, and their families. These artists, with names like Giuseppe Donati, Lambruno Sarzanini, Antonio Soprano, and Giuliano Cecchinelli, created distinct monuments, from morbid to majestic, from classical to cartoonish. There's a dignified replica of Michelangelo's *Pieta*. Not far away you'll find a statue of a married couple holding hands, permanently tucked under the stony covers of a double bed. This is Hope's only R-rated memorial.

There's a replica of a stock car in white granite, recalling someone's passion while remembering his undoing. You'll also find a tractor-trailer, a basketball, an armchair, a globe, and more, reminding us, I suppose, that we can die anywhere and anything can be lethal.

Praise for the Stonesmiths of Hope Cemetery

Coming from New Hampshire, the Granite State, I had heard rumors of the famous monument carvers from Barre, VT. But I was unprepared for the astonishing tombstones of Hope Cemetery. Opened in 1895, this graveyard is an art gallery, celebrating life in the midst of death with some of the most compelling and quirky tombstones in the nation.

I arrived on an appropriately gray and threatening day in July and toured, first by car and then on foot, moving from stone to stone— touching and marveling. While the average New England tombstone evokes a dull finality, these sculptures speak volumes about both the deceased and the carver.

One final resting place is a stuffed armchair. In another, a couple lie in their granite double bed, together as in life, pajamas on. In Hope Cemetery, the angels sometimes look bored with eternity, while massive gravestones rise like Greek temples nearby. No subject is too offbeat, personal, or creative for the carvers of Barre, the Granite Capital of the World, from soccer balls and airplanes to cars and trucks. One carver evokes an image of the dead man's wife in the smoke of his cigar. In another stone, reminiscent of Michelangelo's *Pieta*, a woman clasps a turn-of-the-century workman. We from New Hampshire salute the stone carvers of Vermont who refuse to give death the final word. Bravo!—*J. Dennis Robinson/ SeacoastNH.com*

Blood Cemetery

Another New England necropolis with a spooky reputation is Pine Hill Cemetery on Nartoff Road in Hollis, New Hampshire. Locally it is known as Blood Cemetery, but not for any sanguinary reason. It's only because a family named Blood is interred there.

Since the cemetery is the last known address of many of the town's founding fathers (and mothers), enough time has passed to create some pretty scary stories. For example, the ghost of Abel Blood is said to prowl the grounds at night while the finger on his headstone—normally pointing heavenward—will supposedly change direction after dark. Beware if it points at you!

Anyone trying to photograph these phenomena is likely to find unexplained orbs in the pictures. Ghosts, perhaps? Some people, using tape recorders, claim to have picked up strange tapping sounds on their recordings. Morse code from reanimated corpses? Or maybe ghastly ghouls trying to escape their burial boxes?

Truth? Rumor? Hoax? Only the dead know for sure.

Center Church

Probably the weirdest, eeriest, and most unusual cemetery we've seen is in a churchyard that is not next to—but rather under—the church. The Center Church, on the town green in New Haven, Connecticut, was built over an existing graveyard. So to visit the graves, you have to enter the church and follow the signs that direct you to the crypt. There, where you would expect to see Sunday school classrooms and a space for church suppers, are rows of ancient tombstones embedded in the earthen floor. It's an underground cemetery with stones dating back to 1687. There are 137 identified bodies in this puritanical underworld, including those of New Haven founder Theophilus Eaton, Yale founder James Pierpont, Margaret Arnold (Benedict's first wife), and the grandparents of Rutherford B. Hayes. Some estimates suggest there are another thousand underchurch bodies left to be identified.

Grass doesn't do very well here in this damp, lightless environment, but at least the stones are protected from the elements, vandals, and the ravages of time. Still, it can be a dangerous place. Visitors have to watch their heads and feet at the same time—no easy task: The crypt's ceiling is low, while many headstones are small and easy to trip over.

Dreary Dennis

New England chronicler Edward Rowe Snow claims that the cemetery in Dennis, Massachusetts, on Cape Cod is the ugliest graveyard in the East. He says, "It is hard to conceive of the diabolical ugliness of some of the stones here." He then points out the monument of Major Micah Chapman, who stands forever dressed in full military regalia—wig, waistcoat, buttons, and blouse. The major seems to be guarding his own grave—from what, we don't know. The aesthetic police, perhaps? Or cannibals?

Not far away, Mr. Snow tells us, we can view the "rather ghastly" grave of Joseph Hall, who died in 1787 at age sixty-three. His monument depicts a human skull ghoulishly sinking its upper teeth into one of the (human) crossbones we often see associated with pirate flags.

With more oddities in the background, this seems just the spot to inspire ghost stories and other weird tales.

The Phantom and the Madonna

St. John's Roman Catholic Cemetery in Northfield, Vermont, has a ghostly gravedigger who cares for it and its haunted statue: a tomb-top effigy of the holy Madonna. If you decide to go looking for her, you may find that she's also looking for you.

One lifelong Northfield resident tells of a spooky Halloween night in the late 1960s. He, along with some high school friends, grabbed a few illegal beers and headed out to the cemetery for some Halloween fun. They got more than they expected.

Hiding among the stones, the boys growled and moaned, trying to scare each other and anyone else who might be lurking around. Today the Northfield man recalls the ensuing events:

"It's pitch black and windy, and I'm near this huge statue of the holy Madonna. The other guys are down at the other end hiding. Then I hear these noises, like digging. I turn and see this old guy shoveling away. There was this weird glow around him. Then—I swear this—I saw the head of the Madonna turn slowly towards me. That's when I got the hell out!"

Smart move.

Confrontations with the disapproving Madonna are relatively rare, but Northfield's Phantom Gravedigger has been on the scene for decades. Generally he's spotted at night while his corporeal colleagues are safely snoozing in their beds. He'll be toting his pick and shovel or carrying his glowing lantern as he walks among the dark headstones.

White Lady of Union Cemetery

Easton, in southwestern Connecticut, is the home of what may be the most celebrated cemetery phantom in the country. She is the famous White Lady. For more than half a century, she has been putting in unscheduled nighttime appearances at Union Cemetery, near the Easton Baptist Church. Literally hundreds of people have met her. Some witnesses perceive her as a refugee from another time as she drifts about in her white ruffled nightgown, bonnet, and long, braided hair. Certain witnesses have reported frightening dark, shadowy figures clutching at her from behind trees and tombstones.

This extraordinary phantom will, on occasion, exit the cemetery for solitary sojourns nearby. About a decade ago she was strolling along the road when local fireman Glenn Pennell accidentally rammed into her with his truck. His vehicle passed right through her!

This very haunted cemetery boasts even more spectral occupants. Visitors frequently report conversations with what seem to be people. They look, talk, and act like living human beings—until they abruptly vanish before the witnesses' startled eyes.

Photographers have been able to get pictures of Easton's cemetery phantoms. Graveyard photos often disclose shapes that were not visible when the picture was snapped.

But BEWARE! Easton's White Lady has become something of a local celebrity. Her happy haunting ground is closed from sunset to sunrise, and town police see it as their duty to ensure that the dead rest in peace.

A Graveyard with a Sense of Humor

The newer of the two town cemeteries on Faxen Hill Road in Washington, New Hampshire, is not such a grave place. In fact, it seems to have more than its share of entertaining gravestones. There's the grave of the leg for instance.

Seems that one Captain Samuel Jones lost a leg in a construction accident and decided to give it a dignified burial, complete with a funeral and its own head-, or maybe, footstone. It reads CAPT. SAMUEL JONES LEG WHICH WAS AMPUTATED JULY 7, 1804. When the rest of the captain died some years later, he was interred in Boston, Massachusetts, making him one of the few people buried in two states. In Captain Samuel Jones's case, R.I.P. means "Rest in Pieces."

If you look up from Mr. Jones's footstone, you might get a kick out of what you see. There, near the top of the hill, is a perfect stone sphere. Nothing funny about that, you might say. Well, not until you read the family name: It's Ball. Could that humor have been intentional?

There may be nothing really funny about this third grave; however, it is a true rarity in this part of the world. If you can locate what is probably the biggest stone in the cemetery, you'll see what we're talking about. It proudly brandishes the Soviet hammer and sickle. This is the final resting place of Fred and Elba Chase (died 1933 and 1967). Their stone recalls them as "courageous and devoted fighters in the class struggle." As far as we know, this is the only tombstone in New England bearing such an insignia and epitaph. One suspects the town is not too happy about it; the Chase grave seems more overgrown and hidden than the rest.

Happy Face or Sad Face?

If you don't know whether to laugh or cry at the Washington gravestones, you'll face a similar dilemma at the Chester Village Cemetery in Chester, New Hampshire. In fact, the stones themselves seem equally confused. Look for a number of pre-1800 tombstones with faces carved upon them. Now look again. Some of the faces are smiling; some are frowning. Exactly what determined who got a smile and who got a frown has long been the subject of conjecture.

One story maintains the stones are the work of two carvers, Abel and Stephen Webster. Supposedly, the brothers carved a smile or a frown depending on how they assessed the deceased's chances of achieving eternal salvation or damnation. Those who have studied the matter guess that all Abel's effigies are smiling, while all Stephen's frown. Different temperaments? Sterner religious convictions? The why of it is still a mystery.

Another explanation holds that Chester had but one stone carver, who was continually in the habit of creating happy-faced effigies. Then he got religion. After trying unsuccessfully to convert his neighbors, he packed up and left town in a huff. But since he was the only stonecutter around, the townsfolk still required his services. However, after his exodus, he would carve only disapproving frowns.

The Chester Village Cemetery also has another unrelated oddity worthy of mention. It may record an early example of what we now call near-death experiences. On the grave of Lydia A. Webster (died 1862, age thirty) is etched circumstantial evidence of an experience described by many who claim to have returned from death's door. Her tomb bears her actual last words, "It is all light now."

Alas, Lydia didn't return.

Okay, so maybe it was just a misspelling, all right?

The Mysterious Finger

If you enjoy graveyard puzzles and mysteries, there is no better spot than the Methodist Cemetery in Whitefield, New Hampshire. During the 1860s and '70s it was fashionable to carve gravestones with a finger pointing heavenward. The meaning is obvious: "Going home," "Going up," "Gone above," "Gone to God," whatever.

But Whitefield's Cemetery offers a perplexing variation. The stone of Ira Bowles (died January 10, 1863, age sixty-two) has a pointing finger, all right. But it's pointing straight down!

What does it mean? Who would want to mark their final resting place with a finger pointing hellward? Nobody seems to have the answer.

And while you're trying to figure that out, factor this in: While no other New England town has such an aberration, Whitefield has a second such finger! Look at the grave of Henry A. Lane (died September 17, 1866, age twenty-two) in the Pine Street Cemetery. Could the interred have been a suicide or criminal? It's hard to believe that grieving parents would spend a lot of money on a marker alerting the community to their son's presumed damnation.

Why do such stones exist here and no place else? It's beyond us.

Pampered unto Death

It used to be more aptly named Bow-Wow Villa. Now it's part of K-9 Instincts Kennel on Wapping Road in Portsmouth, Rhode Island. But whatever you call it, it's still the spot where the rich and famous from Newport and thereabouts buried their tiny dead loved ones. Not their children, their pets. This is a graveyard for elite animals, a pet cemetery full of terminally cute headstones. Fluffy, Phydough, and Phi-phi rest eternally beside parrots and ferrets, continually receiving the special treatment they were so accustomed to in life. A distinguished monument is that of Pookie, a departed pooch once belonging to the Duke and Duchess of Windsor. Pet lovers may enjoy the excesses of such lavish animal adoration. Animal haters may enjoy spending time in a pet-crowded place that is pleasantly quiet and where you don't have to watch where you step.

Persecuted for wearing the beard.

Looney Tombs

People can demonstrate their eccentricity just as well after death as they do while they're alive. In the following stories we will look at some odd individual graves, often the last known address of some who once populated the vast territory we call weird New England.

Bearded Bad Man

Right in the front of Evergreen Cemetery in Leominster, Massachusetts, there is a conspicuous stone on which is carved a handsome bearded face. The beard is large, full, and well groomed. Below, a caption reads, PERSECUTED FOR WEARING THE BEARD. The portrait is of Joseph Palmer and the beard that got him into trouble; he chose to wear it during a time when most men were clean-shaven. His nonconformity so enraged his neighbors that they perceived him as not only antisocial but overtly sinful. He was mocked on the street and castigated by his clergyman at the communion rail. After that, Mr. Palmer was physically attacked.

But he, not his attackers, was thrown into jail, judged guilty of "disturbing the peace by wearing a beard." Still, he refused to shave. A year later, when his sentence ended, he refused to leave the jail, insisting upon an official proclamation assuring his right to wear a beard. In 1831, his captors tied him to a chair and threw him out of the pokey.

By then, local newspapers had rallied to his defense, and public opinion began to shift in his favor. Today the whole unsavory incident is recalled in marble on Mr. Palmer's grave, assuring us that such intolerance will never happen again. Yeah, right.

DeWolf and the Door

The grave of Captain James DeWolf (1764–1837), in the family cemetery in Bristol, Rhode Island, is an out-of-the-way oddity in a historic and prosperous town. The affluence of the aptly named and unsavory Captain DeWolf came from the slave trade. He used a portion of his wealth to provide for his postretirement years (that is, his death) by converting a peaceful deer park into a private burying ground. There he had constructed an earthen mound some twenty feet high—a tomb for himself and his wife, Nancy. An iron door allowed family members to look into the crypt.

"As long as any of you are around," he told his children, "you'll see my gold teeth, even when the rest of us is dust." The captain died on Christmas Eve of 1837. Within a week, his wife followed him into the great beyond.

But he was wrong about the gold teeth. They didn't outlast him.

On the night of May 11, 1842, grave robber John Dickinson blasted open the door and pulled the captain's teeth. He also swiped a few gold buttons and an engraved coffin plate, but failed to discover the treasure that local legend swore was stashed within.

The mound, however, did outlast the captain and may be seen in the DeWolf family cemetery on Woodlawn Avenue. You can't miss it; it's the only mound there and has a tree growing out of it. Thirty-three other bodies—only a fraction of the huge DeWolf pack—are buried alongside the captain.

Penniless Pauper

The town of Ashford, Connecticut, didn't pay much attention to Lucas Douglass when he was alive. He never married, lived as a recluse, and died at seventy-two with neither friends nor family to mourn him. But folks got a big surprise after they found his lifeless body frozen on the street on a cold December night in 1895. The man they believed to be a penniless pauper had somehow squirreled away thousands of dollars, enough to erect for himself an imposing monument in the Westford Hill Cemetery. It is thirty-four feet high, carved from Italian marble, includes a headstone and sculpted urns, and bears a portrait of Mr. Douglass with the epitaph I HAVE HEARD THY CALL. There is a hundred-and-forty-foot-long stone wall around the entire plot. Today people pay more attention to his grave than they ever did to him. Each year hundreds of tourists spend a fair amount of money to visit the "pauper's" grave.

Stained in Maine

Right in the middle of the town of Bucksport, Maine, is a graveyard commemorating the town's seventeenth-century founder and leading citizen, Colonel Jonathan Buck. But the stone is imperfect. Directly under Colonel Buck's name there is a blemish in the shape of a foot and part of a leg. According to local lore, the stain cannot be removed. It is there, people say, as the result of a curse. Supposedly, Colonel Buck sentenced an innocent woman to death. Her last words were something like, "I'm innocent, and you know it. And I'll be back to dance on your grave."

After the colonel's own rendezvous with the grim reaper, townsfolk erected a monument in his honor, a giant stone obelisk befitting a man of such distinction. Though the stone was perfect at first, a shadow soon fell across it, a shadow that couldn't be erased. Clearly, it was a leg and foot. Had the doomed woman come back to dance on Jonathan Buck's grave? The question has been debated for centuries.

Grave of the Vampire

Forget about those plane tickets to Transylvania; if you want to see a vampire's grave, just head to Rhode Island. There, Mercy Brown, the most celebrated Yankee vampire, rests behind the Chestnut Hill Baptist Church in Exeter.

In January 1892, at age nineteen, Mercy was the third member of her family to die from a debilitating wasting disease. Folks began to suspect the deaths were the work of a vampire's cold kiss. To be certain, the Browns dug up their fallen family. Two had been properly reduced to skeletons, but Mercy was still looking pretty good. Worse, it was clear she had somehow moved in her coffin. And—horror upon horror—there was still "fresh blood" in her veins and heart!

Case closed. Mercy was the vampire.

Village elders knew exactly what to do. They cut out her heart, burned it, and used the ashes to concoct a grisly homeopathic remedy for the survivors to ingest. Evidence would suggest that the cure worked; there were no more vampires reported in Exeter. But something weird still visits the old graveyard. People continue to tell of a mysterious floating ball of light that hovers around Mercy's grave or drifts among the other headstones.

The Light Fantastic

The people of Portsmouth, New Hampshire, may be enjoying a one-of-a-kind phenomenon. Trouble is, it's in a graveyard: the South Street Cemetery. Weird as it seems, one of the gravestones appears to glow. Regardless of the temperature or weather conditions, it shines while its neighbors remain unrecognizable shadows. The glow stone is one of three nearly identical markers standing in a row, but only the middle one lights up. It can be seen from at least two hundred yards away. This inexplicable luminescence has persisted now for more than twenty years. Hundreds of people have seen it, but no one has successfully explained it.

Some say it's supernatural, that it must be the grave of a murderer or murder victim. Others say it's natural, that the stone must contain luminous properties, like uranium. Or maybe it is simply a reflection of a streetlight, electric sign, or traffic light (though everyone agrees it can't be the moon because it reliably glows, even on moonless nights).

Local writer George Hosker sums the mystery up rather nicely. "I'm always amazed," he says, "that people who doubt the glow have no trouble accepting that light can bounce two hundred yards from the street, reflect off the pond, and hit one particular tombstone."

The Tomb of a Selfish Snob

In Brownsville, Vermont, is a remarkable mausoleum. It is atop Strawberry Hill, not part of any cemetery, and contains but a single occupant, Daniel Leavens Cady. Dan is alone by choice—not even his wife was allowed to join him—and positioned so he can continue his lifelong habit of looking down on the village and its inhabitants.

Mr. Cady did have impressive accomplishments. He was a prominent lawyer, then a judge. And after retirement wrote a popular newspaper column. But folks knew the truth: The long-haired, rotund, and egomaniacal Cady was an arrogant, selfish sot.

Grave Stone

Hiram Smith of Chester, Massachusetts, was repulsed by the notion of being buried in the ground. Perhaps he never stated precisely why, but it's easy to guess the possible reasons: worms, insects, rot, bloating, and grave-disrupting floods. Hiram wanted more secure conditions, so he commissioned a unique tomb. He found a huge boulder, ten feet high by thirty feet wide, on a ridge far from any waterways. He had its face smoothed and had two coffin-size cavities, one above the other, dug into the solid rock.

After Hiram died in 1873, his remains were sealed up with slabs of the original stone. The other cavity was filled with the body of Sarah Toogood, who may have been his wife or sister. Whatever the case, the couple will spend eternity together, properly stacked in bunk beds within their stone duplex.

Intended to resemble Napoleon's tomb, his enormous self-designed monument bears a lengthy epitaph he composed in Latin. There are two copies cast in bronze, one outside the mausoleum and—for some reason—the other within. But his departing swipe is composed in English. It says, in effect, if you can't read Latin, you have no business here.

His neighbors, however, got the last laugh: Cady died on April Fools' Day. Even his Roman numerals can't disguise that.

A Rhode Island Rose

Pioneering oddity collector Charles Fort wrote about Rose Ferron in his book *Wild Talents*. He said, "Rose Ferron, aged 25 . . . had, since March 17, 1916, been a stigmatic. . . . The hysterical condition of this girl—in both the common and the medical meaning of the term—is indicated by the circumstance that for three years she had been strapped to her bed, with only her right arm free."

She was a rare Rose indeed, an American stigmatic, perhaps the only one New England has ever produced. Wounds, said to replicate those of Jesus Christ, spontaneously appeared on her hands, feet, and forehead. When she died on May 11, 1936, at age thirty-three, her mystical crown of thorns was visible and photographed. Though essentially ignored by the Roman Catholic Church, Little Rose still has a devoted following who attest to the many miracles she caused to happen. Eleven years after her death, when her remains were

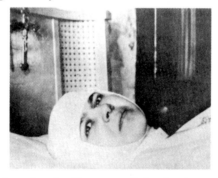

exhumed, they were found to be "incorrupt"; her body had not decayed (which must mean something).

The Ferron house, at 302 Providence Street in Woonsocket, Rhode Island, is where the family lived after Rose died. They resided across the street at Number 271 when her earthly death occurred. Today Rose, corrupt or incorrupt, rests in Woonsocket's Precious Blood Cemetery. Her grave, many believe, has miraculous attributes. Lately her relics, said to be equally miraculous, have been for sale on eBay.

Time Capsule or Tomb?

This little-known and most intriguing grave site may be just what you're looking for . . . if you can find it. It's lost somewhere on the slopes of Deer Mountain, not far from the Maine town of Wilsons Mills. Historian Richard Pinette says the unusual entombment is "especially bizarre!" And his adjective could not be better chosen.

The tomb, hidden somewhere in the north woods, is gigantic! And what it is said to contain is nearly unbelievable: an entire B-17 Flying Fortress, a colossal World War II bomber.

The story is that the plane took off, heading for England. But as the humongous craft reached the vicinity of Deer Mountain, something went horribly wrong. Pilot error? Equipment failure? No one knows. All that is certain is that the Flying Fortress lost altitude and crashed. There were no survivors. A military mission was dispatched into the wilds to retrieve the bodies, and they brought out a few. But after the fact, civilian curiosity-seekers made a series of sickening discoveries: severed limbs, body parts, and other gruesome bits and pieces too morbid to mention.

A second cleanup crew went in. Since the plane was too big to extract, they acquired the use of a giant bulldozer from a nearby logging crew, dug a huge trench, pushed the bomber and its contents into the hole, and buried it.

So it's still up there, buried somewhere on Deer Mountain, rusting, overgrown, waiting like a forgotten time capsule.

Who knows what mysteries—or horrors—it might contain?

Big Jim's Busts

Big Jim Fisk was born in Brattleboro, Vermont, on April Fools' Day, 1834, but he went on to prove himself anything but a fool. From humble beginnings, he evolved into a flamboyant showman-salesman. After a brief stint with the circus, he bought a garishly painted wagon and began a peddler's route that eventually led him to Wall Street. There his fortune expanded, as did his waistline. In 1869, he and the infamous financier Jay Gould attempted to monopolize the New York City gold market, a ploy that brought about Black Friday, the financial panic of 1869.

Jim's greed, cunning, and insatiable appetites culminated in his murder. He was shot to death by his mistress's lover on the staircase of the Broadway Central Hotel in New York City. (Jim's love life was, shall we say, complicated.)

Dead at thirty-eight, the New England native was returned to Vermont for burial under that state's most ostentatious monument. In Brattleboro's Prospect Hill Cemetery you can see a bust of James Fisk and a number of other busts as well; the grave is surrounded by statues of naked women. Each bare-breasted beauty is intended to symbolize some phase of Mr. Fisk's far-reaching career: railroads, steamboats, commerce, and the stage. Or at least that's the story.

End of the Road

Retired police matron Rose Martin had a true passion for her 1962 Corvair. Rose loved that car, drove it for thirty-six years, and before her death in 1998 at age eighty-four she decided to be buried in it. Her permanent parking place is in the Pocasset Hill Cemetery, on the main drag of Tiverton, Rhode Island.

After first removing the engine from the trunk, the pallbearers—six sturdy police officers—shoved Rose's wooden coffin into the rear of the Corvair. Then car and cargo were lowered by crane into the ground, where it takes up four parking places . . . er, burial plots. Rose's picture and that of her beloved car are displayed on her big, booklike marker. Perhaps the tomb tome is intended to represent the Bible, or the owner's manual—anything but Ralph Nader's *Unsafe at Any Speed*.

Mummy's Grave

In West Cemetery in Middlebury, Vermont, there's a headstone bearing highly unusual markings. They are not the typical icons of a Colonial grave. Rather, they look vaguely like hieroglyphics. Upon closer examination, you'll discover that the grave's occupant passed away in 1883. But that's 1883 B.C.! Can this be the oldest gravestone in New England? Did the stonecutter make a transcription error? What's going on?

Actually, this is the final resting spot of Vermont's only royalty, the two-year-old son of an ancient Egyptian king. And how did the mummy of Amun-Her-Khepesh-Ef come to be buried in Middlebury, Vermont?

More than a hundred years ago local oddities collector Henry Sheldon purchased the little prince from a New York dealer. The remains were stored away and forgotten in the Sheldon Museum until 1945 when the curator found them and decided they weren't in very good shape. The kindly George Mead, president of the museum's board of directors, in effect decided to adopt the little lost soul. He had Amun-Her-Khepesh-Ef cremated and buried the ashes in his own family plot.

The Bowman Mausoleum

Many people driving through Cuttingville, Vermont, swear they have seen a ghost. In reality it's a pure white marble statue, the likeness of John P. Bowman kneeling on the steps of one of New England's most melancholic monuments. The statue, steps, and mausoleum are directly across Route 103 from Laurel Hall, an ornate Victorian mansion that was to have been the summer home of Mr. Bowman and his family.

Sadly, death had other plans for Mrs. Bowman and the two Bowman daughters. All passed away, leaving the grieving millionaire alone in his grand house. Each morning he could look out and see the statue of himself kneeling before the crypt that held his family.

Local legend holds that Mr. Bowman pursued occult secrets to bring his family, and eventually himself, back from the dead. His will is said to provide for the mansion's maintenance. For years, a maid and butler were kept on staff to clean, change the bed linen, and prepare and serve fresh meals every night. Who knew? Perhaps one of the deceased Bowmans would amble over from the crypt at suppertime and be hungry. There are also stories of ghostly children, hidden treasures, and the kneeling statue creaking to its feet and patrolling the property by night.

For those more interested in graves than ghosts, the Grecian mausoleum is a true wonder. According to its builder, it is "destined from the solidity of its construction, to endure till the ruthless hand of Time shall have reduced to viewless atoms the massive blocks of granite of which it is built."

In other words, it was built to last. Construction involved over a year's work by one hundred twenty-five craftsmen, costing an exorbitant $75,000 (about $1.5 million today). It consists of 750 tons of granite, 50 tons of marble, over 20,000 bricks, and more than 100 loads of sand. Take a peek through the barred entrance; the interior looks far larger than the outside—an optical illusion done with mirrors. Several statues detail exactly how everyone looked during life. But don't forget, the Bowman bodies lie nearby, resting forever on "A Couch of Dreamless Sleep."

Defiant in Death

Authors of New England epitaphs often used the surface of a gravestone to get in a final good word. Who knows, the right sentiment might open the doors to paradise. But not so for G. F. Spencer of Lyndon Center, Vermont. His last words are famous because of their defiance.

Though the tomb he designed and cut for himself before his death in 1908 (at age eighty-three) is partly defaced, it can still be read. The old philosopher's final thesis says, in part:

SCIENCE HAS NEVER KILLED OR PERSECUTED A SINGLE PERSON FOR DOUBTING OR DENYING ITS TEACHING, AND MOST OF THESE TEACHINGS HAVE BEEN TRUE; BUT RELIGION HAS MURDERED MILLIONS FOR DOUBTING OR DENYING HER DOGMAS AND MOST OF THESE DOGMAS HAVE BEEN FALSE.

ALL STORIES ABOUT GODS AND DEVILS, OF HEAVENS AND HELLS, AS THEY DO NOT CONFORM TO NATURE, AND ARE NOT APPARENT TO SENSE, SHOULD BE REJECTED WITHOUT CONSIDERATION.

BEYOND THE UNIVERSE THERE IS NOTHING AND WITHIN THE UNIVERSE THE SUPERNATURAL DOES NOT AND CANNOT EXIST.

[O]F ALL DECEIVERS WHO HAVE PLAGUED MANKIND, NONE ARE SO DEEPLY RUINOUS TO HUMAN HAPPINESS AS THOSE IMPOSTERS WHO PRETEND TO LEAD BY A LIGHT ABOVE NATURE.

THE LIPS OF THE DEAD ARE CLOSED FOREVER. THERE COMES NO VOICE FROM THE TOMB. CHRISTIANITY IS RESPONSIBLE FOR HAVING CAST THE [FABLE] OF ETERNAL FIRE OVER ALMOST EVERY GRAVE.

Needless to say, certain God-fearing townsfolk tried to obliterate these blasphemous words. Apparently Mr. Spencer anticipated that; he inscribed them too deeply to be erased.

Window on the World

At the front of Evergreen Cemetery in New Haven, Vermont, there's an incongruous mound of earth. It is obviously not the work of nature and seems more like a landscaper's faux pas. If you mount the mound and look down, you'll see, of all things, a window in the ground! Peer inside. If visibility is good you'll be looking face-to-face with the long-deceased body of Timothy Clark Smith. During life, he had an elevated fear of being buried alive—not an unreasonable concern in the days before embalming.

When Mr. Smith seemed to pass away in 1893—on Halloween—a special grave was constructed for him: the grassy mound. He was placed with his face directly under a cement tube that led to the surface. The tube was covered by a fourteen-by-fourteen-inch square of heavy glass. In his hand was placed a bell he could ring if he woke up to find he'd been buried in error. Meanwhile, he could look out the window and wait for help to arrive.

There were many ingenious graves built during the nineteenth century to guard against premature burial. This is one of the few survivors. We can't say the same about Mr. Smith.

Witch's Grave

The Old Burying Yard in York Village, Maine, is said to contain a witch's grave. It may be the only grave of its kind in New England, and its unique design makes it not only easy to spot, but also a mystery. For all the world, it resembles a narrow bed. A flat horizontal slab is positioned where the mattress would be, while vertical stone markers stand at either end, like head- and footboards.

The likeness to a bed may be unintentional, since this is apparently not the final resting place of the lady buried below. Locals have been encountering her ghost ever since she passed away in 1774. In any event, below the slab lie the earthly remains of Mary Nasson.

The slab, according to dark tales, is to keep the witch underground where she belongs. But this may be misinformation. Perhaps it was placed there by a loving family to protect the body from predators or to keep grazing cattle away.

Other questionable reports say Mistress Nasson's monument radiates warmth when touched and is guarded by crows. However, history seems to paint a more comfortable picture of Mary. Apparently, she was a respected herbalist. Her medical treatments were in great demand, and she was much loved by those she helped. Her epitaph calls her "A loving Wife" and "A tender Parent dear."

In death, her temperament seems to have changed little. Locals tell how her invisible form plays with the local children, pushing them on nearby swings or plucking wildflowers to give as gifts. No one has ever reported being frightened by this gentle spirit.

While you may not see her ghost during a visit, you can have a look at Mary. Supposedly, that's her portrait carved at the top of her headstone (or is it her footstone?).

Putting a Spin on Things

In the Grove Street Cemetery in Putnam, Connecticut, is a six-foot granite pillar on top of which sits a solid granite ball about three feet in diameter and weighing some four thousand pounds. This upside-down exclamation point marks the Houghton family plot. What's weird, and one would think impossible, is that the two-ton stone ball seems to be rotating. Between 1930 and 1970, it turned some two feet.

But why? What could move an object that size when gravity should hold it firmly in place?

In 1971, four members of David Philips's folklore class at Connecticut State University decided to get to the bottom of things. Margaret Blanchard, Susan Brierton, Pauline Deragon, and Barbara Cook tried to consider all possibilities in a paper called "Stories on Stones."

Theories—other than supernatural—include:

1. Expansion from the hot sun.
2. Water trickling under the ball and freezing, thus moving it slightly.
3. The earth's magnetic fields tugging on the ball.
4. The ball's inertia keeps it in place as the earth turns under it. Thus it's the pedestal moving, not the ball. (However, the authors point out that this theory contradicts the law of a left-hand universe, that is, objects in the Northern Hemisphere should rotate counterclockwise. The Houghton ball rotates clockwise.)
5. The whole phenomenon is just seismic shenanigans: the result of vibrations from heavy trucks or earth tremors.

So far, no explanation seems to satisfy. Maybe the solution is supernatural, after all.

Black Agnes

A grave in Green Mountain Cemetery in Montpelier, Vermont, has been terrifying residents for years. It is believed to be cursed. This especially elegant monument was supposedly erected around 1930. Part of the extensive burial plot includes a five-foot dark bronze statue of what appears to be the Virgin Mary. She's seated, shrouded, with her sorrow-filled face upturned toward heaven. For some reason she has picked up the nickname Black Agnes. While no one seems able to say why she is called that, many will tell you she guards the grave of a murder victim. The curse is that anyone who sits on Black Agnes's lap in the light of the full moon will suffer seven years of bad luck, most likely resulting in death.

A fair-sized collection of stories illustrates the validity of the curse. One tells of a brazen high school boy who defiantly plopped

himself down on the statue's bronze lap. Shortly thereafter he died in a canoeing accident on the Winooski River—drowned within half a mile of Agnes.

However, upon closer examination, much of the story doesn't hold water. First, this is not the grave of a murderer or murder victim; it's the final resting place of a local philanthropist. Second, he died in 1899, not 1930. And third, the statue is not of the Virgin Mary at all. In fact, a perfunctory anatomical examination will quickly reveal that it is male. He is Thanatos, the Greek personification of death. While some might consider it risky to sit in the lap of death, I suspect that the curse, if there is one, is generated by Thanatos' anger at being mistaken for a woman.

Graveyard Humor
Repartee with the Grim Reaper

Cheshire, Connecticut:
Dr. Isaac Bartholomew, 1710, age (39?)
He that was sweet to my Repose
Now is become a stink under my Nose.
This is said of me
So it will be said of thee.

Hatfield, Massachusetts:
Here lies as silent clay
Miss Arabella Young
Who on the 21st of May
1771
Began to hold her tongue.

Topsfield, Massachusetts:
Mary Lafavour, 1797, age 74
Reader pass on and ne'er waste your time,
On bad biography and bitter rhyme
For what I am this cum'brous clay insures,
And what I was, is no affair of yours.

Winslow, Maine:
In Memory of
Beza. Wood
Departed this life
Nov. 2, 1837
Aged 45 yrs.
Here lies one Wood
Enclosed in wood
One Wood
Within another.
The outer wood
Is very good:
We cannot praise
The other.

New Shoreham, Rhode Island:
Captain Thomas Coffin, 1842, age 50
He's done a-catching cod
And gone to meet his God.

Hollis, New Hampshire:
Here lies old Caleb Ham,
By trade a bum.
When he died the devil cried,
Come, Caleb, come.

North Attleboro, Massachusetts:
Here lies the best of slaves
Now turning into dust
Caesar the Ethiopian craves
A place among the Just.
His faithful soul is fled
To realms of heavenly light,
And by the blood that Jesus shed
Is changed from Black to White.

Milford, Connecticut:
Mary Fowler, 1792, age 24
Molly tho' pleasant in her day
Was suddenly seized and went away
How soon she's ripe,
how soon she's rotten.
Laid in her grave and soon forgotten.

Martha's Vineyard, Massachusetts:
Caroline Newcomb, 1812, age 4 months
She tasted Life's bitter cup
Refused to drink the portion up
But turned her little head aside
Disgusted with the taste and died.

Orient, Maine:
William Deering, 1839, age 49
For me the world hath had its charms
And I've embraced them in my arms,
Counted its joys and sought its bliss
Although I knew the end was this.

Chilmark, Massachusetts:
Jonathan Tilton, 1837, age 66
Here lies the body of Jonathan Tilton
Whose friends reduced him to a skeleton.
They robbed him out of all he had
And now rejoice that he is dead.

Ryegate, Vermont:
Alden Work, 1856, age 80
I lived on Earth
I died on Earth
In Earth I am interred
All that have Life
Are sure of Death
The rest may be inferred.

New Boston, New Hampshire:
Sevilla,
Daughter of
George & Sarah
Jones
Murdered by
Henry N. Sargent
Jan 13, 1854.
Aet. 17 yrs & 9 mos.
Thus fell this lovely blooming daughter
By the vengeful hand—a malicious Henry
When on her way to school he met her
And with a six self cocked pistol shot her.

Fletcher, Vermont:
Lurana Nichols, 1863, age 51
Here lies the remains of H. P. Nichol's wife
Who mourned away her natural life.
She mourned herself to death for her man
While he was in the service of Uncle Sam.

Duxbury, Massachusetts:
Asenath
Widow of
Simeon Soule
Died
Feb. 25, 1865.
Aged 87 years, 11 mo.
& 19 days.
The Chisel can't help
her any.

Stowe, Vermont:
I was somebody.
Who, is no business
of yours.

Guilford, Vermont:
Henry Clay Barney, 1915, age 82
My life's been hard
And all things show it;
I always thought so
And now I know it.

Putnam, Connecticut:
Phineas G. Wright, 1918, age 89
Going, But Know Not Where

Pawtucket, Rhode Island:
Inscribed on a boulder
William P. Rothwell M.D.
1866–1939
This is on me.

Rainsford Island in Boston Harbor:
Near by these grey rocks,
enclosed in a box
Lies hatter Cox who died of small pox.

Kittery, Maine
We can but mourn our loss,
Though wretched was his life.
Death took him from the cross,
Erected by his wife.

Enosburg Falls, Vermont:
Note: Mr. Church outlived four wives
and decided to move all their remains
closer to his home. During the
digging, the remains of the four
women became hopelessly entangled.
The undated headstone says:

Stranger pause and drop a tear
For Emily Church lies buried here
  Mixed in some perplexing manner
    With Mary, Martha
      and probably Hannah.

Abandoned in New England

in New England there is a saying, "You don't tear a barn down when it can fall down." This says something about the Yankee character. We are thrifty. (Why expend energy and money to get rid of some structure that isn't bothering anyone anyway?) And we are generally oblivious to what others might consider eyesores. In consequence, not only barns but also houses, hospitals, hotels, amusement parks, and vehicles sit derelict in our midst. That's fine by us; they recall vanished times and conjure fascinating stories.

But in the event that some of our treasured "barns" might in fact fall down—or worse yet, be demolished—a few of our favorites are preserved here, derelict and abandoned forever.

Before you explore any of these forgotten treasures for yourself, however, a word of caution. Check out the sites for NO TRESPASSING signs first. If you find them, they're there for a good reason. Many of these old places are crumbling and unstable and therefore dangerous. And if that's not enough, the police are often trolling by, looking for people to arrest.

FORT MONTGOMERY
NAMED FOR AMER. GEN. RICHARD
MONTGOMERY, REV. WAR HERO
KILLED AT QUEBEC 1775. THIS
FORT BEGUN 1844. ARMAMENTS
REMOVED 1900.

Fort Blunder: The Mistake on the Lake

In the northwesternmost corner of New England, standing like a dark sentinel against the Canadian horizon, is a massive, mysterious, almost medieval-looking structure known locally as Fort Montgomery. To the casual eye, it appears like a great stone castle magically floating on Lake Champlain. But where exactly is it? In Vermont? New York? Quebec? Or possibly perched atop some uncharted Lake Champlain island? As it turns out, its exact location has always been part of its mystique.

From a historical standpoint, there is good reason to have built this imposing stone castle exactly where it is. This is a strategic point: New York, Vermont, and Canada all intersect at Fort Montgomery. During the American Revolution, British troops moving down from Canada passed this spot on their way to invading the colonies in 1775 and again in 1776. During the War of 1812, England's bid to take back America, this was again a vulnerable point of entry.

In 1815, before the English—or Canadians—got any more ideas, the Americans decided to erect a fifty-cannon fortress at this strategic point. But logic and intelligence are not always the same thing. By 1819, when construction was well under way, a seemingly peaceful land survey proved to hold devastating news for the fort. Turns out the Americans had built their stronghold in Canada. In short, the British took Fort Montgomery without so much as firing a shot. Since then, for obvious reasons, everyone has taken to calling it Fort Blunder. In 1842, the Webster-Ashburton Treaty restored the land and fort to the United States, but the Blunder name stuck.

In spite of its imposing aspect and strategic location, Fort Montgomery has never seen action. Men have been garrisoned here, and there are persistent rumors that it served as a prison for Confederate soldiers during the Civil War. Its military usefulness, however, has always been a little out of sync with reality. Nonetheless, the fort is a perilous place. Locals have hauled off many of its stones to use for their own homes and churches, so it's a ruin in the process of collapsing. Walls are falling; invisible holes lurk beneath innocent-looking patches of wildflowers. Today the fort is locked, posted against trespassers, and regularly patrolled.

But there is a final little ironic twist to the story. This crumbling piece of neglected American history is once again the property of Canadians. One Victor Podd bought the fort in 1983. Now his descendants own it as Fort Montgomery Estates. And they'd be willing to sell it if the price were right. They'd even sell it to an American.

Touring Tunnels at Fort Adams

One of the most fascinating places I ever went to while I was living in Rhode Island was an abandoned military installation called Fort Adams, located in Newport. It dates back to Revolutionary times. In order to run munitions secretly back and forth, and to make quick getaways into the sea, there are a large number of underground tunnels that criss-cross beneath the fort. In the mid-1980s, my friend and I had the guts to sneak under the unguarded fence and conducted our own private tour of the fort.

We found large brick barracks with vaulted ceilings and many old decrepit buildings pretty much falling to rubble. We went down into one of the tunnels, and it wound up being a seemingly endless creepy black hole, about five and a half feet high. The tunnel was lined with brick walls and an arched brick ceiling (luckily we came prepared with flashlights). Often there were areas where the bricks had fallen in, and much evidence of rats!

We came to quite a few underground intersections, with various tunnels going off in unknown directions. We even came to one section where there was a stairway going down to a second level beneath the fort. Since Fort Adams is not very far above the sea level of the Narragansett Bay, this passage was flooded up to our level with water. We continued to go on and eventually came up in a small cement guardhouse, in a totally unexpected ending point, considering where we started.

I have recently checked it out, and today only one of these fascinating tunnels is open to the public. Fort Adams is now a sanctioned state park and less creepy than when we took our self-guided tour.–*Bob Brunke*

Dreams and Demons in Hell's Half Acre

It started with the persistent concussion of metal on stone.

A group of boys ran off to investigate. What they found was an odd-looking man, a solitary stranger, digging on South Mountain. He was like nothing ever seen before in the Bristol, Vermont, of 1800. The boys approached with timidity, only to be repelled with menacing gestures and a barrage of foul, foreign-sounding epithets. Bewildered, terrified, they ran off to tell their fathers.

Soon citizens gathered to discuss what might be happening on South Mountain. The local storekeeper recalled a "rough and uncanny" stranger who had entered his establishment, purchased some supplies, and vanished into the hills. The boys' fathers and older brothers set out to confront the mysterious intruder. The impact of his axe against stone led them directly to the lone laborer. Hardly fearful, the old man commanded them to leave at once. They refused, reminding him that he was the trespasser. He'd better explain himself, they said, or they'd run him out of town.

The tale he told changed the history of the region.

He said his name was DeGrau, that he was Spanish, and had visited the area many years ago as a child. His father and a group of associates were miners who had been prospecting throughout New England. On South Mountain, they'd discovered a rich vein of silver and begun a mining operation.

Eventually they accumulated a massive amount of high-grade ore, which they smelted into silver bars. In the fall, while preparing to leave, they discovered they had too much wealth to carry away. They walled their treasure up in an oven-shaped cave and disguised the entrance with earth and vegetation, planning to return for it later.

Before departing for their faraway homes, the miners agreed that in order to reclaim the loot they must all travel together. For various reasons they never coordinated the return trip. Presumably, they had carted off so much wealth that they never needed to refill their coffers. Over the years, the original miners died off until Señor DeGrau was the only one left.

But, he explained to the visitors, the land wasn't exactly as he remembered it, a fact no doubt attributable to altered topography resulting from a 1755 earthquake. Still, he dug and poked and prodded and eventually wandered off into oblivion, apparently without finding his prize.

Canadians Continue to Dig

In the years to come, an array of Bristol locals picked up where the Spaniard left off. They discovered some ancient signs of a mining operation, a few nondescript odds and ends, but no mine and no silver. For decades, Bristol treasure hunters were joined by opportunists from far and wide, all determined to find the Spaniards' horde.

In the mid-1800s, a group of Canadians arrived and organized a stock company. An affable sixty-year-old, florid-faced giant known as "Uncle Sim" Coreser directed the operation. He spurred the diggers on with humor and charisma, taking his directions from trusted fortune-tellers, whose paranormal visions allowed them to identify the spot where the treasure lay. The amount that would eventually be unearthed, they promised, was $3,100,000—over $50,000,000 in today's coin.

From 1840 to 1852, Sim's company dug shaft after shaft, some through solid rock, some forty and fifty feet deep. One sank to well over one hundred feet! Still the silver remained out of reach. After more than twelve years and thousands of dollars, Uncle Sim and his team deserted their mining camp. About a decade later, Uncle Sim, inspired by a new conjurer, returned alone. But this effort was short-lived. A defeated and broken man, he abandoned his dream.

The Diggings Today

Intermittent efforts to find the treasure followed over the years, all, as far as we know, without success. The forlorn remnants of Bristol's Big Dig remain on South Mountain to this day. If you can traverse the inhospitable terrain (as nasty as any in the state) you can still discover the rough

rock caves where Uncle Sim's crew lived during their twelve years on what has become known as Hell's Half Acre. You can locate the filled shafts and—if you're brave enough—descend into the only pit that remains open. It drops at a precarious forty-five-degree angle into, so they say, a hand-dug cavern large enough to hold a dance hall. From there, three additional shafts burrow into the bowels of the mountain. But be careful. It is a dangerous spot, perhaps more so because of the hellhound and demon boy Uncle Sim swore will eternally guard the true path to the treasure.

The amount that would eventually be unearthed, they promised, was $3,100,000—over $50,000,000 in today's coin.

South Mountain's Supernatural Side

*"I will not take you far or detain you long.
But I will lead you into what at first sight
would pass for a region of enchantment."*
—Franklin S. Harvey, "The Money Diggers"

There seems to be a law: Where there's buried treasure there are also fortune-tellers, ghosts, and possibly demons.

Between 1888 and 1889, newspaperman Franklin S. Harvey chronicled the South Mountain "treasure affair" in a vastly entertaining series of articles for the *Bristol Herald.*

Mr. Harvey actually spoke with old-timers who remembered the mysterious Spaniard DeGrau. And he had personal recollections of Uncle Sim Coreser. He recorded his last meeting with the old prospector this way: "He had a few tools and was digging and prying around in his feeble way among the loose rocks. I pitied the poor old man, and freely forgave him for all the awful frights he had given me during my boyhood; for hiding behind a rock and growling like a bear; for telling me bloodcurdling stories that made my hair stand on end; for ridiculing my odd and bashful ways; all doubts I may have had of his present or former sincerity were scattered in the winds."

No doubt those bloodcurdling stories first appeared as warnings from Uncle Sim's consulting conjurers. For Bristol's treasure was known to be cursed, protected by demonic guardian spirits who would inflict vast harm on anyone who ventured too close to the cave or touched the treasure. (For a price, of course, the seers were quick to offer mystical immunity from the dangers of digging for "enchanted" loot.)

When the silver was originally placed there, the story went, a savage dog was sacrificed. Its blood was then sprinkled over the cave floor and onto its precious contents. The hellhound was assigned to spend eternity patrolling the cave, listening for intruders, sniffing at fissures, and preparing to tear trespassers to pieces.

But, as Mr. Harvey writes, there was more to fear than demon dogs. "A boy, with a frightful gash across his throat, paced round and round the glittering pile with a red hot iron upraised to smite with vengeful force the sacrilegious hand that dared to touch a single bar of the guarded pile."

Apparently, our gentleman journalist considered it too indelicate to state overtly that the boy had also been sacrificed. Anyway, as the treasure-seekers "hewed their way through the ledge and drew nearer to the object of their search, they could hear the boy sigh and groan. . . ."

As a youngster, Mr. Harvey had often watched the Canadian diggers. He writes, "I can't say I ever heard the howls and groans, but who is to dispute the statement of a dozen gray-haired men, all of whom were ready to say they did hear them?"

Over the years, the saga of the demon-boy and his hellhound has evolved a bit, taking on less sinister and far more poignant overtones. Today folks tell of a young Bristol lad who went walking in the woods of South Mountain. As boys will, he entered the forbidden zone with his dog at his side. But something happened; neither returned home. At nightfall, his worried parents organized a search, but to no avail. The boy and his dog had vanished completely.

Some months later, when the deep snows of winter ran off South Mountain, a lone hunter made his way through

the soggy earth and sharp outcroppings of Hell's Half Acre. There he noticed something near the opening of the single remaining mineshaft. It was the skeleton of a dog.

In a moment, the hunter realized what had happened. The lost boy had fallen into the fifty-foot shaft, from which he was unable to escape. Alone, terrified, he had died there.

His dog remained at the rim of the pit, refusing to leave his young master. The faithful animal stayed until starvation silenced him, just fifty feet above the boy.

Even today, on certain calm fall nights, residents of Bristol swear they can hear something strange among the natural sounds of woodland and wind. Some folks report a far-off cry for help; others hear the unearthly baying of a dog.

Enough people have heard the mysterious cries so that locally that particular excavation has come to be called the Ghost Shaft of Bristol Notch.

Holy Land Awaits Resurrection

It all started out rather covertly—possibly supernaturally. In 1956, Waterbury, Connecticut, lawyer John Baptist Greco met with a small group of associates. The names and exact content of that original gathering have never been made public, but the effects can be seen till this day. Some say Mr. Greco revealed that God had given him a task to perform. Others say he made an appeal for a community project. In any event, a plan resulted and apparently went something like this. Mr. Greco, a lifelong Roman Catholic, had just returned from a visit to the Holy Land. He lamented that everyone could not enjoy the same uplifting experience he had had there. Since it would be too expensive to fly pilgrims to the Holy Land and more expensive still to relocate the Holy Land to America, the best solution was to build a vast, minutely detailed replica on Pine Hill in Waterbury. This ongoing effort would become Mr. Greco's inspiration and avocation.

Blueprints for the construction were developed from studies of the Bible, maps, photographs, and other authoritative sources (including, some say, divine revelation). Over the coming years, John Baptist Greco would watch with satisfaction as a twenty-acre village—the Holy Land in miniature—grew up before his eyes.

Mr. Greco and his helpers fashioned buildings from anything they could find: plywood, tar paper, car parts, old sinks, blown-out boilers, refrigerators,

metal drums, bedsprings. Inadvertently, they also created a grand piece of outsider art full of Lilliputian pyramids, tombs, grottoes, tunnels, and tableaux of religious instruction like "The Pictorial Life of Christ—From the Cradle to the Cross." Somehow, they even located a "photograph" of Jesus and a replica of the shroud of Turin. Underneath it all lay the legendary catacombs.

By 1970, nearly two hundred buildings sprawled across the site, beneath a sixty-foot stainless-steel cross (some locals say Christ was electrocuted on that cross). Now multitudes could rewalk the dusty paths of Jesus' life and death, only in miniature.

During its heyday, the 1960s and 1970s, Holy Land attracted some fifty thousand visitors a year, but its lifespan seemed mysteriously linked to that of its creator. At age eighty-eight Mr. Greco could no longer care for his creation. In 1984, the site officially closed to visitors. Now, twenty

years later, it's still there, a diminutive ghost town. Weather and vandals have taken their toll, but somehow Holy Land survives. While city fathers decide whether to raze it, restore it, or turn it into a hilltop park, people continue to visit. In secret. Just like the place began.

The miniature city was so extensive that now it is ripe for archaeological exploration. Can some of the treasures it contained be rediscovered or restored? Could we excavate the photo of Jesus? Locate the giant fiberglass Bible that seems to have disappeared, or find the remains of miniature popes and Garden of Eden progenitors?

For some odd reason, the rubble and ruins of Holy Land hold a peculiar fascination. The eye may perceive junk, but perhaps the soul sees something else. Whatever may be its fate, Mr. John Baptist Greco, who died in 1986 at age ninety-one, will be watching over us from high above the cross, smiling down from his miniature heaven.

Holy Land U.S.A.: The Well-Lit Ruin on the Hill

The enormous cross at the peak of Holy Land has become Waterbury's signature icon, similar to the Jesus statue above Rio de Janeiro. The electricity bill (which keeps Holy Land aglow through the night) has been prepaid for the foreseeable future. Years of erosion (due to the natural elements as well as the unnatural activities of local teenagers) have reduced Holy Land USA to a well-lit ruin. However, the dilapidation has added an intriguing postapocalyptic aesthetic to this formerly pristine folk art creation.

Greco's work is reminiscent of Southern Baptist folk art representations of biblical stories. It looks like a cross between the Holy Land replicas of Brother Joseph's miniature Ave Maria Grotto in Alabama and the full-scale interpretation of the Holy Land in Bedford, Virginia. —*Ben Osto*

Teleported Trains?

Do you know how big Maine really is? Certainly it's the biggest New England state, but to say it covers over thirty-three thousand square miles doesn't effectively convey its vastness. You don't begin to realize the immensity of the place until you head north, into the wilderness, to just south of the Canadian border. There, roads are few, trees are many, and swarms of mosquitoes and black flies compete for your very last drop of blood. There are no villages near enough to be called "near," and cell phones are as useless as tin cans with broken strings attached.

Now imagine yourself making your way among the thick-trunked trees of this wilderness sheltered by a canopy of green leaves. You're bathed in a surreal glow while stories of Bigfoot and Windigo are racing through your imagination. Suddenly you see something that looks like a structure. You cautiously move forward, wondering who would build a big metallic shelter out here in the middle of nowhere. You sneak from tree trunk to tree trunk, remaining as quiet as possible. Images from *The Texas Chainsaw Massacre* flash in your head as the *Deliverance* theme twangs in your ear. Just exactly what are you seeing? A hermit's condo? A crashed spaceship?

And when you realize what it is, you realize just as quickly that it is utterly impossible. There are no roads, no tracks, no spaces big enough between the trees, but there they are, two huge steam locomotives out in the middle of nowhere. No cars, no other machinery. Just the engines, swaddled in vegetation, plunked down in the middle of the most inaccessible country in all New England.

Have you stumbled upon proof of teleportation? Are they abducted locomotives jettisoned from a passing UFO? How in the world did they get here?

Well, as is so often the case, the explanation is far less interesting than the puzzle, so stop reading here if you don't want to know the secret of this magic trick. Years ago, in the glory days of the logging business, the two locomotives were dragged in on sleds. It was a monumental effort, to be sure, but necessary for the labor it saved. The two trains served a short-line railroad running the ten miles from Eagle Lake to Umbazooksus. Their cargo was pulp hauled out of the deep woods to the water, where it could be floated down to the Bangor paper mills. But, over time, things changed. The loggers pulled out. The tracks were pulled up and recycled. The trains, however, were too old and too heavy to salvage. So they remain here, two out-of-place locomotives, rusting at, and until, the end of the world.

Inside New England's Abandoned Insane Asylums

There is no experience that compares to the exploration of an abandoned insane asylum in terms of eeriness. Not knowing what, or who, might lay in wait just around the next blind corner or down the next darkened corridor is enough to make any spine tingle.

Wandering the vacant hallways of these spooky old buildings, one cannot help but imagine the suffering once endured by the unfortunate souls whose fate it was to spend their lives within those walls. These feelings are made all the more tangible by the artifacts that can often be found, left behind when these institutions closed their doors for good. In some buildings, patient records, fingerprints, and mug shots spill forth from overflowing file cabinets. In others, antiquated surgical tools litter the floors of operating rooms where fragile minds were once tinkered with. Padded cells, electroshock tables, human cages, and draconian restraint devices with leather straps are all part of the abandoned asylum tour.

In more recent times, many of our country's mental facilities have had less than stellar reputations, with histories of patient neglect, abuse, and escape. Eventually most of these troubled institutions would end up abandoned, quietly falling to pieces in silence and solitude. There is a plethora of these abandoned or partially abandoned mental asylums wherever you turn in New England. They stand on the outskirts of our towns, massive, sprawling monuments to instability, often comprised of dozens of buildings, expansive grounds, and networks of underground tunnels connecting the complexes.

Though they may be long dead, the power these magnificent buildings possess over those who visit them has not diminished. In fact, in their abandoned incarnations these ancient asylums seem to be even more potent as places of inspiration and personal reflection. They radiate a weird, almost supernatural aura—dark and somber, melancholy and mournful—which is not likely to be found anywhere else. Perhaps the most magnificent and awe-inspiring of all of these structures is Danvers State Hospital in Massachusetts, the dark castle on the hill.

The Castle of Lost Souls *Story and illustrations by Michael Ramseur*

For the past seventeen years, I have been obsessed with an abandoned lunatic hospital. Perched on a hill north of Danvers, Massachusetts, on Interstate 95, stands the foreboding tree-shrouded silhouette of Danvers State Hospital, its distinctive Gothic architecture now far along the road of decay.

Parents used to threaten disobedient children with a corrective trip to the "Witches' Castle," probably unaware of the connection between Danvers and witches. The Salem witch hysteria and trials did not occur in Salem, but in Salem Village, which is present-day Danvers. The most fanatical judge of the witch trials, Johnathan Hathorne, lived exactly where the hospital was later constructed.

I first encountered Danvers State Hospital on a hot and sultry evening in the summer of 1986. I was a residential counselor in a nearby group home, returning a resident who had been out on a pass. I sat in the van at the Castle, and the main hospital building, which had been shut down for four years, cast its dark shadow across the curving brick driveways and the burned-grass campus. My imagination fed on the texture and pattern of Danvers—its time-stained brick, rusted mesh screens, decaying vents and turrets; its tar-stained roofs with their green copper valleys and their elaborately designed brick eaves. As I sat transfixed, a man's head suddenly appeared in the car's passenger window. His face taut with anxiety, he repeatedly asked, "I'm not going to die, am I?" I told him no, and apparently that was good enough for him, because he then wandered off.

Since that first encounter, I have tramped the grounds, drawn the buildings from every angle, explored the hospital's labyrinthine depths, pored over its records, and interviewed former employees and patients. This is a very brief look at its story.

Danvers Lunatic Hospital was built during the 1870s—a time of deep social commitment to the mentally ill. The noted Boston architect Nathaniel Bradlee designed the massive domestic Gothic structure, drawing inspiration from the "guiding spirit of the model-hospital building," Thomas Story Kirkbride. The superintendent of the Pennsylvania Hospital for the Insane, Kirkbride pioneered an institutional design that he believed would help cure eighty percent of its patients. Lighting and ventilation were essential elements of the Kirkbride plan. Hospitals featured wings radiating off a center section, so that each ward had proper ventilation and an unobstructed view of the grounds. By leaving open spaces at the end of each wing, Kirkbride believed "the darkest, most cheerless and worst ventilated parts" could be eliminated.

At Danvers, this complex design featured a mile-long foundation wall made of fifteen hundred tons of stone, arranged into more than 240 angles. The floor area totaled 700,000 square feet, and the roof surface topped 325,000 square feet. And the exorbitant construction cost of just under $1.5 million drew public criticism. People in the town called it the Castle not just because of its architecture, but out of envy and bitterness. Danvers seemed vastly superior to the conditions in the almshouses and prisons—and the town itself.

When it opened in 1876, Danvers was considered a leader in humane treatment. The patients' regimen involved exercise and the creation of elaborate gardens. The patient-run farm produced large harvests that kept the institution's kitchen busy. But some difficult patient populations brought problems with them. A large and unwanted influx of criminals stirred things up, though the 1886 construction of a hospital for the criminally insane in Bridgewater, Massachusetts, helped stem this tide. Another difficult group to treat were those suffering from intemperance and dipsomania—the nineteenth-century

terms for substance abuse, or "the ancient enemy," as administrators called it. In addition, mentally retarded patients mixed in with the general psychiatric population—it was not until around 1980 when they were moved to their own unit.

By the 1920s, the hospital's overcrowded wards and the prevailing psychiatric "faith-cure artists" took their toll. Around 1930, the hospital's formerly expressive annual reports became statistical repositories supporting the clinical triad of psychotherapy, hydrotherapy, and occupational therapy. These reports hid a sad fact: The hospital's founding tenet of moral treatment had completely dissolved. Danvers was becoming just another "snake pit." Its superintendents had seen this sad state of affairs well in advance, but their warnings of "the evils of overcrowding" and requests for state funding went unheeded.

The hospital had been designed for 450 patients, 600 if the attics were full. By the 1940s and 1950s, it held up to 2,600 patients. Danvers had become overcrowded and understaffed. To keep its burgeoning census under control, the staff used shock treatment, hydrotherapy (including continuous baths), insulin-shock therapy, psychosurgery,

and industrial therapy. Crumbling plaster, wall stains, and holes created a general sense of physical decay. Poorly clothed and sometimes naked, legions of lost souls paced aimlessly on the wards, lying on the filthy cement floors, or sitting head in hand against the pockmarked walls.

Danvers continued its downward spiral until it was shut down in the summer of 1992.

I've had several opportunities to study this gargantuan wreck after the hospital closed. The "A" wing on the eastern side continually drew my attention. It was a ghostly section of the Castle, located next to a beautiful field of colorful flowers, majestic, gnarled trees, and high grass (which, according to my interviewees, used to supply cover for patients having sex). Out of the bucolic splendor rose dark and stained turrets with forlorn barred windows. On a late afternoon visit, I watched the sun's rays reflect from an arched attic window in a ravaged section of the slate roof. Sinewy tendrils of ivy crept inside the window, disappearing into the inky depths. I wondered, What energy dwelled in that forgotten part of the world? Who once inhabited that remote room?

On another visit, the snow was piled several feet deep on the ground and clung to the dilapidated slate roofs, so that their white shapes stood out starkly against the leaden-grey winter sky. I was struck by the sight of one particular window. It rose as a small point directly behind a rectangular addition built in 1920. It was not a prominent window—it was small, not high off the ground, and the frozen snow provided me with a base on which to stand and look inside. I felt as if I were peering into the soul of Danvers, contemplating the myriad tragedies, fears, hopes, and dreams contained within.

In an effort to understand the bedlam, I interviewed a number of ex-employees and ex-patients. The one irrefutable conclusion is that people either loved or despised the place. Both points of view were held with equal passion. One person would tell me, "Danvers was a beautiful place, so peaceful, and what a view!" Another would say, "That place is the Witch's Castle—right out of Edgar Allan Poe. There were maggots in the food there!"

In an article titled "Too Many Patients to Treat, Human Flood Turned Hospital into Madhouse," which appeared in the September 6, 1987, *Lynn Sunday Post*, reporter David Marrs wrote: "Stories like the tale of a boy whose mother could not discipline him anymore and decided to place him at Danvers State for 'treatment' are not unusual. Forty years later, when asked to sign his name, he held the pad and pencil, and in a rough free-hand sketch, drew a picture of the hospital."

After it was shut down, an organization of ex-patients and their allies formed to close a final chapter on the hospital. For more than thirty years, graveyards stood untended on the grounds, marked with numbered stones and no names—and the state had lost records of which name went with which grave number. The Danvers Memorial Committee dedicated itself to remembering those former residents interred there. They researched the death certificates at the respective town halls in order to identify the buried. And in November 1998, they held a service to commemorate the grave sites. The day was cold and blustery as some sixty members of the committee, a state representative, and several members of the media convened to witness the blessing. At one point, they released balloons to symbolize "the letting go of the stigma of the past and the beginning of a new age of respect and dignity for people with mental illness," according to a pamphlet published by the Danvers State Memorial Committee.

A tour of the two graveyards followed the ceremony. It was an unforgettable experience, walking through the recently cleared site, looking at the rows of circular stone markers, each with a number on top. I found myself reading the numbers as we walked past the remains of more than seven hundred people. Each had been a unique individual in life, yet here they were unnamed and unacknowledged in death. Like many of the complex issues at Danvers, it went far beyond my ability to convey. My obsession with the place continues.

Asylums of Connecticut

Located high on a hill overlooking all of Middleton, Connecticut, is Connecticut Valley Hospital, a mental institution constructed in 1868. The facility's buildings range in age from forty to one hundred thirty years old. Some of the older buildings have been slated for renovation and others for demolition. I was invited to document these places before they were lost.

Before I started this project, I thought it would be a great adventure to explore these old and eerie abandoned mental hospitals. After I had spent several days photographing, I began to feel that these places had a lot to teach me. When I am in these places, I have learned to quiet my mind, my own idea of what this place is, and as clearly and compassionately as possible see what these buildings have to say.

This project has opened my life to a topic that I assumed I understood—mental illness. My reeducation led me to feel and see the legacy of ignorance and presumption that caused further suffering for those seeking refuge from their already difficult lives. These places are a statement of how the mentally ill were treated in the past, and yet these spaces would not be unfamiliar to a patient today.

Norwich Hospital for the Insane

The Norwich Hospital for the Insane opened its doors in 1904. Originally designed to hold just a few hundred patients at most, the hospital quickly grew into one of the most infamous in all of New England, known for the neglect and sometimes outright abuse of its vulnerable charges.

As patients flooded into the facility and the number of employees grew, so did the hospital itself. It opened as a single patient building set on just under one hundred acres. By the time of its abandonment, it sprawled over nine hundred acres and encompassed dozens of buildings. The complex included over twenty patient buildings, an administration building, a greenhouse, industrial buildings, and an employee clubhouse.

The peak of the hospital's use was in 1955, when 3,186 patients were living on premises. During the '70s, the usefulness of the hospital was brought into question. Those confined there were staying for shorter and shorter stints. During this same time frame, public opinion began to shift to the view that patients should be treated by their families and communities, not sent away to hospitals.

For the duration of its time in operation, Norwich adapted to the shifting attitudes of the public toward mental health. Some years saw dozens of patients pass through, while others saw thousands. Nowadays it stands in ruins as a reminder of the past.

Fairfield State Hospital, Newtown, Connecticut

The Fairfield State Hospital, more recently called Fairfield Hills, was established in 1932 as an institution for mental patients. The campus sits on eight hundred acres on the outskirts of the upscale village of Newtown, near Danbury. Facilities included a dozen major buildings as well as staff housing, a sewage treatment plant, and a large farm. In 1998, Fairfield Hills consisted of one hundred buildings on a 185-acre campus. The institution is now closed, and the Newtown community is currently considering options for new uses for the complex.–*Chad Kleitsch*

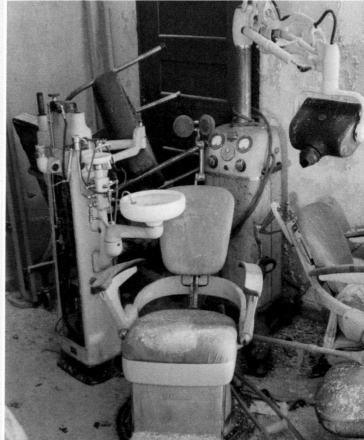

Going Mental in Newtown

In my town of Newtown, Connecticut, there is an abandoned mental institution called Fairfield Hills Hospital. A few of the buildings are still occupied, but most of it is abandoned and in disrepair. A few years ago, part of the movie *Sleepers* was filmed there, with Robert De Niro, Brad Pitt, and Kevin Bacon.

It was rumored that the entire hospital was connected underground by tunnels. My senior year of high school, my friends and I decided to check it out. We found a building, called the Cochran House, where one of the first-floor windows was broken. We went inside. It was damp and dark.

We made our way to the basement and found the entrance to a tunnel. We kept walking and came upon a door, which opened up into what appeared to be an old movie theater. The screen had a huge rip down the middle of it, and it was really eerie. We continued down the tunnels for a while and came across a lot of weird stuff. We didn't stick around too long, because we were afraid of getting arrested.

A kid that I worked with somehow obtained a copy of a map of the entire hospital. He told me that he and some friends found the morgue. Apparently, there is some real crazy stuff in there. There is a lot that I haven't explored yet, which I plan to see this summer.—*Randy Calderone*

Bloody Screams at Fairfield Mental Hospital

My friend and I went to her boyfriend's baseball game, and while we were waiting on the bleachers close to a building, we heard a scream. We were the only ones on the bleachers. My boyfriend plus some other friends of mine went to the building, but the scream was not the worst part: It was the blood on the windows. The thing is, we saw shadows in some of the windows and then heard another scream.

When I did some research on this, I found out the building is a former mental hospital. The hospital was named the Fairfield Hills Mental Hospital.—*Chloe*

Running in Tunnels with Weirdos

As a teenager, I used to run around in the tunnels under the Fairfield Hills Mental Facility. We ran into lots of weird people down in those tunnels, but never any Melonheads. There was some really strange stuff down there, like little classrooms set up behind chain-link fences and crazy people alone in dark rooms and halls. —*Skot Olsen*

The Dilemma of Dudleytown

There is good reason certain things are abandoned: Fort Blunder was never used, the Bristol Treasure was never found, and those darn trains were just too heavy to move. But why would a whole town become abandoned? What is the real reason that Dudleytown, which is situated on beautiful and valuable real estate in the northwest corner of Connecticut, has remained a ghost town since the 1920s?

Local Connecticut demon-chaser Ed Warren calls the place "cursed." New England writer and folklorist Robert Cahill says, "Probably it's the spookiest place in New England." And Hollywood ghostbuster Dan Aykroyd claims Dudleytown is the "most haunted place on earth." Scores of other people with less recognizable names will readily tell you that Dudleytown is spook-filled, demon-infested, and damned.

The story that has grown up about it goes something like this. The original settlers who colonized it in the 1600s, the Dudley brothers, were offspring of evildoers who had tried to seize the English monarchy and failed. Since in those days people believed that monarchs had a divine right to the throne (a belief strongly endorsed by the monarchs themselves), usurpers risked more than royal retribution: They risked a curse. And so it is said the Dudley family was put under a hex by the English royals.

Circa 1639, Robert Dudley transported that malediction to the New World. Like a contagion, it contaminated Dudleytown, launching a history of sudden inexplicable deaths, weird animal sightings, mysterious disappearances, horrible mutilations, epidemic insanity, and ghastly demonic confrontations.

Supposedly, people didn't so much leave as escape. The last citizen to vacate, John Brophy, became a raving maniac, shouting about terrible green spirits and giant animals with cloven hooves that had tried to enslave him.

If all the scare stories were intended to keep people away, it's not working. Recent visitors who've explored the forests and foundations of the ghost town continue to report odd sights, terrifying sounds, and sensations of general unpleasantness.

Since the release of *The Blair Witch Project* in 1999, hundreds of thrill-seekers have descended on the town, looking for everything from proof of the supernatural to the chance to cut a deal with the Evil One. The result, as you might expect, has not been pretty. Littering, loitering, and lollygagging have expanded into burning and vandalism.

As a result, NO TRESPASSING signs have sprung up like wildflowers. Local police routinely respond to complaints about drinking and wild parties. Arrests are commonplace, with $77 trespassing fines the norm, which seem a steep admission fee to a "haunted forest."

Locals readily give outsiders the stink eye, discouraging inquiry. If questions are asked, they clam up. This "town with a secret" sounds like something directly out of a horror movie. So what are we dealing with here? A cover-up? An attempt to kill a curse? Or is it something else?

The Man Who Bought Dudleytown

At the beginning of the twentieth century, at about the same time the last of the original Dudleytown dwellings was tumbling into its cellar hole, Dr. William C. Clarke and his wife, Harriet, were motoring around Connecticut when they stumbled on this seemingly desirable piece of property. Dr. Clarke, a successful surgeon and professor at Columbia College of Physicians and Surgeons in New York City, was also a nature lover. He and his wife decided to buy one hundred acres or so and build a summer cottage.

Apparently, it was Harriet who was targeted as the last victim of the curse. While Dr. Clarke made an emergency trip back to the city, Harriet stayed alone at the cottage.

During the thirty-six hours he was away, something dreadful happened to poor Harriet. No one knows what it was, but when Dr. Clark returned, she had gone irreversibly insane and eventually took her own life.

Now here's something else weird. Rather than flee Dudleytown forever, Dr. Clarke remarried and returned. In 1920, he and some of his colleagues purchased eight hundred and fifty additional acres and formed the Dark Entry Forest Association, which owns Dudleytown to this day.

So now it's off-limits. The association has turned it into a kind of Yankee "Area 51." Predictably, the same secrecy and rumors associated with that storied piece of government real estate in Las Vegas also hover around this place. The owners call Dudleytown a "nature preserve," but some speculate that it is more of a supernatural preserve. If so, we might ask if there is some peculiarity of the land itself that produces weird phenomena.

Well, maybe. For one thing, it is always dark in Dudleytown. That's because it's always in the shadows of the surrounding mountains. Visitors who do not experience major fright-show confrontations invariably complain of feeling ill at ease. They say it is too quiet, that insects and birds are unnaturally absent. Their watches stop; their tape recorders malfunction or pick up sounds their ears had failed to detect.

It is a fact that the topsoil of Dudleytown conceals rich deposits of iron, lead, and who knows what else. Perhaps the village was inadvertently built over a strong, naturally occurring magnetic field. Watches would stop. Puzzling audio anomalies might imprint themselves on recording tapes. And since many birds use the earth's magnetism to navigate, they might well detour around Dudleytown.

But the big question is: How would these magnetic mysteries affect the human metabolism? Could they cause certain vulnerable folks to hallucinate ghosts and demons? Could they inspire mania? Or maybe that's attributable to the lead that leaches into the drinking water.

To take a step farther out, maybe the mysterious alchemy of minerals and man could in fact attract beings from some parallel dimension, one that intersects with ours at that cursed crossroads in Connecticut.

Dudleytown as New England's Area 51 is a way-out notion to be sure. But is it any odder than the idea of a curse?

Camping in the Shadows of Dudleytown

I am twenty-one and have lived my entire life in Cornwall, Connecticut. When my friends and I were about eighteen, we planned to camp out overnight beside the foundations of the homes of the allegedly "cursed" former residents of Dudleytown. We got a late start, and we were all on edge by the time darkness fell. After about an hour of cursing the damp kindling and rotten firewood, we finally got a campfire started. It was early autumn, and as night fell, the temperature dropped considerably. We all huddled around the small fire and passed around bags of chips.

It was then that I realized that aside from the crackle of our little fire and the rustle of the snack bags there was no other sound in the forest. There were no crickets or frogs or anything, just dead silence. One of my friends said that it was just too late in the year for crickets, though he seemed to be trying to convince himself of this as much as us.

As dark as Dudleytown may be in the day, it is nothing compared to the night. If there was a moon in the sky that night, it could not be seen in the hollow where we were camped. The light from our feeble fire didn't extend far and seemed to be absorbed by the blackness that had closed in all around us.

Then all of a sudden we heard a noise, and we all jumped up. It was a low muffled tone coming from somewhere off in blackness.

"Owl," someone said. "It's just an owl! That's all it is."

We all stood with our backs to the flames, staring off into the woods and listening. Suddenly a breeze kicked up that gave the dwindling fire new life. Now our shadows seemed to take on a life of their own and danced across the rock walls of the foundation and in and out of the cellar pits. It was the eeriest thing I had ever seen. I was just about to say something about it when the owl sound shattered the silence once again, only this time it was so loud and close it sounded like a shriek, and we all let out startled screams simultaneously.

At just that moment, the fire suddenly went out. It was as if somebody flicked a light switch off and extinguished it, leaving us standing there in the absolute blackness. I swear, I felt as if I'd just gone blind—I couldn't see my hand right in front of my face!

We all stood there for one long moment, breathing heavily and not saying a word. All of a sudden the forest was not so quiet anymore. The owl (or whatever it was) was sounding off repeatedly and at close range, and there seemed to be a rustling in the leaves all around us. I definitely felt a presence of some kind out there in the darkness, and it was everywhere!

"That's it," someone finally spoke up, "I'm outta here!"

We scrambled to gather up any belongings we could find, threw our packs on our backs, and started walking away—fast! The forest seemed to be alive with sounds now as we trampled through the dry leaves, tripping over rocks and branches all the way. We all just stared down at the dim flashlight beams before us as we beat a hasty retreat out of the Dark Entry Forest. We walked faster and faster and tripped and fell time and time again. It was every man for himself as we raced down the rocky trail. We all just wanted to get the hell out of Dudleytown.

It was about midnight when we emerged from the woods, and life was going on in Cornwall just as normal. People wandered in and out of convenience stores and bars, and cars were gassing up at the all-night service station. It all seemed strange to me that everything was so business-as-usual here in town. It was almost as if Cornwall existed in a different reality, the modern-day world, while off in the woods outside of town there was something much older, darker, and weirder.

We returned from our foray with about half of our equipment, but we brought back a strange and unexplainable feeling with us. Perhaps we were just scared by our own shadows, but that's not how it felt. Though no one said it, we all knew that none of us would be going back to retrieve our abandoned gear anytime soon. As far as I know (or care), it is still there to this day.—*Ryan M*

Stay Out of Dudleytown, Unless You're a Devil Worshipper

One time, with my sister and a bunch of others, we went to walk the trails and see what all the fuss was about at Dudleytown. Well, we saw some of the old foundations and some old roads, but we were like, what's the big deal about this place? Of course, it was the middle of a brilliantly sunny summer day, not at night. We saw an old foundation and cut through the woods to check it out more closely. When we got there, we found the complete skeleton of a dead deer on the edge of the foundation and evidence of a fire in the base of the foundation. Right next to this was a tree that had been split right down the middle into three charred pieces by lightning. It was all so freaky we just ran to get the heck out of there!

We now understand a little more about Dudleytown. Don't go in there . . . it is an evil place. Just leave it alone! Especially don't bring children there. We think devil worshippers like to go in there, so unless you want to join in with them, just stay away!—*Amy B*

Demonic Encounter on Dudleytown Trail

In July of 1998, my fiancé and I, as well as two other friends, went up there to check out the so-called curse. We pulled up Bald Mountain Road around 11:30 p.m. and parked our car and got out. We grabbed the flashlights and cameras, and started walking toward the trail entrance. We heard nothing. Dead silence. No wind, no animals . . . nothing. We walked only a few feet and heard this noise. The sound is difficult to describe, but it sounded like a huge metal dumpster dragging against asphalt. At this point we were freaking out, but we kept going.

When we got to the entrance, we started reading the sign, and all of a sudden I took the flashlight and shined it at the ground where we just walked, and we saw the words in huge letters NEVER RETURN. . . . SATAN.—*Sarah, Torrington, CT*

The Rock

This imposing-looking structure is the U.S. Naval Prison in the Portsmouth Naval Shipyard, situated on an island in the Piscataqua River, which separates Maine and New Hampshire. The prison was closed in 1974 and has been abandoned ever since. Known as the Rock, it was the nation's most feared military lockup for more than half a century. At capacity, it would hold up to 86,000 inmates (hard to believe there could be so many bad guys in the American navy). For movie buffs, this was the destination of Jack Nicholson's prisoner (Randy Quaid) in Hal Ashby's 1973 film *The Last Detail*.

The marines who guarded the prisoners also had good reason to fear: If anyone escaped, the guard would have to complete the escapee's sentence. Local lore tells of a prisoner being transferred to the Rock from Boston. In an escape attempt, he hit the guard's face with his

handcuffs, leaving a deeply gashed lip. Nonetheless, the prisoner was subdued and safely handed over to serve his sentence, but the marine carried a dual souvenir for the rest of his life: a scar and a lisp. That marine—so the story goes—was Humphrey Bogart.

There are many other grisly tales of the Rock, the worst of them, no doubt, forever classified. But you can create a horror story of your own if you try to visit the place. In fact, you might find yourself locked up. Because the abandoned fortress is situated in the navy yard, it is seriously off-limits, especially since the towers tumbled. This is one case where such easily dismissed phrases as Keep Out and No Trespassing should be taken in earnest.

Roadside Oddities

New England is dappled with roadside oddities. Sophisticated and somber, primitive and elegant, tacky and tasteful, natural and—perhaps—supernatural, they're all here in their multitudinous splendor. Some can be seen from your car. Some may involve a short walk.

The trouble is, there are far too many oddball objects to chronicle in this short chapter. Just to whet your appetite, we'll share a few of our favorites. Let's start where the first rays of the sun touch down on New England every morning, the great state of Maine.

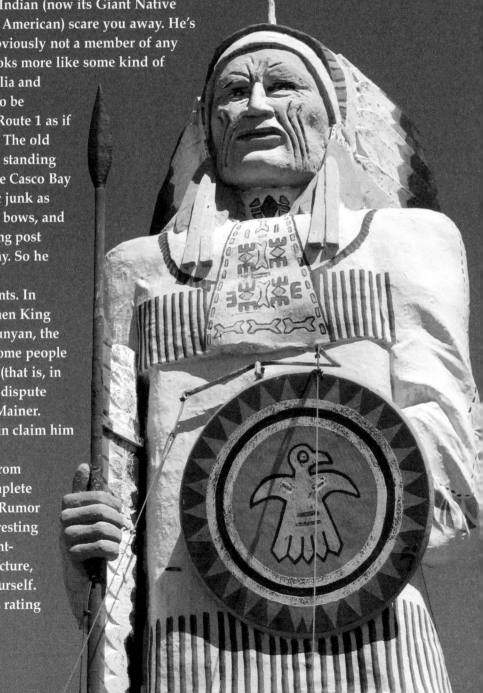

Monumental Mainers

If you're traveling up the coast in Freeport, don't let Maine's Giant Indian (now its Giant Native American) scare you away. He's obviously not a member of any Maine tribe, but looks more like some kind of Plains Indian. In full headdress regalia and standing some forty feet tall, he appears to be watching the highway, looking south on Route 1 as if guarding against imminent tourist attack. The old fellow is getting along in years; he's been standing there since the 1950s. He used to guard the Casco Bay Trading Post (purveyors of such authentic junk as beaded belts, smelly pillows, fake Indian bows, and Steve Martin arrows). But when the trading post closed, the giant Indian refused to go away. So he stands there, still on the lookout.

Maine is also home to a few more giants. In Bangor, in addition to literary giant Stephen King there is a thirty-one-foot statue of Paul Bunyan, the legendary logger, with peavey in hand. Some people say both logger and peavey are life-sized (that is, in Paul Bunyan proportions). There is some dispute about whether Mr. Bunyan was a native Mainer. Other states like Minnesota and Wisconsin claim him too.

Yet another monstrous Mainer hails from Boothbay Harbor—a giant fisherman complete with yellow oilskins and sou'wester hat. Rumor has it that this oversized salt is most interesting when viewed from the starboard (i.e., right-hand) side. Normally we'd show you a picture, but perhaps it's better that you see for yourself. The illustration would kick this chapter's rating from a PG to an R.

Sylvia Hardy

Don't get the idea that Maine giants are all artificial—or all male. A quick stop at the Wilton Farm and Home Museum will put an end to those sexist notions. There you will meet Sylvia Hardy, who was well named, she being a robust and sturdy sort. In fact, when she traveled with P. T. Barnum, she was billed as the Tallest Lady in the World, allegedly standing some seven feet ten and one-half inches tall and weighing over four hundred pounds. After her circus career, she returned to her native Wilton, where she became a spiritualist and, in 1888, a spirit. Her eight-foot coffin is buried in Wilton's Lakeview Cemetery. Maybe you won't meet her ghost at the Farm and Home Museum, but you can see a life-sized mock-up of Sylvia herself and a lot of personal memorabilia.

Perhaps Ms. Hardy wasn't as big as Paul Bunyan, but she was tall enough to store personal items on the casings over doorways; she could cradle an infant in one hand or spread her fingers and completely conceal a newspaper. One of her gowns measures six feet eight inches long. Ironically, her best friend was the minuscule Mrs. Tom Thumb, whom you'll meet later.

An Idol Threat

During the Chinese Boxer Uprising (1898–1900), the brothers Charles and Ruben Hill swiped some large golden idols from a Buddhist temple and hightailed it back to their home in Naples, Maine. They thought luck was

with them when they discovered a stash of jewels in one of the statues. Using their newfound fortune, they built a grand house, where they lived in high style for a short time.

Alas, their luck quickly changed. Soon they came to believe that the purloined statues were cursed. After the brothers died mysteriously, their relatives tossed the statues into a lake, but until this day, bad luck—death, disease, madness—has continued to plague everyone who has owned the Hill property. One of the statues was recovered and is displayed in the Naples Historical Society Museum. The museum itself is a rickety old shed behind the Methodist church. There is no real security system, but the little museum remains oddly undisturbed by vandals and thieves. Even though the statue—among other things—may be of great value, those who know the story won't take the risk involved with boosting it. They remember what happened the last time it was stolen.

Where to Go When It Rains

This is not so much a roadside oddity as it is a seaside oddity. You have to travel to Peaks Island, Maine, to see it, but it has nothing to do with the ocean. And it will appeal to only certain types of individuals—though we're not sure what type. In any event, the whole thing is surreal and, in its own way, wonderful.

You enter the tiny museum at 62-B Island Avenue to the sound of accordion music. The curator and instrumentalist are one and the same: Nancy 3. Hoffman. (Yup, that's her real middle name all right: 3.) You can sightsee while she serenades. And just what are you looking at? A whole museum dedicated to sheaths, sleeves, pockets, or, as they are most commonly called, umbrella covers. This place is unique; it is the world's one and only Umbrella Cover Museum.

Who but Nancy 3 would think to celebrate those flaccid, fleeting items that most of us lose instantly? Some are nylon, plain black, or blue. Some are multicolored and

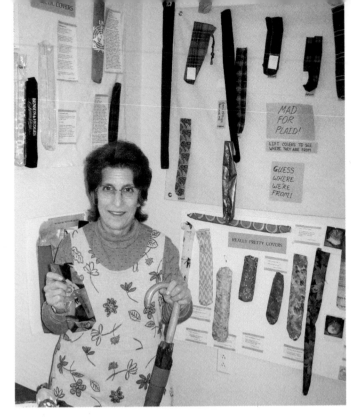

made of more exotic materials like gum wrappers or bulletproof 2,000-denier Kevlar.

After the visionary Ms. Hoffman swiped her first exhibit from a store display, specimens started to arrive from all over the world. Now covers from thirty-five countries are plastered over the walls and dangle all around. Each has its story posted beside it.

The point of all this may seem a little elusive, but the museum's Mission Statement clarifies everything: "The Umbrella Cover Museum is dedicated to the appreciation of the mundane in everyday life. It is about finding wonder and beauty in the simplest of things, and about knowing that there is always a story behind the cover."

Thank God someone thought to collect them. Ms. Hoffman's unique compilation includes about four hundred and fifty of what may be an endangered species: Certain manufacturers are beginning to package their product in throwaway plastic wrappers with no umbrella cover at all! This, Nancy 3. Hoffman says, "is a highly regrettable industry practice."

Someday our children or our children's children may have to venture to Peaks Island to see what we so blissfully take for granted. But before you cast off, better be sure the umbrella is open by calling 207-766-4496 or emailing Nancy3@PeaksIsland.com.

War of the Worlds

Eartha is the name given to the largest rotating globe in the world, and that's according to the *Guinness Book of World Records.* It is conspicuously situated at the DeLorme Map Store in Yarmouth, Maine, where its creator, David DeLorme, took a good deal longer than seven days to bring it about. Diameter: 41 feet. Circumference: 130 feet. Surface area: 5,300 square feet. Weight: 5,600 pounds. Scale: 1:1,000,000; at one one-millionth of the earth's actual size, the thing seems almost big enough to support life.

Combined rotation and revolution occurs every eighteen minutes, driven by two computer-controlled electric motors. Nearly 140 gigabytes of data—that's about 214 CD-ROMs—went into designing its surface. To put that into some sort of useful perspective, the average person reads about one CD-ROM's worth of text in an entire lifetime.

Eartha is tilted 23.5 degrees, just like the earth, with one inch equaling nearly sixteen miles. Maine is as big as a welcome mat. The state of California is three and a half feet tall!

One thing's for sure: That's one mother of an earth.

The Wedding Cake House

Anyone interested in weird architectural artifacts would do well to take a drive down Summer Street in Kennebunkport, Maine. We guarantee you've never see anything quite like the ornate house at Number 105. Although it doesn't look like any wedding cake we've ever seen, it definitely out-gingerbreads gingerbread. There are multiple explanations for why a basic brick Federal-style house should be adorned with such Gothic frosting.

The most romantic holds that its original owner, a sea captain, got married but had to cast off before he got to sample his bride or his wedding cake. So, to pass the long, lonely hours at sea, he took to carving elaborate decorations for his existing home. The Maine chapter of the Daughters of American Colonists tells a slightly different and perhaps less fanciful tale. They say that in 1825 shipbuilder George Washington Bourne (1801–1856) moved into the house with his new bride. Inspired by Milan's Gothic cathedral, Mr. Bourne began decorating late in life, in 1852, using only hand tools. He completed the work shortly before his death. (Isn't that always the way?) A variation holds that shipbuilder Bourne, aided by his apprentice, Thomas Durrell, constructed the house, then designed and carved the adornments in 1826 to please his bride.

So why is it called the Wedding Cake House? Avarice, plain and simple. Around 1900, a Kennebunk businessman published a postcard of the place, dubbing it the Wedding Cake House—he probably sold millions.

Moving On to Massachusetts

Babson's Ball

Until Eartha came into being, the largest globe in the world was in Apecchi, Italy, measuring thirty-three feet in diameter. Here in the U.S.A., our grandest globe was the twenty-eight-footer at Babson College in Wellesley, Massachusetts. The Babson ball is still there and is well worth a look.

While Eartha is indoors, Babson's Ball is entirely outside, making it the biggest outdoor planet on the planet. The idea was to represent earth as it would be perceived from 5,000 miles out in space. Roger Webber, grandson of the college's founder, came up with the idea in 1947. It took him seven years to create this mini-earth from 578 enameled panels. At a weight of twenty-five tons, it was nonetheless designed so it could rotate on its axis.

But dark days were ahead. Within thirty years, the globe began to fall apart, showing all the symptoms of a dying planet. Yet our story has a happy ending. Friends stepped in, and the globe was rescued and restored. Today it's a new and better world, which may mean there is some hope for its prototype.

Mini Miss Middleboro

Only a world champion Trivial Pursuit™ player would be able to identify Lavinia Warren Bump. But in her day, she was known and loved by millions the world over. She married a general and was entertained by royalty in the great capitals of Europe. When she retired, she returned to the town where she was born: Middleboro, Massachusetts.

Today, in the town's modest historical society museum, amid memorable and historic postings, you can get the whole story. A short distance from there you can see the house where Lavinia grew up—to thirty-two inches tall and a weight of thirty pounds. She was a midget, a living doll, perfectly formed, intelligent, witty, and talented. When showman P. T. Barnum heard about her in 1862, he convinced Lavinia's parents to let her join his theatrical company. There she met, fell in love with, and married Mr. Barnum's diminutive superstar General Tom Thumb. When not traveling the world, the couple rested in Middleboro, where they had a mansion built, all to scale. And it was there that they eventually retired. After the general's death, Lavinia married an Italian papal count—also a midget—and they opened a snack bar in town.

Today you can examine the minuscule memorabilia of the Lilliputian lovers by visiting the museum. It will take only a little while.

The Man Who Saved the *Titanic*

What a casual observer driving through the town of Indian Orchard, Massachusetts, might dismiss as simply Henry's Jewelry Store is in fact the *Titanic* Museum. Curator and collector Ed Kamuda has been preoccupied with *Titanic* memories and memorabilia ever since he saw the film *A Night to Remember* in 1958. Since then, he has amassed what is probably the world's biggest private collection of *Titanic* flotsam and jetsam. At the same time, he has become one of the world's leading authorities on the doomed vessel and that impossible-to-forget night — April 14–15, 1912 — when it sank into its watery grave. Mr. Kamuda even consulted with James Cameron about the making of the 1997 film *Titanic*. His assistance earned Mr. Kamuda and his wife, Karen, small roles in the movie, allowing the jeweler from Indian Orchard to stroll the replicated decks of his dream boat.

The contents of this tiny, crowded museum are too vast to list, but there is everything from flags to bells to uniforms and life vests. Mr. Kamuda even has the telegram warning the *Titanic* that a lethal iceberg was in its path (too bad it was delivered here by mistake).

Some people have called Mr. Kamuda's preoccupation morbid or even disrespectful to the fifteen hundred lives lost. Such critics know nothing of true passion and historic reverence. Though it is all done with humility and modesty, by assembling his museum and founding the eight-thousand-member Titanic Historical Society, Mr. Kamuda has unwittingly built something of a monument to himself: the man who saved the *Titanic*.

Skull Rock

This is one of those elusive mysteries that might appeal more to treasure hunters than to armchair adventurers. We have an oddity, but we don't know exactly where it is. As correspondent Jim Moskowitz writes:

"I want to share with you the most astonishing moment of my vacation, which luckily I have photos of. While traipsing around a woods in northeastern Massachusetts, I stumbled on one of the most breathtaking murals I've ever seen, partly so for its design and message, partly for how difficult it must have been traversing the rockface, but more because it's hidden away, something found only by chance—the artist simply put their mural where they wanted and left it there to be noticed or not. The subject is rather intense: It's a thirty-foot-high wall of multicolored bones and skulls, with a message to one side: TAKE THE KNOWLEDGE THAT YOU WILL SOMEDAY BE THESE BONES, AND ENJOY NOW ALL THAT IS PRECIOUS."

This is one of those cases where a picture is worth a thousand words, but a map would be worth a lot more.

And in New Hampshire . . .

The Luckiest Town in the World

Some people believe the town of Hopkinton, New Hampshire, may be the luckiest place on earth. While we cannot analyze the pros and cons of that assertion, we can cite the motivating evidence: a big pile of lucky horseshoes. It was placed there in the 1920s when a local lad discovered the discarded equine footwear under the floor of the village blacksmith shop (now the Sandy Heino & Associates real estate office). He stacked them up outside, where it quickly became a local custom for people to keep adding to the pile. But bad luck often follows good. Furtive folk wishing to improve their own good fortune (or diminish the town's) began swiping horseshoes. The solution was to weld the pile together, creating, presumably, the luckiest sculpture in the world. The effort did not escape notice. Hopkinton made the *Guinness Book of World Records* for having the biggest pile of horseshoes in the world.

Rockets Away!

For a real *Twilight Zone* moment, drive into Warren, New Hampshire. As you approach, it's likely you'll be overcome with a pleasant sense of nostalgia as you anticipate Warren's quaintness, its air of another era. Admire the dignified old buildings on the outskirts. Then move closer, check out the white colonial houses scattered among lush foliage. And, true to form, poking through lofty treetops, you'll see the pointed tips of stark white church steeples — the peaceful beacons of competing congregations offset against an ultra-blue sky.

Then unreality hits.

One of those steeples isn't a steeple at all. It's the nose cone of a giant rocket ship! Has Warren gone a little overboard with its homeland security?

The fact is that the centerpiece of the town green is a seventy-foot Jupiter-C rocket identical to the one that zapped the first American, New Hampshirite Alan B. Shepard Jr., into space on May 5, 1961.

This unusual ornament was transported here by native Ted Asselin. In 1971, he was stationed in Huntsville, Alabama, where unused Redstone missiles are stored. Authorities let him cart one away, and Warren authorities were delighted to let him set it up. Though some may call it overkill, it sure beats a pyramid of black cannonballs or an effigy of the town founder.

Rock of Ages Church

No one would say religion isn't big in New Hampshire, but you couldn't prove it by this North Woodstock church. It is, in fact, a real church. But at just eleven feet by eleven feet, it is probably the grandest cathedral that could be constructed on this peculiar and precarious bit of real estate. Nonetheless, it supports a steeple topped with a cross, and inside there's an altar and wide, welcoming windows. Its door is never locked. Services are held here from time to time. The trouble is, a capacity crowd, we're told, is only twelve and one-half people (or twenty-five half-people, which would be really weird), so the congregation doesn't have much opportunity to expand.

Perhaps the important thing about the Rock of Ages Church is its symbolism: The church is built upon a rock, literally. And also on that rock you'll find stenciled such inspirational messages as ROCK OF AGES; A WEE, FREE KIRK; and VIA DOLOROSA. When we last visited, there were other symbols crowded around it as well. Junk cars, for example, perhaps placed there to suggest the transitory nature of our modern mobile culture. And a garish plastic manger scene, no doubt reminding us that though the Rock of Ages Church may be small, the institution originated in much smaller quarters.

The Tomb Room

It's hard not to stop to stare at the columned mansion at Nine School Street in Hanover, New Hampshire. Older Dartmouth alumni may remember it as Phi Sigma Psi, as it was known during much of the nineteenth and twentieth centuries. Today the 1835 edifice houses Panarchy, one of Dartmouth's two undergraduate societies.

In the old days, it was a private residence owned by a wealthy physician with a dark secret: He kept his crazed daughter locked in the attic. Ill treatment, loneliness, and anguish eventually pushed her to suicide. But she didn't quite complete the job. Something of her still lingers. Certain house members swear they've heard or seen an ethereal female presence, about high school age, in the attic.

But this is not a ghost story, for Panarchy holds another disturbing mystery, this one in a secret basement. It is one of the oddest sites you'll find anywhere on campus—the so-called Tomb Room. This subterranean chamber, rimmed with concrete "thrones," could be the setting for a horror film involving satanic invocations. Noting the names etched on these seats and the accompanying years (from 1897 to the 1940s), one might guess that the Tomb Room was for fraternal rites or initiations, but somehow it seems too elaborate, too expensive, and too secret for that. The "altar," a freestanding stone sarcophagus near the front, suggests darker applications. No one today knows why the secret room is there or how it was used, but the blood-colored candle wax splattered all over the altar sets the imagination racing. Could the "ghosts" upstairs have been conjured by unholy activities in the Tomb Room below?

Madame's Maison de Joie

Madame Antoinette Sherri blew into the tiny New Hampshire town of West Chesterfield from the dance halls of gay Paris. She took the locals by storm; no one had ever seen the likes of this painted lady in a topless Packard limousine. She had married well and was widowed, so she had money to spend. In 1931, she built her grand retreat, Maison de Joie, a castle in the wilderness.

Though Madame didn't mix socially with the locals, she did offer employment, so they learned to tolerate her lascivious ways, her pet monkey, and her fondness for conspicuously younger men. In fact, she continually scandalized the citizens of two states by being chauffeured across the Connecticut River into nearby Brattleboro, Vermont, wearing nothing but a fur coat and a satisfied smile. In time, her looks faded and her fortune dwindled. Little by little she had to sell her possessions: her furniture, her Packard, and eventually her home. Her abandoned mansion attracted thieves and vandals, finally succumbing to fire in 1962. Arson or accident, we don't know.

In her old age, her lavish life behind her, Madame became a ward of the town of Brattleboro, where, at age eighty-four, she died penniless in 1964. But her legacy is a magnificent ruin, her Maison de Joie, which still generates rumors of sordid city sins, a Parisian-style bordello in the wilds, and the "good life" as rarely sampled by staid New Englanders.

Then there are the ghosts. Madame Sherri's castle is known as a haunted place where the laughter of parties long gone can still be heard occasionally and where Madame Sherri herself will still put in the occasional appearance, descending the curved stone stairway that leads from the great beyond to the solid ground of West Chesterfield.

Vermont Oddities

Land Shark!

Well, they're whales, actually. You can spot them cavorting in the field along that stretch of Interstate 89 near Burlington between exits 12 and 13. Because Vermont is New England's only landlocked state, you may be surprised to see a pod of whales in a pasture where cows ought to be grazing. But remember, 10,000 years ago most of Vermont was sea bottom. But we're not going to tell you that you were seeing the ghosts of prehistoric whales. The I-89 Whale Watch is in reality a novel bit of statuary placed there by Randolph sculptor Jim Sardonis. Officially, it's called *Reverence,* to symbolize the planet's fragility. So keep your harpoons holstered.

Whale Tales

I was driving to Vermont when I came across this odd and wonderfully weird site. Along the fields and mountains, I came across these "Whale Tails" on Rt. 89 by or in Burlington. Is it some whale cemetery? All I kept asking myself is WHY?? It made me laugh, and I just wanted to share my road site attraction. Enjoy.—*Rose Newton*

Printed in Stone

It is a Vermont curiosity that has all but vanished from local guidebooks. In olden days, it was considered a remarkable puzzle and people flocked to see it. But in today's faster, less contemplative quest for entertainment, few venture to South Woodbury. At least not to see the footprints.

Admittedly, dinosaur tracks are plentiful in New England. But it is rare indeed—here or anywhere else—to see human prints embedded in stone. Especially in a vertical cliff. In South Woodbury, if you find the right spot on Cranberry Meadow Road, you'll encounter two distinct footprints in the face of a boulder. There is a handprint just above them.

How did they get there? What could have formed these seemingly impossible permanent impressions? Are they natural or supernatural?

The prints have been there longer than anyone can remember and would be totally incomprehensible if the locals hadn't concocted legends to explain them. One asserts they were made by angels. Nowadays, some probably blame extraterrestrials. But most folks just say they're "Indian footprints" and leave it at that.

Over the centuries, rain and Vermont winters have eroded the stone impressions, so in 1958 a local man, fearful the puzzle would be lost, took chisel in hand and sharpened the existing footprints. Bad move in terms of archaeology. Good move in terms of preserving legends. But then again, the archaeologists were doing nothing to preserve them on their own.

Queen Kong

Who says there's no Bigfoot in Vermont? Just north of Brandon on Route 7, near, or possibly in, Leicester, there's a monster that would make even Bigfoot take to his heels. It looks like a still from a *King Kong* remake, poised with a VW over its head, ready to hurl it at the next tourist who stops to take its picture.

Known locally as Queen Connie, this prospective bride of Kong stands about twenty feet tall. Being feminine, perhaps she is of a more docile nature than the King. If not, she has plenty more ammo scattered at her feet. She's standing on the grounds of Pioneer Auto Sales Inc. The Queen is a popular local attraction with everyone but professional watchdogs. No need for them here.

Setting Limits

Before the invention of speed limit signs, it took Yankee ingenuity to get people to slow down on dangerous curves. In Bristol, Joseph Greene came up with a novel idea. It may not observe the proper separation of church and state, but it seems to work: He had the Lord's Prayer carved on a rock outside town.

There are many variations on the reason he did this, but they are minor. In effect, it's this: As a boy, Greene drove logs down a dangerous mountain road to a sawmill in Bristol. When he got to Bristol Rock, he had to observe a last bit of caution. Take the curve too quickly, and his load could shift or tumble. When he had made it safely past the rock, he'd say a little prayer of thanks. In 1891, as a successful physician in Buffalo, New York, he commemorated his Vermont boyhood by commissioning the carving. Hopefully, he thought, seeing the prayer would remind others to slow down. A secondary effect, according to some, is that it warns people to clean up their language before entering town. We've seen much evidence of the former, but very little of the latter.

We've Got a File on You!

It's a fact. Vermonters don't like to throw anything away. Rather than shred or burn out-of-date files, Vermonters simply erect skyscraper-high file cabinets and store everything. Burlington, the state's largest city, boasts the world's tallest file cabinet. Since no building is high enough to contain it, you can find it in an open space just off Flynn Avenue between Pine Street and Lake Champlain. It seems to tilt a little, reminiscent of the lesser but still Leaning File Cabinet of Pisa, Italy. So don't stand too close during a windy day, or Vermont will have a file on you.

The Thing About Things

The Main Street Museum of Art in White River Junction is not to be missed. It has often been called the strangest museum in Vermont. We can't disagree. It pushes any conceivable definition of museum. Or art.

David Fairbanks Ford, the creator, curator, and artist-in-residence, is an amiable curiosity himself, an engaging hybrid of historian and humorist, with a dash of P. T. Barnum showmanship thrown in. Somehow, he has magically synthesized something all new; yet it feels old—a throwback to the grand old days of the nineteenth-century private museums and personal cabinets of curiosity.

What Mr. Ford has created is somehow greater than the sum of its eclectic parts. If we were to look at the components individually, we would see, for example, a mink in a bottle, the preserved carcass of a sea monster allegedly pulled from the Connecticut River, stuffed deer busts, MACBA (Modern Art Created by Accident), and a real show-stopper—a carefully mounted blue bottle containing what's left of the salve used to treat Phineas Gage's celebrated head wound (see page 130). One illuminated bottle even displays the gallstones of Elvis Presley.

If you are easily offended, it might be well to avoid the infamous Virgisaurus, half Madonna, half dinosaur that one-ups the half-woman, half-fish mermaids of yesteryear.

All this apparent clutter, chaos, and incongruity forces one to contemplate the nature of museums and curating. Why do we save what we save? How do we decide what to discard, what to display, what to hide away, and what to destroy?

Who knows? Often, compulsive savers experience a peculiar fascination with objects connected to specific events or associated with famous people. Artifacts presumably create a more tangible, albeit imaginary, link with the past. In the 1930s, a woman donated a glass tumbler to the Fleming Museum in Burlington, Vermont. A glass tumbler? So what? Then she explained that it had arrived on the *Mayflower*. Suddenly it took on additional allure. A curator long-gone wrote on its label, "But can she prove it?" It doesn't seem to matter; today the original tumbler has disappeared—but a stand-in is exhibited in its place.

The notion of the stand-in has opened up myriad possibilities at the Main Street Museum. And myriad questions: What's real, and what isn't? And what difference does it make?

As curator Ford says, "We can decide the value of things ourselves. We can decide what the meaning of an object is ourselves. We must never let some corporation, some academic, some curator—especially some crazy alternative curator from some alternative museum—decide the value of objects, of things, for us. Do not let the roadside-ization of America take over."

Spoken like a true Yankee. And that said, the art of this somewhat subversive, egalitarian, and independent collection is that it challenges the very concept of the "museum" or the "gallery." It's also a pleasant reminder that none of us should take it, or ourselves, too seriously.

South to Connecticut

Little People Village

There's a tiny place somewhere in the wilds of Middlebury, or maybe Waterbury, Connecticut, that is more shrouded in mystery and legend than in legitimate history. It could be a place of elevated paranormal activity; then again, it may simply be an ancient roadside attraction from the early days of touring cars. Or it could be something else altogether.

What you see is a collection of diminutive dwellings, mostly ruins at this point, but still capable of evoking a strong sense of wonder. The question is, How do we explain them?

Well, it depends on who you talk to. One person will tell you that a nearby, full-sized house was once occupied by a man who had married a witch (or perhaps a seer). She commanded him to build the tiny village as rent-free housing for the wee folk who frolicked in the surrounding woodland.

Another version holds that the man lived alone in the big house (today nothing but a cellar hole). In time, his isolation led to either heightened mystical sensitivity or overt mania. He began hearing voices. Perhaps they were fairy voices. In any event, he commenced the construction of miniature homes for his invisible guests, presumably hoping to move the voices out of his head and into proper housing. One voice, purporting to be a king, even demanded a throne, which the man obligingly carved from solid rock. (A variation holds that the man built the throne for himself to lord over his personal population of wee folk.) In time, the persistence of the voices and their nonstop demands drove the unfortunate man insane. He died, some say by his own hand, in the house. Local legend holds that by visiting Little People Village you too can hear the voices if the conditions are right. If you do, we hope you'll get the real scoop on the history of this unusual place.

A Visit to Lilliput

I was thrilled to find this place because it's not only a haunted spot, it's also a famous old roadside attraction from the 1920s and a folk art site, which satisfies my wife's interests. I have to admit I was driven to visit this place because I had a dream about a similar place many years ago that was so frightening I never forgot it.

When I looked over the layout, I thought it might have been a large religious grotto, similar to the amazing Ave Maria Grotto. But I heard from a former resident of Middlebury that it was an old service station from the 1920s that was located near the trolley tracks that ran to the Quassy Lake resort area. It was indeed run by an old man with a white beard, and even then it was in disrepair. –*Ben Osto*

Permanently Parked

Hamden Plaza on Dixwell Avenue in Hamden, Connecticut, was once the site of a most unusual parking lot. It appeared as if an overzealous paving crew had tarred the whole plaza without first removing the cars parked there. Some twenty vehicles were forever preserved in a coating of macadam like insects suspended in amber. At twilight, they looked like three-dimensional shadows of automobiles emerging from the tar, like dinosaurs bubbling from the La Brea pits. But day or night they were an eerie, puzzling sight.

Created as an artistic project in 1978, the Ghost Cars dared us to assign meaning. Did they signify the end of a mobile America where car and tar had permanently merged? Was their intent to frighten, comfort, or confront? Who can say?

Inevitably, local legend clicked in where explanations eluded. Certain individuals explained that they were an underground junkyard, the partially buried carcasses of cars in which accident victims had died. Others went a step farther, saying actual bodies were concealed within car-coffins. We were all set to nominate Hamden Plaza as *Weird New England*'s official parking lot when we got word that the community had decided to bulldoze the whole thing. The Ghost Cars are gone now. If you see them, they really will be ghosts.

Skulls or Skullduggery?

It may look like a tomb, but this brown stone, windowless structure on High Street in New Haven, Connecticut, is in reality a clubhouse for very rich and privileged boys. It houses a highly secret fraternal order founded in 1832 at Yale University, known as the Skull and Bones club. And the grisly fact is that there really are skulls and bones inside. Past and present rulers of this country, including captains of industry and finance, have spent time within these sepulchral walls, swearing oaths, forming allegiances, and behaving in ways the rest of us can only imagine. John Kerry was a member. So was George W. Bush. George W.'s father, George the First, was also a member, as was his father, Prescott Bush.

It was with Grandpa Bush that one of the most enduring mysteries of the Skull and Bones club began. It has to do with the club's exhibit of real skulls and bones, which may be those of Geronimo, the last great Apache warrior. The story is that Grandpa Bush led an expedition to Fort Sill, Oklahoma, to rob Geronimo's grave and that he

transported the relics back to the New Haven repository as a kind of trophy.

Is it true? Right now an agency of the federal government that oversees the Repatriation Act is investigating. (The Repatriation Act sets up a process for the return of Native American burial items to the tribes.)

Meanwhile, evidence is piling up. Yale graduate Alexandra Robbins considered the matter in her 2002 book *Secrets of the Tomb.* She cites a letter from a Skull and Bones whistle-blower who informed Apache leaders that Geronimo's bones were not in Fort Sill as the tribe believed, but rather in New Haven. His message included a photograph showing a glass case displaying Indian artifacts and the bones and skull that the informant claimed were Geronimo's. Also included was a copy of a diary entry—allegedly part of the Skull and Bones' archives—describing the

Geronimo as prisoner at Fort Sill, Oklahoma

322

grave robbing: "[Prescott] Bush entered [Geronimo's tomb] and started to dig," it said. "The skull was fairly clean, having only some flesh inside and a little hair."

Prescott Bush was a 1917 Yale graduate who was stationed at Fort Sill after World War I. If he in fact robbed the grave, his ghoulish motives are a bit puzzling. Sometimes Indians were said to be buried with gold and other valuables. Then again, the future senator from Connecticut may have just wanted a prize, though a gruesome one, to display in the secret confines of his club. After all, who would object but womenfolk, and they were not allowed on the premises until 1991. (Interestingly, Ms. Robbins notes that the vote to allow women inside the club passed by the narrowest of margins. The old boy network, led by alumnus William F. Buckley Jr., fought the change in court, asserting that admitting women would lead to date rape. Doesn't say much for the club's perception of its own members.)

Henrietta Stockel, an Apache historian, believes the skull is there, but suspects it may belong to another Apache leader, Managas Colorados. The U.S. Army suckered him into surrendering in New Mexico, then murdered and decapitated him. His skull has never been located. Unless it is in New Haven. Alone. Or with Geronimo's. We may never know.

Admittedly, George the elder signed the Repatriation Act into law in 1990. This might imply that he had nothing to hide and gave no credence to the Geronimo story. However, the law applies only to human remains maintained by institutions that receive federal funding. The Skull and Bones club considers itself tax exempt and nonprofit by virtue of its alleged educational affiliation. Yale, on the other hand, maintains that the club is independent.

Other grisly trophies are said to be secreted away within: Hitler's personal silverware, the gravestone of Yale's founder, and even a third prized skull, that of Mexican hero Pancho Villa.

A final oddity that we have verified via a reliable, undisclosed source is that the Skull and Bones club consistently has the highest water bill in all of New Haven. Think about it. That may be the weirdest thing of all. What could they be doing with all that water? Cleaning consciences? Laundering money?

George H. W. Bush (at left of clock) with Skull and Bones members at Yale University, New Haven, circa 1947

The Smallest Show on Earth

The Barnum Museum in Bridgeport is worth a look for a number of reasons. First, from the outside, it's a weird building reminiscent of the time the magnificent Barnum built it as the Barnum Institute of Science and History.

Science and History? Yup. There was a lot more to this flamboyant nineteenth-century Renaissance man than many of us give him credit for. For one thing, he was once mayor of Bridgeport.

A pathetic scattering of relics from his "Odditoriums" in New York City can be viewed here in all-too-modern display mode. You can see an authentic mummy, a human footprint embedded in rock (how'd that happen?), wood

from Noah's ark (yeah, right), memorabilia of Barnum's midgets (Tom Thumb, Lavinia Bump, Commodore Nutt, and the rest), and an authentic reproduction of a bogus Feejee Mermaid (from A&E's biopic about Barnum).

After two of Barnum's New York museums burned, he turned his attention from curating to creating circuses, and that is how he is generally remembered. The same promotional superpower that turned Jenny Lind into America's first superstar transformed tawdry traveling troupes into three-ringed wonders. Of course, the Barnum Bridgeport Museum can't house a real circus, but it does contain something that is, in its own way, every bit as magic and magnificent: a scale model (three quarters of an inch to the foot) of a 1903 Barnum and Bailey five-ring tent. It measures 1,100 square feet and depicts every minute detail of old-time circus life.

This microscopic marvel, in which even Tom Thumb would appear a colossus, is the handiwork of lifelong circus fan William R. Brinley. Over a span of thirty-six years, he designed and created this mini-masterpiece, comprised of over five thousand hand-carved figures and the wagons, tents, rings, trapezes, and other colorful contraptions that make up a circus.

In a sense, the lavish creation is a reconstruction of the way Mr. Brinley remembers the circus from his boyhood. In the old days, a circus created an instant holiday when it hit town. How the pomp and circumstance of the parade wagons and calliopes must have enlivened the drudgery of New England life. What wonders the big top contained: clowns, elephants, scantily clad babes on tightropes, wild man-eating animals from exotic locales. And what mysteries the sideshows concealed: bearded ladies, sword swallowers, magicians from the faraway Orient, and the ever-popular half-man/half-woman often referred to as the "morphadite."

Tiny, unexpected details make Mr. Brinley's circus a true wonder. He includes a false bottom in the ticket wagon so the clerk can stash money and an extra bit of bed so the giant can sleep comfortably. A hidden door in the dining car leads to a secret room where illegal gambling proceeds regardless of local legislation.

To truly appreciate Mr. Brinley's life's work, you must study it. It is a three-dimensional book that must be read. To flip through the pages, pausing for only an occasional glance, would be to do yourself and Mr. Brinley a true disservice.

The Smallest Show on Earth may not be quint-essentially weird, but it is a true wonder.

Can You See the Jesus Tree?

The Lord works in mysterious ways. He may be putting in an unusual appearance in, of all places, Milford, Connecticut. Over the years, many residents have said they have bumped into Jesus as they traveled along Hawley Avenue. He's on a maple tree rather than a cross.

The tree, higher than eighty feet, lost a limb when Hurricane Gloria blasted through in 1985. The scar where the limb was once attached quickly assumed some pretty peculiar properties, and that's what's got everybody so worked up. To some it looks more like a human face than a scar. More specifically, they say it looks like Jesus' face. Avenue resident Claudia Voight was among the first to see it, and she said it took her breath away. Soon other Hawley Avenue residents were gawking at the unusual sight. Parades of autos quickly followed, and for a while, this roadside oddity (or apparition) made the route between Anderson and Beach avenues a very popular thoroughfare.

If you're in the neighborhood, you might want to take a cruise down heavenly Hawley. Who knows, you could just bump into Jesus. Just try not to bump into a tree.

Jesus in Connecticut Trees

There is a small park at the corner of Chapel Street and Wooster Place in New Haven where people claim to see the face of Jesus in the bark of some of the trees. When we visited, we came to the conclusion that looking at tree bark is a lot like staring into ink blots: The patterns are largely open to the interpretation of the viewer. Sometimes people just see what they want to see. Though I didn't find the Savior on any of the arbors that I pondered, I did recognize a formation that bore an uncanny resemblance to a thick T-bone steak and a tall mug of beer. But I was pretty hungry at the time.—*MM*

The State of Rhode Island

The Big Blue Bug

It's a standoff. The New England Pest Control Company in Providence is poised to do battle with a giant termite. If they can't control this pest, we're all in trouble; a swarm of these monsters could take over the world. But not to worry, the bug is a phony, though the company is real (perhaps giving it an unfair advantage).

The Big Blue Bug, also known as Nibbles Woodaway, is the world's largest scale model of a *Reticulitermes flavipes,* 920 times life size. What can only be called Rhode Island's weirdest landmark was created in October 1980 by the Avenia Sign Company. It's 58 feet long, 9 feet high, 6 feet in diameter, with 40-foot wings, 7-foot antennae, and legs 11 feet long. Good thing it's not real. Mere humans would never stand a chance.

Looking at it from Route 95—a good, safe viewing distance—we can't imagine this monstrosity pinned to an entomologist's display board or squashed by an oversized flyswatter, which, when you think about it, might have made a more effective mascot for a pest control company.

Trailing the Devil

South Beach in Middletown, Rhode Island, is home to a yawning abyss called Purgatory Chasm. Legend says this gaping slash in the landscape was created by a powerful downward swing of the devil's axe. He was chopping at an Indian woman who had brought out his homicidal tendencies. This wasn't the Christian devil, mind you, but rather Hobomoko, the Indian devil. His target, the poor Indian woman, had apparently murdered a white man, though why Hobomoko should care is one of the many mysteries associated with this strange place. Anyway, after leaving a fifty-foot gash in the rock, Hobomoko took another swing, chopped off the poor woman's head, and tossed her severed body parts into what is now called Purgatory Chasm.

Her ghost is said to walk the treacherous cliffs overlooking South Beach, but exactly how she keeps from falling in again without benefit of a head is an ongoing puzzle. Anyway, after Hobomoko did his dirty work he leaped away, propelled by stomping his footprints into the rocks, where they can be seen to this day, along with spatterings of the Indian's blood. The scene of the crime is ten feet wide, one hundred twenty feet long, and more than fifty feet deep. Exactly why it's called Purgatory Chasm is perhaps the last mystery of the place. Maybe it is because a bit of evil—Christian or Indian—still hovers there. People are known to leap across the chasm to demonstrate their bravery or, more precisely, their stupidity. Others, with equally solid nerves but more brainpower, inch their way to the edge to get a view of the cave at the base of the cliff. Regardless of the state of your nerves, Purgatory Chasm is a scenic and haunting spot. Price of admission: your soul.

Newport's Mystery Woman

For decades, chroniclers of Newport, Rhode Island, have loved to drop the names of the wealthy people who built extravagant mansions along the coast, the various superstars who performed on Newport stages, and the ultrarich who have vacationed in this New England über-resort. Such star-struck chroniclers like to crow about what an exclusive community Newport has always been.

It certainly excluded Beatrice Turner. She was wealthy, beautiful, educated, poised, an extraordinary artist, but perhaps she was just too strange.

Although she was knockout gorgeous, she never married—never even had suitors or close female friends. Until her death from cancer in 1948, when she was fifty-nine years old, she was always seen in clothing from the Victorian Era. During the roaring '20s, her hems never lifted. In the 1940s, she still dressed like a grandmother.

Who was this mysterious Miss Turner who summered in Newport? Why did she wander the tall cliffs by the sea alone at all hours of the day or night?

We may never know.

Though she is gone now, you can still see her house, called Cliffside, today one of the Legendary Inns of Newport, a meticulously restored Victorian delight. But in Beatrice's day it was known as the Haunted House, for she had painted it jet black.

The story of Beatrice Turner is the stuff of legend, a classic mystery that haunts the imagination. There is something gothic about her life, something tragic about her passing, and something irresistible about her afterlife.

Perhaps the story best begins when Beatrice's life ended. The first people to enter her black, ramshackle, seemingly abandoned mansion probably got the surprise of their lives. It was filled, top to bottom, closet to attic, floor to ceiling, with paintings. For more than forty

solitary years, she had created thousands upon thousands of them, the majority—more than one thousand—self-portraits.

Vanity? Only at first glance. Apparently never courted, seemingly friendless, the retiring artist spent the years after her parents' death painting her most accessible model.

Although she willed her lifework to the local historical society, nobody wanted it. Twelve large trucks hauled everything away to the Newport dump to be incinerated. Luckily, a local lawyer, Nathan Fleischer, rescued many of her paintings and a few diary pages.

From these puzzle pieces we begin to assemble a new portrait of Beatrice.

She was the only child of wealthy Victorian parents, Adele and Andrew Turner. In late-nineteenth-century excess, the girl was overprotected, not permitted to form any real friendships. However, her considerable artistic talent could not be ignored. She was sent away to art school, but her stay there was brief. When her father learned she was sketching nudes, he summoned her home, where she was required to stay. "You should spend your time painting yourself," he is said to have told her, "for you'll never discover a more beautiful subject."

Perhaps Turner's affection for his daughter exceeded Victorian or any other propriety. He doted on her and wrote her poems, one of which suggests what may have gone on behind those heavy Victorian drapes. He wrote:

When looking at thy form divine
Perfect in each curve and line
And gazing at thy silken hair
And basking in thy orbits rare
A misnomer 'twas in naming thee
Aught else but Venus.

Mother had a different set of claws into Beatrice. According to nineteenth-century mores, a daughter's

primary duty was to care for her mother. So Beatrice became companion, servant, and eventually nurse. When the two women were seen in Newport together, they would be dressed in the style of the late 1800s: long dresses, high collars, wide hats. Beatrice never modified her outmoded attire until the day she died.

It is difficult to imagine what sort of impact these anachronistic and perhaps slightly demented parents had on their only daughter. Surely, unhealthy bonds were formed.

Her father passed away in 1913. Because of his morbid fear of being buried alive, his corpse was kept in the home. During that time, Beatrice propped him up and painted his portrait. He is seen looking directly at the viewer. The painting's title, *Daddy in Death*, is the only indication of his condition. It was shortly after his burial that Beatrice had her mansion painted black, instantly creating Newport's Haunted House and giving folks all the more reason to avoid the place.

In the sequence of self-portraits, we can literally watch Beatrice age. When she was in her fifties, after her mother's death, she began to paint herself in the nude. Her lifework was a unique vision that nobody wanted.

Today Beatrice Turner's house is the Cliffside Inn. The late Winthrop Baker, who bought the place after viewing one of Beatrice's paintings, hung about one hundred of her remarkable self-portraits. They look out at you from every wall. Her house is now her art gallery.

And Beatrice herself may be there too. People have reported seeing a specter in a dark blue full-length dress with a high collar. One second she's there; the next she's gone. Other guests, mostly men, will wake up to see a beautiful woman standing at the foot of their bed, a woman with a sad smile and wide, beseeching eyes. Then she'll fade away. Even in death, no one will ever get to know her.

NO COMMENT !
A *Weird New England* Scrapbook

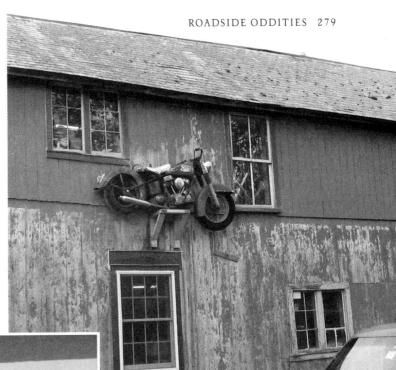

Which state is it in? Which town? A treasure hunt through the wilds of *Weird New England.*

INDEX Page numbers in **bold** refer to photos and illustrations.

WEIRD NEW ENGLAND

By
Joseph A. Citro

Executive Editors
Mark Moran and Mark Sceurman

ACKNOWLEDGMENTS

The following people and organizations—though not weird themselves—helped tremendously in the creation of *Weird New England.* The author wishes to thank Ted Asselin, Winthrop Baker and Legendary Inns of Newport, Emerson Baker, Jack and John Barwick, Tony Basiliere, Roderick G. Bates, Steve and Marge Bissette, Jae Burton, Jerry Carbone and the staff of Brooks Memorial Library, Allison and Brian Citro, Howard Coffin, Loren Coleman, Steve Conant, Jim Defilippi, Mike Dobbs, Art Donahue, Joe Durwin, George Earley, David Fairbanks Ford, Diane E. Foulds, Gene Fox, Partick Gray, Paul Grzybowski, Jeff Hatch, Elliott Hersey and the Patten Lumbermen's Museum, Betty Hill, Nancy 3. Hoffman, Charlie Jordan, Ed Kamuda, Cheryl LeBeau, Peggy Leite, Ted Lylis, Gary Mangiacopra, Jim Millard, Al and Holly Molinaro, Mark Moran (for his editorial wisdom and good humor), Jim Moskowitz, Cornell Nash, Anthony Nevico, Ben Osto, Panarchy, Pigman, Charlie Powell, Steve Scanlon, Susan Reid Shepherd, Linda Smith, Mariella Squire, Cathy Taylor, Charles Upton, Jack Weiner, and Eugene Winter. Certain individuals, due to request or my Swiss-cheese of a memory, must remain anonymous.

No thanks to the Skull and Bones club.

Publisher:	Barbara J. Morgan
Assoc. Managing Editor:	Emily Seese
Editor:	Marjorie Palmer
Production:	Della R. Mancuso
	Mancuso Associates, Inc.
	North Salem, N.Y.

SHOW US YOUR WEIRD!

Do you know of a weird site found somewhere in the United States, or can you tell us about a strange experience you've had? If so, we'd like to hear about it! We believe that every town has at least one great tale to tell, and we're listening. It could be a cursed road, haunted abandoned site, odd local character, or bizarre historic event. In most cases these tales are told only in the towns in which they originated. But why keep them to yourself when you could share them with all of America? So come on and fill us in on all the weirdness that's lurking in your backyard!

You can e-mail us at: Editor@WeirdUS.com,
or write to us at:
Weird U.S., P.O. Box 1346, Bloomfield, NJ 07003.

www.weirdus.com